ACT
NATURAL

ACT

NATURAL

HOW TO SPEAK
TO ANY AUDIENCE

KEN HOWARD

RANDOM HOUSE

NEW YORK

RANDOM HOUSE and colophon are registered trademarks
of Random House, Inc.

Martin Luther King Jr.'s "I have a dream" speech is reprinted by
arrangement with the Estate of Martin Luther King, Jr., c/o
Writer's House as agent for the proprietor, New York, New York.

Excerpts from Sir Winston Churchill's speeches are reprinted by
arrangement with the Estate of Sir Winston Churchill, c/o Curtis
Brown, Ltd., as agent for the proprietor, London, United Kingdom.

Alan Jay Lerner's lyrics from the *My Fair Lady* song "You Did It" and
Seesaw's "Nobody Does It Like Me," lyrics by Dorothy Fields, are
reprinted by permission of Warner Bros. Music Publishing.

Library of Congress Cataloging-in-Publication Data

Howard, Ken
Act natural : how to speak to any audience / Ken Howard
p.   cm.
Includes index.
ISBN 0-375-50736-1
1. Public speaking.   2. Acting—Psychological aspects.
I. Howard, Ken.   II. Title.
PN4129.15.H68 2003
808.5'1—dc21   2002030693

Random House website address: www.atrandom.com

Printed in the United States of America

2 4 6 8 9 7 5 3

First Edition

Book design by Jo Anne Metsch

For Jeannie Epper,
who gave me the gift of life,
and for Linda, my wife,
who makes each day worth living

CONTENTS

ACT
NATURAL

INTRODUCTION

In 1985 I was master of ceremonies at a fund-raiser for the Manhattan Theatre Club, a small theater founded in 1970 on the Upper East Side to showcase the work of new playwrights. The theater had launched a number of plays that went on to Broadway, including *Ain't Misbehavin'*, *Mass Appeal*, and the Pulitzer Prize–winning *Crimes of the Heart*. The fund-raiser was staged at the New York Hilton, featuring performances by several stars from Broadway musicals. In the audience were even more stars of stage and screen, as well as writers, directors, and producers. Scheduled to appear onstage to explain why they believed this theater was important to the cultural life of the city and therefore worthy of big checks were the theater's founding artistic director, Lynne Meadow, and the actor Robert De Niro. After I welcomed the crowd and filled them in on what to expect over the next couple of hours, I walked offstage, and Robert De Niro, whom I had met once briefly, collared me. "How do you do that?" he asked with a grin, alluding to the fact that I had spoken without any notes. He confided that he was extremely uncomfortable with such personal appearances and was dreading his turn. De Niro then showed me a typewritten page of what the PR people had prepared for him and, with a twinkle in his eye, asked, "Any advice?" I said, "Well, first of all, whatever you do, don't read that." I reminded him that the audience had come to see *Robert De Niro,* the justly world-famous actor, and he should go onstage and simply tell them why he thought the Manhattan Theatre Club was so wonderful. "As if," I advised, "you were telling a friend."

When I introduced De Niro, he walked up to the podium, displayed his script, and announced, "Ken Howard said not to use this." He crumpled it up and tossed it over his shoulder. Then he bent over the microphone and proceeded to tell the audience what the Manhattan Theatre Club meant to him—in his own words. Charming, self-effacing but passionate, informative but in no way perfectly crafted, he gave a performance that was pure De Niro, and the audience loved it. As he came offstage with the applause ringing through the Hilton ballroom, he looked at me, nodded in that De Niro way, and said, "It worked!" At the end of the evening, it seemed all anyone could talk about was how "honest" and "real" Robert De Niro had been.

All De Niro had done was act natural. In this book, I will show you how you, too, can step into the limelight and impress any audience. Nothing is more important for making your way in the world than appearing confident, articulate, and comfortable in a public setting. Yet in survey after survey, people confess that the thing they fear most in life is speaking in public. Just the prospect of such moments can bring on feelings of absolute terror. Who hasn't been there?

Act Natural will help you deal with that terror; it will show you how you can turn it into your ally. Based on courses I taught at Harvard College ("The Self and the Role") and Harvard Law

School ("Public Speaking for Lawyers"), this book will take you through a series of steps, techniques, exercises, and a few secrets from the acting trade that will help you learn how to be the person you want to be in public. In preparing these courses, I noticed that most of the traditional texts and manuals on public speaking are full of useful tips—how to build self-confidence, look professional, outline your message, write your speech, improve your memory, look 'em in the eye, and so forth. Some even stress how important it is to be "real" in front of an audience, but they never quite explain just how you get there and pull off the very thing that made De Niro's little talk such a big hit. He seemed like a real person talking about something he really cared about. Did we actually get the real De Niro? I can't say, because I do not know the man. The audience thought so. We certainly got someone who was different from what we see on-screen, and we didn't get a person reading a canned speech to us. It seemed like an extemporaneous conversation. But he wasn't really winging it, either. Yes, he threw away the script, but the experienced performer in him knew that if he tossed it onstage, he'd get a nice laugh and the audience's attention. He also knew that it was his job to deliver the information that the PR people had provided him, which he'd had plenty of time to look at; he told us a bit about the history of the Manhattan Theatre Club, the playwrights and young actors it had nurtured, and its budgetary needs. Then he added his own memories of how important such small theaters were to him as a young actor. All in his own words. The audience loved him for showing up, for caring about the theater—as we all did—and for not speaking *at* us but *to* us, like a friend.

In fact, De Niro was playing another role: himself as public speaker. Like any good actor, you must appear spontaneous and real when you speak in public, whether making a brief introduction or a pitch, whether sitting for an interview or standing in front of large crowd. You must also connect emotionally to your listeners. This is what all good communicators do. Performing well in public (and giving a speech or making any kind of public presentation *is* performing) is not about fancy words, a beautiful voice, or an elevated speaking style. The Hilton audience was riveted by De Niro not because he was a brilliant speaker. He is not even close to that. They loved him because he showed them a De Niro they had never seen before, another New Yorker who shared their passion for the theater. But it was a performance. When I told him that this audience had not come to listen to him deliver a PR person's speech, it did not take De Niro much time to figure out how to play himself giving a speech at a fund-raiser. He was good that night because he applied a lifetime of acting experience to a brief speech.

What, you might ask, is so real or honest about that? My answer: In real life, people are always playing one role or another; in a sense, who we are is the conglomeration of the different roles we play in life, public and private. When I was at Yale School of Drama, my teacher Stella Adler used to say by way of encouragement, "Acting is what you do. That's why you're called actors, not feelers." She meant that in order to create a character onstage, to make a role come alive, you have to be *doing* things from moment to moment in ways that are unique to your character and will achieve his objectives for any given scene. But isn't "acting" what we *all* do? Aren't we always gearing our behavior to the objective at hand? Every day in our life and work, we play many different roles—as friends, lovers, spouses, parents, students, teachers, employees, managers, CEOs, even presidents of the United States. Ronald Reagan was an actor who played the role of president so well that even his political enemies admit he was better at acting that part than any other. During the last presidential campaign, the one thing voters seemed to agree on about George W. Bush and Al Gore was that neither candidate was much of a communicator. Even their closest advisers admitted that each man had difficulty conveying in public the terrific guy they claimed he was in private. People who live in the public eye tend to be more aware of the split between their public and private selves. Actors are particularly self-conscious about the various roles we all play in public, and some of us spend a great deal of time picking up tips about human behavior by watching people go about their daily business.

Psychologists and sociologists have been onto this for decades. Preparing my Harvard lectures, I benefited from Erving Goffman's *The Presentation of Self in Everyday Life,* a book-length analysis of how people in social encounters play different "parts" to create and influence the impressions they wish to make, using, as Goffman points out, some of the same techniques actors do. As dramatists of ourselves, we produce a series of playlets every day. When you talk to your boss, you don't act the same way you do when speaking to your own subordinates. When you meet the head of the mortgage department at the bank, you probably aren't wearing the same face you wear when rendezvousing with your lover. In each setting, you are trying to achieve a particular objective—and act accordingly. *Act Natural* will show you how to prepare your best self for the role of public speaker. How often have you heard someone say about great actors, such as De Niro, Spencer Tracy, Robert Duvall, or Gena Rowlands, "They don't even seem to be acting"? They are acting like mad, of course. That's the skill, and the magic, of it. The hardest thing for actors to do is seem "normal" or "real" while delivering a writer's lines in front of an audience or a camera. Actors are always working on it. There is a technique to creating a sense of spontaneity in a formal situation, and I have come to believe that anyone can learn this technique to inject life into everyday roles (thus the title of my Harvard course, "The Self and the Role"). Yes, you have to learn many different things. But once you get a few things straight, the rest simply falls together. In this book, I will show you:

- How to transform your fear of failing into an advantage

- How you can apply actors' techniques for seeming real and spontaneous onstage to the task of public speaking

- How to structure and clarify your message

- How to train your memory and learn what you want to say so well that you will not forget it under pressure

- How to connect emotionally with an audience—and increase their sense that they are getting a glimpse of the real you

- How to sell your message and persuade your audience to take action

- How to adapt all these techniques to any public situation, from a brief intro or pitch to a major presentation or speech, even a job interview

"Can nonactors really learn this stuff?"

Absolutely. Like many experienced performers, I have taught my share of acting classes. But back in the 1980s, after teaching master classes to actors at Vassar and the American Repertory Theatre in Cambridge and then teaching at Harvard, I realized that I preferred teaching nonactors. Aspiring actors often tend to arrive with a lot of preconceptions and emotional baggage. The Harvard students were not interested in being the next Marlon

Brando. Well, maybe a few were. But, by and large, they were heading in all sorts of interesting directions with their lives. They came to my class hoping to find out how they could take a meeting, sit for a job interview, and, most important, stand up in front of a group of people and impress the hell out of them. *Act Natural* is a combination of what I taught (and learned about teaching), along with the performing techniques I first learned at the Yale drama school from the legendary acting teachers Stella Adler and Robert Lewis, and adapted to my own work and needs over thirty-five years as a professional actor. The ideas, tips, and exercises in this book make up my own approach to helping nonactors prepare for their various roles in everyday life. Some people are just good on their feet, and we have to study them and figure out what makes them appear so relaxed and comfortable in public. Ronald Reagan didn't need this book, but George Bush did. John F. Kennedy didn't, Richard Nixon did. Bill Clinton is a brilliant performer; George W. Bush could use some coaching. In this book, I intend to show you what you can learn from the public personas of politicians and some great American performers. Of course, I can't promise that I'll make you a star. But I will show you how you can walk into a room and do what they do.

"But I don't want to be a phony."

Contrary to some conventional wisdom, acting is not about "faking it." It's about using who you are—your experiences, your emotions, even your terror of performing in public—to create someone people want to watch and listen to. The key to genuine communication, whether you're playing Hamlet, a top job candidate, or VP of marketing, is getting your authentic self before the people in the room. This is not a matter of simply taking yourself public. Frankly, the stakes are too high for only the ordinary you to step forward. You must present the *best* you—a heightened you, a you showing grace under pressure, a you appropriate for the situation, a you who tells the story you want to tell as well as you possibly can to achieve your goals. It is about you *selling* your message to your listeners.

What it is not about is perfection. Winning people over is not about being slick on your feet. I have heard refugees from terrorism and civil war mesmerize audiences in broken English; they are their stories, and that is power and truth enough for any audience. Though a dated example, perhaps, Jack Welch, General Electric's legendary former CEO, can hold a room in awe even though he is a lifelong stutterer. He knows how to step into a room and deliver "Jack Welch," the man who turned GE into one of the most admired corporations in America. Becoming a good communicator is about transferring the relaxed, effortless charm of a private conversation into the public realm. It's about sharing your passion, feelings, and humor. Being good on your feet is about creating a private space in public, the experience that William James called "public solitude." *Act Natural* will hand you that key and help you make sure that when you are called upon to speak in public, the most impressive version of you will show up.

"But I have a rotten memory."

Your memory is better than you think, if you know how to use it. I will show you how my fellow actors and I memorize hundreds of lines in a relatively brief period of time, then stand and deliver again and again before thousands of people with nary a stumble. I will also explain the advantage you have over the actor who cannot stray from the text, whether it's by William

Shakespeare or Neil Simon. The secret is in how you prepare. I will share some age-old memory techniques and show you how to fill the well so high that you'll never come up dry.

"I feel so awkward in public."

We all do, even experienced actors. The quickest route to feeling comfortable in any public situation is recognizing that it's not just about words—it's a physical act. You're not on the radio. How you walk into the room, how you look, what you're wearing, how you stand or sit, what you do with your hands, the angle of your head—it is all part of the whole experience of communicating what you have to say, and you have to prepare what you do as carefully as what you say. I will show you how to make your physical actions and gestures organic, matching your objective rather than seeming like effect.

The thing that provoked the most groans in my classes at Harvard Law School was when I suggested that everyone prepare a song and sing it in front of the class. I have been singing in public since I was a teenager in a church choir. I am convinced that performers at every level can actually learn a lot from professional singers. Frank Sinatra knew it took more than a pretty voice to sell a song. I will show you how a master singer like Sinatra also used his body, his head, and his heart to reach an audience.

"I don't want to be boring."

The best communicators, like the best actors, are able to make an emotional connection to their audience by expressing feelings and humor. That's what made Reagan the Great Communicator. Clinton does seem to feel your pain. Successful entrepreneurs,

CEOs, and leaders in every arena know how to get others emotionally committed to their ideas and strategies. *Act Natural* will show you how you can, in Mark Antony's words, use the "power of speech to stir men's blood" and create a genuine moment the same way that good actors do onstage or in front of the camera. When that emotional connection is made, you cannot be boring.

"Is there a tried-and-true formula?"

No. Since Demosthenes put pebbles in his mouth to cure his speech defect, there has been no shortage of tips and guidelines for becoming a better communicator. Many of them are just plain wrong; dumb, even. So much of what you do depends on who you are, what your message is, and where you're delivering it. For instance: "Dress up." Yeah . . . but that Armani suit, power tie, and $500 tasseled loafers might not go over well with a group of construction workers. (Neither, I should add, will the jeans, boots, and hard hat.) You have to rehearse, as actors say, for the room. Context is crucial. There is no one way to speak in public, because your audience is bound to be different each time, not to mention the setting. Are you making a presentation to a group of colleagues, clients, or bosses? Are you meeting one-on-one with an employee, or with a banker to get a loan to keep your business afloat? Are you selling something, or yourself in a job interview? Are you giving a speech? Is it a happy occasion, a birthday party or wedding, or a funeral? You have to prepare accordingly. "I was great in the shower," people say. That would be useful if you were making your presentation in a shower. *Act Natural* will help you know your audience and the room.

"Aren't actors—and great communicators—
born, not made?"

Some people are certainly more talented than others, but just because you aren't Mozart doesn't mean you can't learn to play the piano well. The inclination is to say that the best performer is the one who seems the least theatrical: Robert Duvall, for example, or Spencer Tracy. "They're just being themselves," people say. Nonsense. They are making all sorts of acting choices that reveal sides of themselves you might not see in real life, even if you were their best friend (for example, desperation, panic, murderous urges, and any other behavior or emotion that might come out in the extremes of a dramatic role). Because they are such good actors, you do not notice the decisions, you do not see the seams; you think they must have just walked out in front of the camera and played themselves. In fact, "being yourself" is extremely difficult, as I suspect you have discovered every time you have to say a few words before an audience, no matter how small or friendly.

But we can all learn to present a better version of ourselves, to bring into public the relaxed and passionate conversationalist that we can be among friends and family. The first step is to realize that every time we try to persuade someone to do what we think they ought to do, we are selling our message and thus ourselves as the messengers. We all strive to make the right impression in various situations. How to do this and sell an idea to others has to be at the heart of any course on communication. To me, the process seems very like the way I work to "sell" a monologue or a song or to make a character come alive. I've had directors say to me, "Okay, that's it. Now sell it!" What they meant was, "You've got the shape of what you're doing; now throw yourself fully into the moment and make it come alive.

Don't worry about the details. The audience is there, you've got them. Just put your heart and soul into it and sell it." Encased in that "just" is a life's work, which was why De Niro was able to turn my simple direction into an impressive moment.

The improvement I saw among my students convinced me of the helpfulness of acting techniques for people who want to overcome their stage fright and enjoy success when presenting themselves and their ideas before a group of people, large or small. I decided that what I taught and, more important, what I learned in the course of teaching would make a useful book. But you also have to do your part. Frankly, this is not a book simply for reading; it is also a manual. And just as acting is about doing things to achieve a particular objective, a good public speaker has to spend time speaking in public. There is no such thing as an armchair speaker (at least outside certain institutions where people talk to themselves). Based on the courses I have taught, this book takes a step-by-step approach. I believe in starting with modest goals and building on the confidence you earn from achieving them. Dealing with a fear of speaking in public is fundamental, so I begin there. True confidence will never come, however, unless you learn what makes a good speech work and how to structure and prepare it. The impact on what you say will depend on how you say it, and that re-quires learning various techniques to appear real and spon-taneous in public. I try to deal with each hurdle as it arises. Finally, effective communication comes through not merely learning what you must do but also doing it—over and over.

At the end of each chapter, I have included an assignment based on the work I required my students to do. I cannot threaten you with a bad grade, but I can emphasize that the only way to get better on your feet is to keep testing yourself. So take my assignments seriously, do the work I advise, and then test the results on friends and family. I never ask for a presentation that is more than a couple of minutes long. I believe that if you can prepare yourself to be impressive in a short speech, the difference between that and being an effective communicator in any arena is only a matter of time and some hard work. You will never improve as a speaker unless you practice speaking.

1

MAKING FEAR YOUR ALLY

Personally, I am always very nervous when I begin to speak. Every time I make a speech I feel I am submitting to judgment, not only about my ability but my character and honor. I am afraid of seeming either to promise more than I can perform, which suggests complete irresponsibility, or to perform less than I can, which suggests bad faith and indifference. —Cicero*

Fear is, perhaps, the ultimate proof that all of us are created equal. Your turn to speak, and suddenly your mouth turns to cotton, your throat is a desert, your voice cracks, your armpits are dripping faucets, your legs are concrete blocks, your heart is running a marathon. In study after study, decade after decade, when people are asked to rate their biggest fears, number one is always speaking before a group of people. You, too, get scared? So what: Everyone does. *Even Cicero!*

Most people assume that professional actors and lecturers have built up an immunity to stage fright. In fact, most actors dread stepping into the lights as much as you do, probably even more, because their careers are riding on it. The great American actress Helen Hayes claimed she used to routinely throw up before making her first entrance in a play. Anthony Hopkins has revealed that he, too, is inclined to get sick to his stomach be-

*From *Cicero* by Anthony Everitt (New York: Random House, 2001), p. 58.

fore going onstage. I recently read an interview with Jane Fonda in which she explained why she was quitting acting: "The older I got and the more experience I had under my belt, the more fearful I got. I don't want to be scared anymore." The daily terror that dogged her brief appearance on the New York stage in *The Vagina Monologues* sealed her decision to pack it in. "I was praying I would be hit by a car," explained the two-time Academy Award winner.

I have been performing in public since I was a teenager, and every single time I'm about to walk onstage or before the cameras, I have been scared. Of what? Let me tell you a story: In 1973 I was onstage in what was then the Uris Theatre on West Fifty-first Street in New York, in one of the early scenes of the opening-night performance of the Broadway musical *Seesaw.* I was standing in a phone booth on one side of the stage, and my costar Michele Lee was standing in an apartment set on the other side. My character was new in town, had just been mugged, and was calling the only person he knew in New York, a girl he had met earlier in a bar. The conversation was supposed to be awkward, but the dialogue was written to be delivered with a quick back-and-forth rhythm: I said something, she said something, I responded, she responded, I reacted, bing-bang. And so it went—until a stage lightbulb popped or flickered as Michele said a line. From my phone booth, there was a pause longer and more awkward than we had ever rehearsed. I had gone blank. That flash of light had derailed me, and I lost my next line. Immediately, I was hit with a wave of stage fright, the worst in my life (this was my first starring role "above the title" in a Broadway musical), and then, mercifully, the line returned to my stunned brain, and I said it. I don't think the audience even sensed that they were watching a career in the balance. After the performance, I asked Michele Lee if she had noticed. "Notice?" she exclaimed. "My heart stopped!" Every actor has forgotten a line, and knows it can happen again. The fear comes from dreading that moment when you are unable to answer the question "What comes next?" You have rehearsed for weeks, you are in the middle of the play, and suddenly something distracts you—a stage light blows, someone is talking in the audience, you look into the eyes of your costar and her nose drips from her cold—and you "go dry" or "go up" or, my favorite, of unknown origin, "go to Cleveland." (Just writing about not knowing my lines onstage is enough to get my own heart pounding.) Many actors have a recurring dream of forgetting their lines or saying them perfectly but in the wrong play. Opening nights always incite the most terror. Producers were often surprised to find me, a few minutes before curtain, perfectly calm and discussing the future of the New York Knicks with a stagehand. What they didn't know was that *after* the show, I would retreat to my dressing room, where I would begin to shake and get very emotional, sometimes to the point of even crying a little. I had survived another opening night as an actor, and the relief was as if I had just avoided a major train wreck. After one opening, I actually threw up. When the comedian Fred Allen was asked why he always gulped down a tumbler of bourbon before his first entrance, he deadpanned: "You don't expect me to go out there alone, do you?"

My goal in this book is to make sure that when you go out there you do not feel so alone. I intend to provide you with so much support that when you appear in public, you will not choke on the pressure. I have devoted this first chapter to the obstacle that everyone must get by in order to be successful in public: controlling the fear. In a sense, this entire book is about dealing with the inevitability of performance anxiety. The ultimate protection from nerves comes from being so well prepared that you will be a relaxed and confident speaker—the subject of the following chapters. But to get from here to there, you first have to deal with the fear. The challenge is to rein in that fear, ride it, and turn it from something that can hurt you into your ally. No matter how scared you may feel at the prospect of stepping into the limelight, you don't have to be wired or medicated. You don't even have to throw up to be good. The primary goal in any performance is to be alive up there, real. Good actors seem to be making it up as they go along, and so should a good speaker, presenter, or job candidate. Performance anxiety stiffens you, makes you seem unreal and robotic. I can help you become more like yourself in public—there are techniques to infuse spontaneity and life into a performance—but I cannot promise to remove the fear.

THE FEAR IS A GOOD THING—HONEST

That tingle taking over your body signals that what you are about to do matters, and if it matters to you, it is likely to matter to your audience. When you're on, you want to be, well . . . *on*. To do that, you will need all the energy you can muster. What distinguishes expert performers and speakers from those who obviously want to be elsewhere is that when they step into the spotlight, they are never alone. But it is not a stiff drink they have on their side; it is their fear. They have learned how to keep the knots in their stomachs from spreading and immobilizing their hands, their throats, or their minds. Instead, they are able to turn the tension into a kind of energy bar from which they can take a bite at any point during a performance. The same anxiety that can immobilize you can also increase your intensity in public. When certain speakers strike you as having more zing, as being so pumped that their enthusiasm becomes yours, they are most probably turning their performance anxiety into an advantage.

To be sure, talented speakers have lots of other things going for them. They are smart, funny, moving; above all, they know what they are doing. I will show you how you, too, can be all of that by breaking down your performance into *what you are doing* from moment to moment. The more ammunition you have, the more relaxed you will be. But you still have to deal with the anxiety to make it useful. Professional performers know that if you aren't scared, you aren't likely to be any good. The better you get at speaking—the more your reputation grows as a skilled communicator—the higher the stakes get, and the more anxious you are likely to become about blowing it. (Athletes, too, feed off their fear of failure. In today's *New York Times* sports page, Tiger Woods says, "The day I'm not nervous when I tee off is the day I quit. In my mind, that's the day you don't care anymore." Those downhill ski racers in the Olympics are amazing, but they are also scared; that's what helps them get to the bottom of the course so fast, and in one piece.)

THE SOURCE OF THE FEAR

What's the big deal? After all, we spend our days talking, and some of us have been known to talk in our sleep. We will bore our families and friends with the details of this project or that, who said what at work, and did you catch that story in the newspaper?—all without the slightest quiver of anxiety. Some stranger on a plane to Albuquerque asks you what you do and three hours later is regretting it. But if you have to answer the same question in front of your daughter's third-grade class on career day, you wish you were dead. Actors are terrified about not remembering their lines, but the public speaker is not likely to have any obligation to a text. So why do we get so scared?

People who cannot face speaking in public are inclined to

think that they suffer from some kind of personality disorder. But nothing is healthier or more rational than performance anxiety, or what is commonly known as "stage fright." Speaking in public will always entail the possibility of failing in public, and there is no feeling in life quite like that of public humiliation. (That is why, I suspect, most people seem to prefer death.) It is one of the ironies of life that when we are about to do something unique to human beings—address an audience—the animal within us takes over. Danger lurks, and suddenly eons of natural selection kick in, the body releases a shot of adrenaline, and we experience a fight-or-flight response. We call it stage fright.

Seasoned performers do not flee; they embrace their stage fright and ride it to victory. I know it sounds like I have just defined masochism—voluntarily putting yourself in the way of pain. But winning over an audience has its own special benefits that can make even the fear seem worthwhile.

WHY DO ACTORS MAKE A CAREER OF TERROR?

There's the prospect of money and fame, of course. And then there's the urge to explore a nascent talent for performing. But I think most good actors would tell you that one of the reasons they face the terror is that on the other side stands an even more remarkable feeling. For when everything works—when the adrenaline, the words, and the charge from a satisfied audience all come together—the result is an experience that even the most nonreligious actors I know can only describe as spiritual. I recently read an interview with the English actor Ben Kingsley (*Gandhi, Schindler's List*), who said that when he is acting, he is in "an ecstatic state of privacy." Athletes call it being in the Zone: a moment when the crowd disappears and you simply cannot miss. The Zone is within the reach of public speakers as well. I cannot promise you nirvana every time, but if you work on the techniques in this book and keep testing yourself in front of various audiences, you will notice how much calmer you are in public; you will even find yourself evaluating the performance and adjusting as you go. My teacher Robert Lewis used to call it "that little birdie on your shoulder." Suddenly, you are able to think faster and more clearly. The presence of others will stir you, and their applause and laughter will give you more confidence, even inspire you. You will move them and you will be funnier. The more you have at stake, the better you will perform. You will appear so confident and at ease that people will think you are making it up as you go along. Indeed, you will get so good at handling yourself and garner enough praise for your skill and charm that you will be eager for the opportunity to do it again.

I guarantee that. But the ticket to getting this good is actually your fear of failure. Therefore, you have to find ways of putting this fear in its place, where it can help you.

DEALING WITH IT

If you've played sports under pressure, you already know what I'm talking about. In 1982 I got my first invitation to play in what was then still called "The Crosby," a celebrity pro-am golf tournament held at three different courses, including the famed Pebble Beach on California's Monterey Peninsula. Bing Crosby came up with the idea in 1937 as a vehicle for his Hollywood pals and professional golfers to hang out together, hit the little white ball, and do some truly professional drinking. In 1947 Crosby moved the event to Pebble, where it stayed. These days the tournament is called the AT&T Celebrity Pro-Am, and though the intimacy and conviviality of Bing's "clambake" are long gone, the one thing that will always remain is the terror among celebrity hackers as they step up to the first tee and hear their names announced.

Back then, although I'd been around golf and played off and on for years, I had only recently taken it up more seriously, joining the long list of what the famous golf writer Bernard Darwin once called "the dogged victims of inexorable fate." When I am acting or singing, my confidence comes from knowing what I am doing. On the first tee at Pebble, I couldn't sing, tell stories, or deliver a monologue by a great playwright. I was required to hit a ball down the fairway, and the prospect of whiffing it or hooking it into the crowd and beaning someone was absolutely terrifying and by no means improbable.

After struggling through three days of practice rounds, I spent the next morning on the practice range, desperately searching for a magical swing to get me through the opening round without major humiliation. For inspiration, I found myself watching Jack Nicklaus hitting balls nearby. He noticed me watching, said hello, and even took the time to say a few nice things about my television series *The White Shadow*. Then he got to the interesting stuff. He had watched me hit a few balls and was kind enough not to point out all my defects; he even warned me about listening to any tips I might receive on the practice range this close to tee-off time. "Thinking about them on the course will just make you crazy," he warned. "Having said that, I'll now give you a tip you can really use." He knew I would be tense playing in front of the crowds, and he served up a technique that would relax me. After my caddy handed me a club, Nicklaus advised me, I should look where I wanted to hit the ball, grip the club, "and then squeeze it really hard while taking a deep breath, then relax your grip and exhale before you step up to the ball and give it a whack." The danger for every golfer playing under pressure, he pointed out, was holding the club so tightly that the tension spread throughout the rest of the body.

I used Nicklaus's relaxation tip during my rounds, and I'm sure it helped me, though not enough to make the cut. But that gave me the opportunity to follow his round on Sunday. I was standing with the crowd near the first tee when he arrived. He noticed me and signaled me to step just inside the ropes to join a small entourage. The starter announced his name, and he teed up his ball and went through his routine. Then I noticed something: As he stared down the fairway at the spot where he wanted to hit his ball, Nicklaus gave the three wood in his hands a hard squeeze and took a deep breath. After exhaling as he relaxed his grip, he stepped up to his ball, performed his famous waggle—and hit the sucker straight down the fairway. Nicklaus then looked over at me with a twinkle in his eye and gave me a gesture with his hands, palms up, that said, "See? Would I tell you to do something that I don't do?" It was a thrill to share this private moment on the first tee with Jack Nicklaus, but it was also instructive to see that the greatest golfer of the twentieth century had to calm his nerves with his own version of the breathing techniques that I learned at the Yale School of Drama.

HOW I AVOID GOING TO CLEVELAND

In the fall of 1985, I was standing in the wings of the ABC studios in Los Angeles, wearing a tuxedo and preparing to emcee a syndicated television show called *Dream Girl USA,* a slightly hipper version of the beauty-pageant format where the beautiful contestants really did have talent. I had two minutes before the announcer said, "Ladies and gentlemen, your host, Ken Howard," before I would walk on the stage into a spotlight and start talking before a live audience of a few hundred people, not to mention millions of others out there in TV Land. As I waited in the wings, a guy with a handheld camera was shooting a behind-the-scenes documentary, and he turned his camera on me. After a few seconds he stopped and said, very politely: "Mr. Howard, I don't mean to bother you, but you *are* about to go onstage. Could you just act a little nervous, pace up or down or something, so we get the idea that something's about to happen? You look like you could doze off." So I did a little pacing and fidgeting to make him happy.

What that cameraman didn't realize was that he had already filmed me in a state of nervous anticipation. Hosting a beauty pageant was hardly the most challenging role of my career, but there were all those people out there, the lights, the cameras, and I had been hired to be good. I was experiencing my customary nerves and working to get them under control. But rather than pacing around and allowing the terror to build, I was in the middle of a series of breathing and visualization exercises that help me relax and lodge the image of a successful performance in my imagination.

For decades medical researchers and psychologists, particularly those who work in education and with athletes, have known that breathing deeply from the diaphragm (also known as "belly breathing") leads to relaxation and increased mental concentration. When we are angry or scared, we tend to breathe more quickly, even pant or choke up (thus the metaphor of "choking" to describe failing to perform under pressure), and our hearts accelerate. Breathing from the diaphragm (the muscle separating the chest and abdominal cavities) involves the entire upper body. As you take a deep breath, the diaphragm moves downward, creating a vacuum in the chest cavity that then draws fresh air into the lower portions of the lungs. As the middle part of the lungs inflates, the abdominal area expands, and then the chest, filling the upper part of the lungs. Full, deep breathing brings larger volumes of air in and out of the lungs, forcing your breathing rhythms to become slower and steadier. The result is a relaxed and soothing feeling in the body. That "knot" of tension you feel in your gut will relax, and so will you. Moreover, this large intake of air will increase the amount of oxygen in the bloodstream, which also tends to increase concentration. When you speak, you have to breathe, and to use your voice forcefully and effectively, you must learn how to control your breath. (A squeaky or nasal voice, for example, will be distracting, and so will speaking too quickly while gasping for breath.) Breath control will come up again and again in this book; good actors and skilled singers can hold an audience on a single breath, and speakers can benefit from the same technique. Here, however, I will limit my discussion to the ways that proper breathing can help you deal with performance anxiety.

Slow, deep breathing is encouraged in exercise and sports (think of a diver taking a deep breath before springing from a board, or a weight lifter inhaling as he picks up the barbell and exhaling as he pushes it over his head). Ancient relaxation techniques such as yoga and tai chi also center upon proper breathing. There are literally shelves of volumes in the bookstores about breathing and stress reduction. If you are fascinated by the subject, I recommend reading a few. Chances are you should be breathing more deeply all the time, not just under pressure. Deep breathing is healthier. Many people tend to breathe through their mouths and throats or high in their chests—the thorax areas—never filling their lungs fully. If you have this tendency, the result is a weak, unsupported voice, general tension, and a decreased amount of oxygen in your bloodstream.

To find out if you are not breathing deeply enough, lie down on your back and place your hand on your stomach, right below the rib cage. Take as deep a breath as you can. If your hand doesn't move or actually moves down, you are breathing totally from your thorax. A proper deep breath—through the nose—will expand your lower abdomen, creating a vacuum in the chest that draws the air into the lower lungs, which inflates the upper part of your stomach, thus raising the hand on your stomach. Further inhaling will distend your chest, drawing in more air until your lungs are completely filled.

Learning to breathe more deeply for its relaxation effect is hardly rocket science. My own breathing techniques will be recognizable to athletes and practitioners of yoga. They also can be learned easily with just a few minutes of practice each day.

BREATHING TO RELAX
Exercise #1

Get comfortable, and focus on some point in the room or on the wall. Then begin counting to ten, emptying your lungs of all the air; push it out as much as possible and then some more. (You will know you've exhaled entirely when you feel you need air.) Now close your mouth and keep it closed, and begin breathing in slowly through your nose, again to the count of ten, slowly and completely filling your lungs. Hold your breath for the count of ten, then release it slowly through your mouth to the count of ten.

This is not as easy as you might think. The inclination is to breathe in too quickly to get the air you need and blow it out too fast after you've held your breath for the count of ten. Concentrate on the rhythm of your counting and keep it consistent while exhaling and inhaling. To make sure you don't exhale too quickly, keep some breath in reserve so that when you get to ten, you can push out this last little supply of air. You might have to experiment a couple of times to get the breathing and counting in sync. I have found it useful to think of my lungs as upside-down ice-cream cones: The point of the cone is the top of the diaphragm. The key is to fill the cones all the way to the bottom and then push the air up from the bottom out of a small opening of your mouth, creating a narrow cushion of air (as if you were blowing on something to cool it).

Sucking in all that air is likely to leave you a bit light-headed, the result of storing up all that oxygen. I recommend sitting down when you first practice this exercise to counter the possible wooziness. Try it: Sit down and release all the air in your lungs—1, 2, 3, 4, 5, 6, 7, 8, 9, 10. Then inhale again through your nose to the same count of ten. Hold it for ten, then exhale for another ten until you've emptied the air from the bottom of your diaphragm all the way up through your lungs and slowly out of your mouth.

Are you more relaxed? There's no way you can't be. If you focus on your breathing, you can sit on it like a cushion that will help relax you and make your nerves vanish.

Exercise #2

This is a simple variation of Exercise #1 that helps you relax a particular part of your body. Some people feel a lot of tension in the neck and shoulders. So instead of breathing into those inverted cones in your midsection, inhale into your neck or shoulders. Use the same procedure as above, emptying the air totally from the part of the body you want to relax, inhaling into that same part of the body, holding the air there, and exhaling from there, each time to the count of ten. As you complete this exercise, you will be amazed at how that part of the body is relaxing. Some people like to work their way up from the ground, breathing into their toes and exhaling, as if the air were contained in their feet. Try that, too. You will find that it relaxes your ankles and feet.

Deep breathing is known to sharpen mental concentration. This is essential to creating the kinds of mental images that will increase your self-confidence when performing under pressure. As I prepare to go onstage, I do the above breathing exercises to relax, but I'm also simultaneously visualizing what I'm about to do in the most positive way possible. If all you can imagine is failure, you will find it very hard to succeed.

GETTING YOUR IMAGINATION TO WORK FOR YOU: THE POSITIVE POWER OF VISUALIZATION

You have to put your fear into perspective. My wife, Linda, is a professional stuntwoman who used to specialize in driving fast, lighting herself on fire, and free falls. Before Linda would jump off the ledge of a tall building (she doesn't do this sort of thing anymore, thank God), she had to release all the tension in her body. She had to relax, but not too much. The adrenaline pumping through a stuntwoman's body keeps her alert to danger, which includes the effects of too much adrenaline. Stuntpeople have been killed because they were so pumped up with adrenaline that they launched themselves too far and overshot the air bag they were supposed to land on.

According to Linda and the other stunt professionals I've talked to, the key to dealing with the fear and getting the stunt right is visualization. The stuntperson can imagine two results— getting hurt or pulling it off. The same goes for performing in public. If all you can imagine is yourself failing, you will never get beyond the shakes. My wife calls it "bad imprinting." The Harvard psychologist Joan Borysenko calls it "awfulizing"— imagining everything that can go wrong. We all do this. What goes through your mind is something like: "I've got to go out there and talk for fifteen minutes before these people, and I have a weak voice. What if the microphone doesn't work and I have to speak more loudly than I'm used to? I won't be able to relate to them properly. And though I am a good salesperson, there are people a lot better than I am. Maybe I'm the wrong person to be making this presentation. Because when I start thinking about what I know, I begin to realize how little I know, and what if people ask me questions I can't answer?" And so it goes.

Once the awfulizing begins, there's no stopping it. Suddenly, you are thinking there's a guy out there in that audience with a gun containing a bullet that has your name on it. In fact, they all have guns, all aimed at you—you're performing before a firing squad! The imagination of disaster is so powerful that even when things are going fine, you find yourself trying to satisfy the one person in the audience who seems to be shaking his head in disagreement. You start saying to yourself, "I know what I'm talking about. I'm good. I'm going to persuade that SOB, too." I have heard the comedian Larry David, who cocreated *Seinfeld,* talk about the comedian's need to persuade the only person in the audience who is not laughing to crack a smile: "Why isn't he laughing? I must've delivered the joke badly." Instead of focusing on the fact that 99 percent of the audience is on the floor laughing, you zero in on the one hard case. This kind of George Costanza view of the universe can be a major obstacle to enjoying speaking in front of people.

To keep from driving yourself crazy with premonitions of disaster, you have to intentionally take your imagination by the hand and walk it in the opposite direction. To visualize yourself being wonderful in front of an audience, you must let your imagination conjure up the moment when your audience is amazed by how relaxed and charming you are. Run a movie of your best possible performance in your head. See their looks of admiration and approval. To be great, you have to imagine the possibility of being great. If the only thing you can see is catastrophe, you definitely increase your chances of fulfilling that prophecy.

I have found that when I'm dealing with fear, I'd better not be bashful. To prove it, I will risk embarrassment by confessing that before I step onstage, I get into a positive mood by employing an internal commentator with a pronounced home-team bias. In my head, I am hearing: "Here comes Ken Howard onstage. From the audience's applause, you can tell people are delighted to see him. He looks great. The guy is positively charming, very funny. Extremely talented. Howard is really on tonight. There is no stopping him." I am also rehearsing my performance in my mind ("Walk slowly out there, couple of easy physical movements, hit the lights, and then say, 'Good evening, ladies and gentlemen, welcome to the premier presentation of . . .'") I also recommend having the first few sentences clearly in mind, and rehearsing any names you might have to say. First impressions are crucial. Recently, a friend of mine from the world of golf, Paul Spengler (executive vice president of the Pebble Beach Company), had to make some introductory remarks at a meeting and asked for a last-minute tip before he went on. Frankly, it was a bit late, but to help him face his audience with a positive image in his mind, I advised: "Whatever you do, glow."

Acting is more than just standing up there and saying the words. Actors are paid to create a role; we are paid to use our imaginations. To succeed at the role of the best possible you, you, too, will have to use your imagination and create a world in which you are happy to be successful. Before you claim that such a feat is beyond your powers of imagination, let me repeat the reason most people are so scared in public: They cannot think of anything but making a fool of themselves. Why is it so hard to see yourself being brilliant? Even if you've never been able to utter a word in front of other people without your heart pounding or your voice cracking, you are bound to be good at something.

We all have had the experience of success. I have always found it curious that people pull off the most amazing feats of skill and courage every day—running corporations, getting into medical or law school, scoring touchdowns, building dams, making a killing in the stock market, having babies—but when they are asked to state their name and where they're from in front of ten strangers, they freeze. I'm pretty sure that improving your speaking skills is nowhere near as hard as having a baby or running General Electric.

Before you are crippled by your lack of confidence in public, start contemplating all the obstacles you have surmounted in life. Think about the times when you were nervous and you were great. Think about your previous successes in school, sports, and at work—when you got the job, won the client, sold your boss on the idea, passed the test, made the shot in the final seconds of the game. Why shouldn't the ability to win over an audience be among those successes? Keep in mind that your audience wants you to succeed; you ought to want the same thing for yourself.

THE CLASSIC "DALE CARNEGIE" TECHNIQUE

There was a time in the United States when training in public speaking was synonymous with the name Dale Carnegie, author of one of the most successful motivational books in publishing history, *How to Win Friends and Influence People,* first pub lished in 1937. But Carnegie's first book was *Public Speaking and How to Influence Men in Business* (1926), based on a course he taught at the 125th Street YMCA in New York City. The book became one of the main texts in his world-famous public-speaking courses. Carnegie was a genuine student of the art of communication, analyzing the work of such great American performers as Abraham Lincoln and Mark Twain for tips to pass along to his students, mainly men looking to get ahead in the business world. Carnegie knew he had to address the issue of fear, and he believed that mental exercises could help. Before a speech or presentation, he advised, even while sitting on the dais or at a table, you should concentrate on relieving tension in your body. Wherever you feel it most, according to Carnegie, you should go there mentally. If your forehead or neck is tightening up, then focus on relaxing it and letting the stress leave you. If it's your shoulders that are stiffening, loosen them.

Psychologists and physiotherapists would certainly agree. Sometimes the easiest way to make tension go away is to tighten that part of the body and then relax it. This is a variation of the Jack Nicklaus trick of gripping the club really tightly, taking a deep breath, and then relaxing your grip as you exhale.

TO BE SELF-CONFIDENT, FIRST TRY ACTING SELF-CONFIDENT

The key to being great in public is self-confidence, and all the breathing exercises in the world will not give you that. You have to be prepared to do some serious work, to push yourself, to expand your imagination. You also have to be prepared to do some acting. "Action seems to follow feeling," William James wrote, "but really action and feeling go together; and by regulating the action, which is under the more direct control of the will, we can indirectly regulate the feeling, which is not." According to James—and many other psychologists since—if you make the effort to act courageous, you will begin to feel courageous. Similarly, to develop self-confidence in front of an audience, begin by acting as if you already have that audience in the palm of your hand. Visualization techniques will help you here, and so will the breathing exercises. Laughing can also help you relax. In drama school, Stella Adler used to show us how, by simply laughing out loud, an actor could transform his mood. How do you make yourself laugh? It is not only a funny story or image that can make you laugh. Breath helps you do it, too. Producing great explosions of breath in the form of laughter will actually create a sense of physical relaxation quite similar to exhaling deep breaths. Manufacture some big laughs, huge Ed McMahon–like guffaws: "HA! HA!" Keep at it, and soon you will be relaxing and feeling better. I find that when I'm a bit down or dealing with some of life's inevitable difficulties, I can start myself laughing and actually transform my mood, at least for a while. (Contrary to the usual warning, *do* try this at home, otherwise people will think you've lost it.)

LOOSENING UP THAT VOICE

One of the first things to go under stress is the voice. Stage fright can cause your throat to constrict, making the voice crack or boosting it to a pitch so high that you sound like a chipmunk. Worse, you can do nothing about it while it's happening. You must work on your voice *before* you go out there. Voice and diction work are an integral part of an actor's training. I entered Yale drama school with a strong natural voice, pretty good diction, experience performing Shakespeare, and classical training in singing. I also naturally breathed deep from the diaphragm. Under stress or in an emotional scene, however, I tended to breathe too fast and more from the chest and neck. My "S" sounds were slightly sibilant, my "T" sounds were splashy, and some of my vowel sounds pegged me as a native of the New York City area. To erase these relatively minor defects, I spent two full academic years at Yale, and three times a week I would lie on my back or sit in the lotus position, humming consonants that opened into long vowel sounds that descended a musical scale: "Ang . . . ah, ah, ah, ah, ah." The exercise forces you to hang on the "ng," feeling its vibration in the mask of your face (the nose and mouth), then releasing it into an open sound —"ah"—that is held and controlled with a relaxed, unconstricted throat as you go down the scale holding the notes evenly. The key is to avoid vibrato and/or breathiness to the final note, a full octave below the first "ah" that came from the "ng" that you originally felt vibrating in the nasal cavity.

I found such exercises extremely effective, but describing them makes for extremely boring reading. Even the little bit on voice improvement that I tried to do with my Harvard students turned out to be a waste of time. To teach anyone almost anything about how to get the most out of your voice requires a detailed analysis of how humans produce sound, and that alone requires diagrams of the head, discussions about middle-sinus resonators and soft palates, experimenting with musical scales, and a vast array of exercises that have to be memorized to be done properly. An on-site instructor is also key, listening and watching and correcting; if you've seen Henry Higgins work with Eliza Doolittle in *My Fair Lady,* you get the picture. (Eliza: "The rain in Spain stays mainly in the plain." Higgins: "Again.") For our purposes, the voice stuff is unnecessary. Effective communicating in the twenty-first century is not about oratory or sounding like a member of the Royal Shakespeare Company. My aim is to help you develop an easygoing, conversational delivery. Most people's ordinary voices and accents will work just fine. Even if you tend toward a dull monotone, my suggestions in the following chapters for how to enliven your performance with feeling will automatically add some colors to your voice.

If you still think your voice needs some serious work, begin with two classic texts: *Freeing the Natural Voice,* by Kristin Linklater, and *The Use and Training of the Human Voice,* by Arthur Lessac.

What you can use are some exercises to help warm up your speaking apparatus before you go on. It is one more way to cope with the fear. In addition to the breathing exercises, I do some things with my voice that help me calm my breathing as well as loosen my tongue before I go to work. Here are several personal favorites that I have been using throughout my career. There are bundles of these that help you get your mouth around various vowel and consonant sounds. Backstage at most plays or musicals can sound like a barnyard, as different actors go through their favorite warm-ups. This one is about practicing the vowel sounds "ah," "eh," "ee," "aw," and "ooh." Repeat them out loud and try to memorize them for future use.

1. PATAKA PETEKE PITIKI PETEKE PATAKA
    PAWTAWKAW POOTOOKOO PAWTAWKAW PATAKA

2. MANALA THAVAZA MENELE THEVEZE
    MINILI THIVIZI MENELE THEVEZE MANALA THAVAZA
    MAWNAWLAW THAWVAWZAW MOONOOLOO
    THOOVOOZOO MAWNAWLAWTHAWVAWZAW
    MANALATHAVAZA

(My wife just looked over my shoulder at this, rolled her eyes, shook her head, and walked away. But try it, and see how quickly it loosens up your tongue and voice.)

3. Now try saying: "Good blood, bad blood" three times, then four times quickly in succession. Then try it again. And again. And maybe again tomorrow. Tough, huh?

4. Here's an easy one that helps wake up the tongue: Trill your tongue so that it makes the sound of a playing card being fanned by a bicycle spoke—"d-r-r-r-r-r."

5. Tongue twisters are also a fun way to loosen up. I had to work hard to deliver this one at high speed when I played Pish-Tush in Gilbert and Sullivan's *The Mikado:*

To sit in solemn silence in a dull dark dock / In a pestilential prison with a lifelong lock / Awaiting the sensation of a short, sharp, shock / From a cheap and chippy chopper on a big black block!

The most efficient and satisfying way to pull this off is to slow down and use repetition until your tongue, teeth, and mind find a way to do it. But have fun with these. The advantage you have over an actor as a speaker is that you don't have to recite a certain phrase or line if it ties your tongue. You're the playwright of your speech. Throw out the offending phrase and replace it with words that are easier to say.

AND WATCH OUT FOR YOUR HANDS

Ideally, you want your hands to be relaxed and gesturing naturally, just as they are when you're talking to friends and family. Many speakers look like robots in an effort to keep their hands from shaking and exposing their nervousness (thus exposing how uncomfortable they are). It is a problem as old as acting itself. As the character Nina in Anton Chekhov's play *The Seagull* laments about her fiasco as an actress: "I didn't know what to do with my hands!" The best actors can stand onstage with their hands at their sides. It is very hard to do. When I am nervous, my hands tend to shake, so I work on coming up with things for my hands to do.

Dale Carnegie advises beginners to clasp their hands behind their backs while wiggling their toes. I'm sure this could help at first, but you will risk looking a bit awkward. Carnegie also suggests carrying a silver dollar or large coin in your hand to squeeze. That, too, could prove distracting to your audience. I find having a lectern to grab hold of is a great help. One of the toughest things to do in public is plant yourself firmly to avoid swaying from side to side. If there is no furniture to hold on to, I would advise beginners to prepare physical things to do during a presentation. Props are useful—charts, blackboards, pointers, anything that will keep you moving like a real person. Such movements will help you to keep focused on the objective of your speech and its structure; they will also make what you're saying easier to remember—all issues I will be addressing in the next three chapters. But for now let's get your fear under control with a little workout.

Your First Assignment

Prepare a sixty-second statement—just your name, what you do, why you want to be a better public speaker, and something about yourself that will make an impression on the audience. One minute with some charm, some humor, even a little emotion. Above all, be yourself. Work on it, try it out on your family or friends—but not before you also spend some time controlling your anxiety with the breathing exercises and visualization techniques.

One minute to say your name and introduce yourself—like a little kid at summer camp? Absolutely. It is not as easy as you think. In fact, I would wager that the last time you were at a meeting or a conference and the host asked you all to introduce yourselves, your heart immediately began to beat faster. Though

stating your name and what you do seems like nothing, introducing yourself to a group of strangers in a relaxed, self-
confident, and charming way adds up to almost everything it
takes to be a good communicator. Whether you are giving a
major address or a small presentation or are just introducing
yourself to a new group of people, your goal is the same: to
make a good impression. That is worth some preparation and
work. Spend at least a couple of days on this one-minute intro.

I first discovered how revealing this exercise could be as I
began teaching the original master class at the American Repertory Theatre in Cambridge. When I asked the acting students
to prepare to introduce themselves to their fellow classmates, a
number of them were contemptuous. After all, they were *actors*
who were expecting to work on scenes from Chekhov and
Shakespeare, and here I was starting off with this summer-camp
stuff. It turned out that most of those aspiring actors could not
hold an audience even for a minute. Some of them tried to be so
cool that they actually failed to state their own names. So the
following year, when more than 150 Harvard undergraduates
showed up for a course that I had designed for 30, I turned to
my summer-camp exercise as a way to separate the serious kids
from those who had come to see if the Hollywood guy could actually talk in complete sentences. At the end of my introductory
lecture (imagine my anxiety about speaking to a roomful of Harvard kids about how I could teach them to be good speakers—
talk about putting your money where your mouth is), I asked
those who were still interested to return the following week prepared to spend one minute in front of the class explaining who
they were, what they were studying, and why they wanted to
take a course in public speaking. I also suggested they include a
remark or an anecdote that would leave an impression on the
audience, a little piece of themselves.

More than 120 came back for more. Some of them were just

great—smart, funny, even touching, and clearly talented. One guy did a very funny bit about living with his name, one of those grand old WASP monikers comprised of three surnames with a Roman numeral after it. Another fellow went on about what an honor it would be to study with someone as famous in show business as the teacher of this course and proceeded to list some of the highlights of "Mr. Howard's remarkable career"—all of which were the credits of the actor-director Ron Howard. A very talented girl gave a street-smart account of what she was doing at Harvard, what her goal was (to be a rock star), and ended by saying, "And on another note"—and then hit a high C! The kids loved it, and so did I. One student caught my attention as he discussed in a lovely, lilting island accent what it was like for a boy from Jamaica to be at Harvard. Intelligent and witty, he was like a young Sidney Poitier. Only later did he reveal that the Jamaica he was from was actually Jamaica, Queens, a few miles from New York City. It was such an impressive performance that I still remember it clearly almost fifteen years later.

Many of the students were awful, scared to death and scrambling to avoid humiliation. But I had decided that my only real criteria for selecting students was whether they could convince me that they really wanted in. After all, the goal of the course was to help people get better on their feet. I could not expect everyone to be brilliant from day one. If they had been, there was no need for the course. I eventually admitted sixty-four students, including a few who cornered me and begged to be let in. How could I stand in the way of such motivation? Two of them emerged among the best in the class, and the third was better than average.

So try out the assignment. Figure out what you want to say and work on it over a couple of days, a few minutes here and there, using the tips and exercises I have outlined in this chapter to control your fear of failure. Then test it out on a few friends or family members. Maybe even talk your significant other or a friend into coming up with his or her own one-minute presentation. Turn it into a game—whatever it takes to get yourself to stand up in a potentially embarrassing situation and talk for a minute, which is, incidentally, a long time. (Stare at your watch for the next sixty seconds, and consider how many words could fill that time.) But don't hurry. And don't go too slow. Go only as quickly as you need to. The great Jack Benny did a run-through for one of his final performances on television, and the young director came up to him to say, "That was great, Jack. The only thing is that tonight, when we do it, if you could just pick up the pace a bit and do it a little faster, it will all be fine. Okay?" After a pause, Benny said "Well . . . sure . . . but it won't be funny."

A couple of tips: Organize what you want to say—a beginning, a middle, an end—write it down, study it, get it clear in your mind. Then throw the paper away. Don't memorize it word for word; that will only tighten you up and get you worried about forgetting what you had to say. If you have a few shiny phrases, they will be there after you've worked on the piece for a few days. Later in the book I will devote a section to improving your memory. For now go with what you're used to. As you prepare, think about yourself delivering this little one-minute speech. Visualize where you'll be doing it, get the room in your mind's eye; go through the motions as if you were an astronaut preparing to be rocketed into space. The space program uses simulators so that by the time astronauts have to do these jobs while hurtling through space, they will have already done them many times before in Houston. Test-drive your presentation so that when you do it for real, it won't seem like you're doing it for the first time. And remember to stay focused on your purpose. (For the Harvard students, their purpose was to get into the class. Your goal is to make a good impression, to be better than you have been before.)

When you practice alone, do it *out loud*. Trust me. I know it may seem a little strange at first, but it makes a big difference. Think of it this way: You're not really talking to yourself, you're talking to other people who just don't happen to be there. I guarantee that if you put in the work, when you deliver your introduction in front of other people, you will be pretty good, maybe even very good. The words will be there, and you will be comfortable with them because you've been practicing. It will be as if there were a tape playing in your head with the whole minute's presentation on it. If you are really well prepared, you might even have the sensation of watching yourself do it, hovering above the event as if you were the novelist of your own speech. Most important, you will discover how useful a few days' worth of preparation is for putting fear in its place.

NOW FOR THE HARD STUFF

Being good on your feet is about more than not being scared. Once you understand how to put the fear in its place, then you can concentrate on becoming skilled. The ultimate way to conquer fear in public is to get good at appearing in public. You want to be calm and cool; you also want to be smart and funny and moving. But what is most important is that you remain alive and in the moment, truly communicating with the audience— relaxed, but making sure that your feelings are still available to you and that your intense desire to communicate is apparent. You want to personally connect with your audience.

That's what the rest of this book is about: showing you how to prepare so well that when you speak in public, not only will you not look scared, you will also be able to do it without notes. You want to look so calm and relaxed that you seem to be making it up as you go along, with humor and emotion. And throughout your entire performance, you want your audience to know that you are speaking *to* them and not at them. To achieve this, you must learn how to be in total control of the entire performance. Your words are connected to ideas, and each idea is tied to an action, which in turn flows into the next action. Every public statement, whether a brief introduction or a long speech, should have a logical shape. When you practice that shape and rehearse the words and actions that inform it, you will step into the room and initiate the first action that will take you all the way to the final one. Just like any good actor.

"But I am not an actor!" you protest. And my answer to that is: Acting is what we all do every day of our lives.

2

"ACTING IS WHAT YOU DO"

(AND SO IS PUBLIC SPEAKING)

This morning I was having coffee with my wife, discussing what we had to accomplish today: I would take the dog to the vet before I went to the studio; she would get the mail and pick up something for dinner. We then discussed other, more intimate matters, and the phone rang. It was my agent. I switched from loving, devoted husband to professional actor concerned about what new projects were in the works and getting paid for the jobs I had already done. Later I went to the set of *Crossing Jordan,* the new television series I'm in, where I became a working actor performing the role of a retired Boston cop whose beloved daughter is a skilled forensic scientist with no social life and a tendency to infuriate her superiors. On the set, I joked with the crew—not as that Boston cop "Max Cavanaugh" but as myself, the actor who enjoys hanging out on the set. After the shoot, as I walked toward my parked car on the lot at Universal Studios, I saw some tourists noticing me. A few nodded or waved as they went on their way, while others couldn't restrain themselves and called out my name or asked for an autograph. I was friendly without trying too hard to play the modest TV star. On the way home in the car, I called my mother and was the dutiful son. Right now I am playing a role that's unusual for me—author of this book.

Does that make me some kind of man of a thousand faces, a person with no center, a pure phony? I don't think so. I like to think I was just being me, dealing with my personal, family, professional, public, and private obligations. My manner, attitude, and feelings may have been different in each case; even my voice, walk, and posture may have changed. But in every case, I was the real me, though playing a different role according to what I was doing (my action), why I was doing it (my objective), and where and with whom I was doing it (my circumstances). Who does not do this?

We all walk around wearing different masks. Who are we, really—the person who exists in our head or the one who lives in the opinions of others? We are all those people. What we do and how we go about doing it in different circumstances is what reveals who we are—our character. After World War II, the sociologist Erving Goffman began to analyze human social interaction, using the metaphor of theatrical performance. According to Goffman, whose 1959 book *The Presentation of Self in Everyday Life* has been a staple of psychology and sociology courses and is still in print, "the part one individual plays is tailored to the parts played by the others present." Often we are both performer and audience member, trying to influence and impress each other. And like actors, Goffman says, we use certain "dramatic effects" to make an impression in our various public roles.

Sometimes we are called upon to play the role of public speaker. Why not learn to play that role extremely well? In Goffman's world, we are actors without knowing it. In mine, once we understand that we are acting all the time, then it makes sense to learn what actors do to make their characters impressive—and the role of public speaker has much in common with acting. The character that you have to perfect is the best version of yourself—for that occasion and that audience. Not a phony version of yourself, just a better-prepared version. Making a presentation, sitting for a job interview, or speaking before a large audience is nothing like chatting at the breakfast table. You must take your daily self, ratchet it up for this new role as speaker, and put it on display. What impression do you want to leave? I am assuming you do not want people to think you are terrified, that you don't have anything to say, that you are a knucklehead, or worse, a poseur, a fraud. Is there something about the way you present yourself that will get so much in the way that you are bound to fail? As an actor often on the lookout for behavior I might use in my work, I am inclined to be very sensitive to the kind of role-playing that most people do just to get through the day. But some of it is transparent to anyone: the salesman who comes on like your new best friend, the doctor who could use a personality transplant, the colleague who claims to have your interests at heart when it is clearly only his own that engage him. We are inclined to say that they are just going through the motions; we might even describe their behavior as bad acting. Why? Well, good salesmen or doctors do not *act* that way.

All audiences have their expectations—of doctors, salesmen, friends, bosses, parents, you name it. When you take on the role of speaker, you have to live up to that part. You want to win the job, get the bank loan, make the sale, raise money, entertain the wedding guests, convey an image of the deceased from the old days, get people to vote for you. Your audience is likely to have heard a terrific version of every one of these performances, and they will judge you accordingly. Your toast to the bride and groom, for example, should be very different in tone and style from the eulogy you deliver at an old friend's funeral. And while that may seem pretty obvious advice, why is it that most folks are equally stiff and unreal in both situations? Too many people think the point is simply to give a speech or to say what must be said. But why are you saying it? What are you trying to accomplish? What kind of show are you putting on? If you plan and orchestrate what you are doing in ways that are as intelligent, charming, humorous, sincere, and moving as you can be, you will appear alive and natural to your listeners. Why? Because they will recognize your actions as the way real people behave in those situations.

Before I can teach you how to match your behavior to your objectives, let me explain what it is that actors do to gain your attention and admiration.

WHAT IS IT THAT GOOD ACTORS ARE GOOD AT?

It has been my experience that even people who are passionate about theater and film—including some directors, writers, and critics (particularly critics)—are a little fuzzy about why certain actors impress them. It is their "stage presence," or their "charisma," their "truthfulness," or even more vaguely, they are "just naturals." But when you watch remarkable actors like Marlon Brando, Robert Duvall, Al Pacino, and Gena Rowlands, what do you think constitutes their brilliance? Everyone seems to agree they are good. But what is it that everyone agrees on? Why is it that such actors are riveting even when they are doing nothing onstage or on-screen but listening to another character talk?

Because good actors are always doing something that makes an impression and holds your attention. That is the definition of acting: *performing tasks to achieve an objective in a particular situation*. In life, we are pursuing goals all the time, and when an actor onstage or in film pursues objectives that resemble those that people might pursue in real life, audiences are moved to say that the performer seemed real. Watch Brando in *On the Waterfront* or in *The Godfather*. He is mesmerizing when he is talking and when he is listening, when he is physically active and when he is still. I have studied Brando in both of these films again and again, and he never looks like he's acting at all. Every bit of his behavior is convincing, including the silences. But try it yourself. When untrained, or badly trained, actors attempt to do what they do naturally every day in real life (performing simple tasks, walking, talking, listening), they look like they're acting; they don't seem real. That is the irony—and magic—of it: Good actors are acting like mad and look real, while bad actors try to be themselves and end up looking phony.

Too many critics seem to suggest that gifted actors simply walk out on the stage and let the magic happen, as if they were inspired by the gods. This is, of course, nonsense. Violinists must practice for hours every day, dancers work on every move of every part of their bodies, painters paint over their mistakes time after time, and writers write and rewrite. Why would anyone think that even the most talented actors could be successful without spending time on their voices, their diction and breath control, their bodies, their relaxation and coordination, and their imaginations? In creating a role, there are lines to memorize and basic blocking to learn, to be sure; but for an actor to make his character come alive and move and mesmerize an audience, the sweat must go into figuring out what he ought to be doing as that character and why. Like the violinist, dancer, painter, or writer, the actor has to find the overall objective in what he or she is doing, and let that objective inform every detail of the work. Above and beyond the greatest technical virtuosity, this is what "technique" is really all about.

"Acting is what you do," Stella Adler used to say to us in her acting class at the Yale drama school. "That's why they call you 'actors' and not 'feelers.'" What she meant was that, as an actor, you must do more than speak your lines, move around the stage, and express emotion; you must always be engaged in an action to achieve an objective. Stella wasn't referring to a mere physical activity such as opening a door, taking off a hat, having a drink, or waving good-bye. She was talking about the moment-to-moment playing out of an overall objective in a scene. For example, if an actor is playing a mother whose home has been invaded by terrorists, the preparation might go something like this:

> *My overall action is to protect the lives of my children. To accomplish this, I will engage in numerous actions, all of which support this overall action. I might try to prevent the terrorists from realizing there are children in the house by keeping them away from the children's room. I might try to distract them by getting them to relax, making them laugh, befriending them, or even going so far as to try to arouse them sexually. Maybe I will try to gain their trust by convincing them that I am interested in their safety, or go the opposite direction and try to scare them.*

And so on. The choices this actor makes are limited only by her imagination and the circumstances of the scene. She can do any one of these things or a combination of them; she might even do all of them simultaneously. For isn't that the way real people act in such crazy, scary situations?

At the heart of this kind of role preparation is performing what Stella called "logical actions" in imaginative circumstances—behavior that serves the overall action of the play. By logical actions, Stella (and Constantin Stanislavski) meant those that serve the overall action of the play and therefore have their own interior logic. Say, for instance, the mother in the play asks the terrorists who have invaded her home, "Would you like something to drink?" Here she is doing something more than offering them refreshment. She might act more obsequious than her character has ever been or with more charm or sexuality. But the last thing a good actor would do in this sort of scene is act scared. For this mother, protecting her children is paramount, and it is this overall objective that breathes life into the line and performance; it is this determination that continues the action of the scene—and holds the attention of the audience, who will be occupied by wondering whether she will succeed in keeping the terrorists from harming her children.

Creating real, believable characters onstage and on-screen is the art of acting. By understanding clearly what their characters are about in the context of that play or film—and doing it as if they are those people in real life—actors are able to peel away everything that doesn't contribute to that impression. This is what it means to inhabit a role. Each action serves the role and its objectives. Stella Adler would warn acting students, "Don't go to the words!" She was certainly not encouraging anyone to paraphrase the text or improvise on it. Stella did not believe in wandering far from the world of the play itself. Her goal was to unite the actor and his part within the boundaries of the text. In discovering the actions and objectives of their characters in a particular scene, actors often find that the words they say are the least of it. Of course, they have to understand what they're saying and never give the impression that they are mindlessly reading from cue cards in their head. But you cannot take your eyes off actors who work this way. They connect to audiences because they seem real, and they seem real because of what is going on beneath their behavior. What they do—how they *act*—is guided by the objectives of the character.

In a recent television interview before a live studio audience filled with actors, Gene Hackman illustrated the challenges an actor faces with a painfully personal story from his childhood. His parents had been having problems, and one day when he was playing with his friends, his father drove by and gave him "a little wave." As soon as the young Hackman saw the wave— the way it was delivered, the expression on his father's face—he knew his father was leaving and would never come back. He was right. It was just a "little wave," but when Hackman re-created it in the interview, that small gesture was informed by human emotions that last a lifetime. For an actor to bring a similar wave into a movie or play, he must understand and feel all the emotional history embodied in the gesture itself. What he does and how he does it will reveal the truth of the moment in much the same way that Gene Hackman did in his interview.

WHERE ACTING AND
PUBLIC SPEAKING CONVERGE

Those of us listening to Gene Hackman were moved by his childhood memory not because he broke down and wept—in fact, he kept his emotions in check. Nor were we impressed by his way with words. His account was quite prosaic, no fancy phrases or exclamation points, just the facts and the wave. What was compelling about his story (his mini-speech, if you will) was that as he described the exact moment he realized that his family had come apart, the pain of a lifetime was present in his voice and face. When he simulated his father's wave, the turn of his wrist summed up the sadness, defeat, and embarrassment that Hackman had felt that day in his childhood or whenever he thought about it throughout his life. He had revealed to us a raw nerve, something that every actor in his audience knew he used in his acting work. But it was that same emotional component, brought to life with a gesture, that made Gene Hackman such a compelling storyteller.

That is the challenge in being a good communicator. You must make an emotional connection to your audience, share a piece of yourself, reveal that you and they are standing on common ground. As he told his story, Hackman was more speaker than actor, but the same thing made him riveting in both realms: his ability to be real and truthful by acting in a way that served his objective and was perceived as real. Every speaker should strive for the same effect. Your audience wants you to succeed. They have come to hear your story and relate it to theirs. But you'd better have your message straight and make sure everything you say and do contributes to it. Like an actor, you must be clear about your objective; you must, in Stella's terms, "play the action." Stella's point was that an actor can achieve reality in a work of fiction only by knowing exactly what his character is doing, what his action and purpose are, within the play's parameters of style and content.

My point—taking Stella's advice into the arena of public speaking—is that as we move through our busy lives, talking to various friends and colleagues, we are switching roles continually. But we always have an overriding purpose in mind that fits the context, and we choose what we say and do to achieve that purpose. A boss who must meet with employees to discuss why sales are down will make his case in a different way from how he explains the same information to his own boss. In the first case, his purpose is to find out what went wrong, maybe even kick some butt. But when he walks into his boss's office, his goal will be to get out of the meeting with his job. Same facts, different objectives, and therefore different actions or demeanor. When Bill Gates introduces a new product to his Microsoft marketing team or to the media, he must convey his enthusiasm and passion for the product so that they will go out into the marketplace and do the same. If he slouches into the meeting, displays the product, and shrugs, he and his product are in trouble. His actions do not serve his overall objective. That wave Gene Hackman described cannot be any wave; it must be a wave with a purpose—the kind a father would give as he says good-bye to his young son, perhaps forever. The pitch you make to the bank manager for a loan is bound to be different from your toast at your best friend's wedding. But the way you make the case for more bank financing to keep the company growing—you're smiling, you're pumped, you can show them the sales graph that looks like a rocket launch—will differ when you need that loan to keep the business from going under: Here you must bury your frustration and doubts and turn on the charm, backed with whatever figures and predictions might prove that with another infusion of cash, profitability is right around the corner. It is conceivable that someone who didn't know you and sat in on both meetings—a bank manager in training, for example—might not even recognize you as the same person. How many times have we failed to recognize someone when we meet them out of context? In the eyes of others, what we do often adds up to who we are. So when the woman coming out of the movies says hello, it takes you a few seconds to realize she's your dentist, because you've never seen her without her white coat, glasses, and drill. Could that man at the end of the bar laughing out loud and with his arm around a beautiful woman really be the local undertaker? All of us are known by the roles we play. (One of the persistent frustrations of the acting life is the director or network executive who won't consider you for a role because you were so convincing in your previous roles. CBS, for example, originally had difficulty seeing me as an ex–pro basketball player turned high school coach in *The White Shadow* because they viewed me through my previous stage and TV roles as an uptown WASP and sometime lawyer. In fact, the lead in *The White Shadow* was less of a stretch for me as an actor than most of my previous work; as a former high school and college basketball player, I had a lot more personal experience about how coaches acted than Wall Street lawyers.)

Matching your behavior and demeanor to your objective is an important lesson anyone can learn from the craft of acting. It is an area where the public speaker actually has a head start on the actor. First of all, you do not have to create a role. The role is you—as public speaker. It is the difference between Gene Hackman playing his father in a movie and Gene Hackman telling the story of his life. The storyteller does not have to work at finding the character; he *is* the character. The character's emotions are his own. His story finds its outline in the events of his life. Will he forget the details of such a story? More likely, his hardest task will be to figure out which details to leave out.

The second advantage that you as a speaker have over the actor is that you are not tied to a playwright's words; you do not have to memorize what you say verbatim. For this playlet—your public appearance—you are the creator. Some of you might see this lack of a script as a distinct disadvantage. Many view the writing of a speech with almost as much trepidation as delivering it. I have some very simple advice for how to deal with the fear of writing:

Never write a speech.

You will never be able to convey any sense of reality by reading a speech. Even if you are blessed with a natural photographic memory, do not write your speech and memorize it verbatim. That, too, is likely to undermine your effort to seem spontaneous and real. In the next two chapters, I will explain how to prepare and remember the kind of presentation that is more likely to impress an audience than the customary recitations or bad readings that most of us are subjected to. For now let me say that the opportunity to give voice to a great writer's thoughts is never what makes an actor impressive. Anyone who has seen an amateur version of Shakespeare or a Tennessee Williams play knows that the words are the least of it. Yes, writers provide the words; but what the actor brings onstage is something for the audience to hear and *watch*. The theater is not radio. Anyone who goes with a copy of the play and keeps his eyes on the text rather than on the stage is missing the point. You have to watch how the actors are making the writer's words come alive. That is what grabs you about Pacino or Rowlands. They communicate what their characters are like as people through what they do from moment to moment. In this way they find the truth in their roles. How can something be "true" when it is played out in costumes and makeup, with fake swords, papier-mâché boulders, or a full orchestra in the pit? That world may be make-believe, but the actor's behavior and expression of feeling are real. The audience can detect phoniness from all the way up in the cheap seats. I'm not sure this detection is even a conscious thing; I think it is more a visceral reaction to what is true and not true. George Burns liked to say that the key to great acting was sincerity, because "If you can fake that, you can fake anything!" But I don't believe you can fake any emotion night after night. And certainly no actor can fake it when her face is projected twenty feet high in an on-screen close-up. The camera photographs thought, and if there is nothing going on behind that big, beautiful movie-star face, audience members will soon be checking their watches or wondering what they should order for dinner.

Your audience will be no less demanding. They will not hold your words against you, but if you are insincere, trying to manipulate their emotions, posing as something you are not, or just plain unprepared, they will hate you for it. Hackman's simple story was effective because it was filled not with shiny phrases but with real life. I know many brilliant writers who are awful speakers. Imagine trying to deliver a transcript of a speech by Winston Churchill or Martin Luther King, Jr. No matter how good you are, you won't be Churchill or King. Ronald Reagan had some very talented speechwriters, but who would you prefer to listen to—Reagan or the speechwriters? Churchill, King, and Reagan all added value to the words. They brought their own intensity and convictions and histories to each speech, along with an actor's ability to put those feelings on display. And here lies the key to being an effective communicator:

It must be just you telling your story.

The audience has to have a sense that they are getting the real you. They have come to hear you talk, and there you are in the flesh, being you, sharing your life or your expertise or your passion for a cause. If you are nervous, uncomfortable, looking stiff or out of place—in other words, if you are not you—they will feel cheated, and you will lose them. This ability to get real in public explains the success of popular talk-show hosts who give a kind of performance that lies between acting and public speaking. For years, every weekday, Oprah Winfrey and Rosie O'Donnell entered America's homes, and who in their adoring audience doubted that they were getting the real Rosie or Oprah? These two women are masters at bringing their best selves in front of the cameras every day—no matter what personal or family problems might be distracting them off-camera. They strike me as naturals in public. Yes, they have done some good acting in film and TV, but their acting success comes at least in part from their instinctive ability to be real in front of strangers. Rosie also has the added value of having spent years on the road as a stand-up comic, playing the wiseass plump girl from a working-class Irish-American family from Long Island. She was that girl, but that was not exactly the real Rosie. For as real as Rosie and Oprah seem on TV, they are also performing under considerable pressure—as we all must in public situations.

To act natural in such pressure-packed situations, you will have to put in the same kind of work that any good actor (or talk-show host or stand-up comic or politician) would do for a role. Actors are not making it up as they go along; nor should you even think of winging it. But to give the appearance of spontaneity, you have to prepare and practice. If you are clear about the objectives—what message you want to convey to a particular audience at a particular time—and if you prepare with those goals in mind, the way you achieve those objectives during your presentation is what will make you an effective speaker—and performer. Remember, if you are awake, you are always, in some sense, *performing*. And when you are performing, you must have a purpose in mind. For the public speaker, this purpose is generally getting a certain message across. And if you are not clear about what that message is, you can't expect your audience to get it.

WELCOME TO THE METHOD

By the time I had the honor of studying with Stella Adler, she had been teaching acting for more than thirty years. Among her students were Marlon Brando and Robert De Niro, who both have made a point of acknowledging the profound impact she had on them. Stella Adler grew up in the theater world. Her parents, Jacob and Sarah Adler, were the reigning stars of New York's Yiddish Theatre in the early 1900s. Stella reported that her first childhood memory was of her mother in a red dress, sweeping her up in her arms and kissing her. At the time Sarah Adler was playing Nora in Henrik Ibsen's *A Doll's House,* with Stella and her brother, Luther, playing Nora's children. By the mid-1920s, Stella had already performed in more than a hundred plays.

In 1929 she became one of the first members of the Group Theatre, founded by Cheryl Crawford, Lee Strasberg, and Harold Clurman, whom she eventually married ("So that I could divorce him!" she would later explain). The Group was a collection of actors, writers, directors, and designers of a distinctive left-wing persuasion, including the successful playwrights Clifford Odets and William Saroyan. Their goal was to bring to New York, and then all of America, a new kind of theater and style of acting that had been developed during the turn of the century at the Moscow Art Theatre, founded by Constantin Stanislavski and Anton Chekhov, the author of at least three of the greatest plays in the history of modern drama, *Three Sisters, The Cherry Orchard,* and *The Seagull.* In Chekhov's plays, the characters just seem to exist. Their inner lives are more important than the plot; nothing and everything seems to happen. In *The Cherry Orchard,* for example, the action never leaves the drawing room, yet Russian history changes before your eyes. Stanislavski sought to create a kind of acting that would inject life into the revolutionary plays that his friend Chekhov was writing. He believed that the actor was responsible for getting the playwright's truth onto the stage. Before walking in front of the audience, every actor had to create a fully rounded character, including a past that existed before the action of the play. "You cannot do the present onstage unless you have ten thousand more pages about the past," Stella used to say in her lectures on Stanislavski, whose method soon became known as the Method, and modern acting was born.

By 1934 Stella was clashing with Strasberg, another strong personality who was also an inspiring acting teacher, over their interpretations of Stanislavski's method. Stella felt that Strasberg's approach allowed an actor to stray from the text and depended too much on the ability to recall emotional moments from his own past during performance, risking an emotionalism that was difficult to modulate and control. She would later concede that such idiosyncrasies might work for movies, in which an editor can cut out moments when an actor gets too carried away. But Stella always insisted that if the actor got out of control onstage, he could sink the whole play. Strasberg also encouraged actors to inject their own personalities into a role; in Stella's opinion, if an actor depended only on his own personality traits, he wouldn't have any range. The actor with a regional accent, for example, or the lanky American hard-guy type, might be great for contemporary roles, but the same mannerisms would be absurdly out of place in Shakespeare or Greek drama. (Think of Paul Newman or Robert Redford, both extremely talented actors, in togas.) The Strasberg acolyte always risked pulling the audience out of the fictional role of the play. ("Why is that Greek hero speaking with a New York accent?")

Stella decided to clear things up with the great man himself. She found Stanislavski in Paris and worked with him every day for five weeks, until he begged her to stop and allow him to spend some time with his family. Legend has it that as the ocean liner docked in Manhattan, Stella could be seen at the railing in a big Parisian hat, her blond hair blowing in the wind, waving to her friends from the Group and exclaiming, "We've been doing it all wrong!" Stanislavski's method had a tremendous impact on

American acting. He always insisted that his system was based entirely on studying what great actors did onstage. "Why does this actor hold my attention more than the others do?" he asked. "What makes that actor so believable?" What good actors had in common, according to Stanislavski, was "the playing of actions," and he made it the bedrock of modern acting technique. It was not just saying the words and expressing emotions, but *doing* what such a character would do as he said those things. What was the purpose of the scene? What was that character's objective? For Stanislavski, the answers to such questions were central to creating a living character.

Though Stella and Strasberg disagreed on how actors should go about creating emotion onstage, they both acknowledged the importance of playing the actions. They concurred that what great actors are great at is coming up with original behavior by using their imagination and focusing on the intentions of their characters. Stella began giving lessons at the Group on Stanislavski's method to actors such as Sanford Meisner, who would eventually start his own successful acting school; Elia Kazan, one of the most influential stage and film directors of the twentieth century (*Death of a Salesman, A Streetcar Named Desire, On the Waterfront*—and thus, according to Marlon Brando, the other great influence in his evolution as an actor); and Robert Lewis, the director and teacher who became the Method's most sensible explicator (I highly recommend a trip to the library for Lewis's entertaining collection of lectures on acting, *Method— or Madness?*). When the Group broke up in 1939, Stella established her own acting school and also taught at Yale, where I first met her, sixty-five years old but still beautiful and a force of nature. Stella Adler died in 1992 at the age of ninety-one, but her influence and her legacy endure. The Actors Studio was founded in 1948, and Lee Strasberg's disciples include such stars as Paul Newman, Marilyn Monroe, Walter Matthau, James Dean, Al Pacino, and Ellen Burstyn, an extraordinary line-up whose work has influenced several generations of younger actors.

THE METHOD OF PUBLIC SPEAKING: FINDING THE "JUICE"

That sense of authenticity you get from the great Method actors, how natural and real they seem, is what you want when you speak in public. I believe that anyone willing to put in the time can learn how to appear spontaneous in a public forum using techniques from Stanislavski—via Stella, Bobby Lewis, and me. But first you must get the hang of the Method's central principle: "playing the action." And to do that, you have to be very clear about the objective of your speech or presentation. I recently read an interview in *The New York Times* with the talented movie director Ang Lee (*Sense and Sensibility; The Ice Storm; Crouching Tiger, Hidden Dragon*), who explained that before he could direct a movie, he had to be clear about its central theme, the heart of the work, what he called "the juice." *Crouching Tiger* can be viewed as an artsy version of the Hong Kong martial arts flick. In addition to the amazing fight sequences and special effects, however, the movie portrays an intense love affair between a man and a woman, both medieval Chinese warriors, equally beautiful, brave, and skilled. They also have something else in common: They cannot express their true feelings. "The repressed emotional wish," Ang Lee said, "that is the hidden dragon."

Very Stanislavski. Stella would have said that the characters in Ang Lee's film were playing the actions of repressed lovers. Everything they did as actors—and Ang Lee did as a director— was filtered through that central theme, "the juice," or, as Stella would have called it, "the spine" of the screenplay. Every time that man and woman were together in a scene, they did things that made you aware of their unspoken love for each other. "Find the key to the role," Stella used to say when she was teaching. Brilliant actors such as Pacino, Brando, Duvall, Hackman, Streep, and Rowlands are particularly skilled at finding the key that lets them into the inner life of their characters, which, in turn, influences how that character will act onstage.*

Actors of this caliber are so talented at preparing and playing their roles that they create a visceral, instinctive connection with the audience, and that makes their talent very hard to analyze. But when you do, you realize that you are responding to some-

---

*I have tried to name actors I admire who are well known to a wide audience, mainly through their film work, so that you will see their faces and pieces of their performances in your mind's eye as I mention them. But I have also tried to cite movie stars who are accomplished stage actors as well. It is what actors do before a live audience that is most instructive to public speakers.

I do not want to suggest that all good actors are only Method actors. The British and Irish theater turn out generation after generation of startling talents who probably never heard of Stella Adler. They, too, achieve an impressive reality onstage. That is every actor's goal; the means you use to create such truth is up to you. My gloss on the Method has worked for me. I also know that it can help nonactors become better in front of an audience. But I certainly do not want to suggest that the only good actor is an old actor. Yes, the actors I keep mentioning may have a lot of gray in the hair, but that's because I am going back to the people who most impressed and influenced me when I was trying to make a career. I am less familiar with the stage work of younger actors, but I would add two who have astonished me with their range: the African-American actor Jeffrey Wright, who has already accumulated an impressive body of work in the independent film *Basquiat,* based on the true story of a successful young artist addicted to heroin; *Shaft,* as a flamboyant pimp; and the TV miniseries *Boycott,* as Martin Luther King, Jr. Mary-Louise Parker was a wonder in the film *Fried Green Tomatoes,* pulled off a very different role as a popular singer who was the mistress of mob boss Sam Giancana in *Sugar Time,* and won the Tony Award in 2001 for her performance as a mathematically gifted young woman in the Broadway play *Proof.*

thing going on underneath their performance, their subtext, the
key they have found to the role. Good acting is about getting at
the truth of the moment—that moment, for that character. It is
true to life, but true in a heightened way, which is why what we
see onstage or in a film often seems even truer than life.

Finding that same kind of truth is no less crucial to the success
of your role as a speaker. You, too, will have your "hidden
dragon"—to get that loan from the bank because your business
is either thriving or going down the tubes; to kick some butt on
the sales team in the morning because numbers are down, or to
break the bad news to the boss in the afternoon without losing
your job. To be as convincing as possible in these roles (not just
say the right thing but *act* in the right way) requires what actors
call "making choices."

MAKING CHOICES

I got my first paying job in an Equity acting company in the
summer of 1968 at the Williamstown Theatre Festival in the
Berkshires of northwestern Massachusetts. The artistic director
at Williamstown was Nikos Psacharopoulos, who also taught directing at Yale, where I had worked with him in several of his
classes, evidently well enough to merit an invitation to Williamstown as a "journeyman." That meant that though I had not yet
earned my Equity union card, I could still perform onstage and
get paid for it ($50 a week, plus a shared college dorm room).
This was a great opportunity for me to put much of what I had
learned from Stella Adler and Bobby Lewis into action. I had already played more than twenty big roles onstage in school and
non-Equity summer stock, ranging from the title role in Shakespeare's *Macbeth* and Jamie Tyrone in Eugene O'Neill's *Long
Day's Journey into Night* to *Li'l Abner* and Billy Bigelow in

Carousel. But Williamstown would be my first chance to work with seasoned professional actors and watch how they went about their business.

In my first two plays at Williamstown, I had the honor of working with Olympia Dukakis, first as Achilles to her Clytemnestra in *Iphigenia at Aulis,* and then in Tennessee Williams's *Camino Real,* in which I played Kilroy and she was the Gypsy Woman. A wondrous stage actress, Olympia is now probably best known for her performances in the movies *Moonstruck* and *Steel Magnolias.* But back then, she was already in a league of her own as a stage actress, performing with great abandon, always truthful, full of passion, pain, and humor. She seemed to be able to laugh and cry at the same time, often causing audiences to do the same. As Clytemnestra, Olympia would implore Achilles to save her and her children from a fate worse than death. My job during this part of the play was to stand perfectly still. "No small moments," Nikos had warned. "No small thoughts, no small feelings, no small gestures, Kenny! You are a Greek god!" The diminutive Nikos would then strike a pose and make a face: Eyes blazing, standing ever so erect, he actually looked a little like Napoleon in casual wear. But I got the point. I stood as tall and as still as possible, like a living, breathing statue, looking into the distance and listening as Olympia played her astonishing Clytemnestra.

Every night she was different, but always incredibly moving. Playing from moment to moment, she would begin with the dignity of a queen, then proceed through a series of subtle alterations in attitude—imperious, threatening, alluring, cajoling, flighty, gritty, pragmatic, insane, brave, petty, weak, and childlike—as she pleaded her case. She would always end by throwing herself at my feet, humbled and broken, a desperate mother who was willing to do anything to save her children. At the time Olympia herself was obviously pregnant, giving the scene even more poignancy. She was so spontaneous and moving every night that my biggest challenge was to keep from being moved by her performance. I could actually hear people in the audience getting caught up in their own emotions. My Achilles looked at Clytemnestra a mere four times in the course of the scene, turning in her direction only once. I don't remember the words of the translation we were using, but I will never forget the clarity and power of all the choices Olympia made to achieve her overall action, saving her children's lives. She was playing the character with all the size and style that such a great classical role required, but what she was doing was so specific and personalized to Olympia Dukakis that she was also always Olympia talking to me. Olympia is an extremely generous actress and a wonderful acting teacher in her own right, so she would talk to me later about how she worked and where some of her choices came from. The main actions she had chosen as Clytemnestra were so much larger than life on one level ("To challenge a god, to rage at the heavens," she explained) and yet on another level so personal ("To get in your face, to make you hot, to strut my stuff, to feel the child I'm carrying"). Everything she did was an act of invention, yet it also had the ring of truth, because it was Olympia as if she were Clytemnestra, doing what any woman might do in the same situation. You cannot take your eyes off the actors who work this way because of what they are *doing*. The fullness of a stage performance might vary from night to night, but if the actor's choices of what her character does onstage are original and memorable and serve the text, that's what we mean by talent. I recognized Olympia's choices as a classic example of Stella Adler's constant exhortation to students, "Make it your own!"—another acting technique that is indispensable to public speakers. You are, after all, playing yourself. Ironically, when most people perform in public, they fail to get themselves right. ("He is so much better in private," your friends assure the other members of your audience.)

MAKING IT YOUR OWN

Acting technique is a very personal matter, cobbled together over time from various teachers and mentors and other actors we might admire. Like a lot of young actors, I sometimes had a tendency to overintellectualize a part. I tried to get the clothes right, the walk, the gestures—what actors call "working from the outside in." English actors are noted for this outside-in style: Laurence Olivier had to get the right nose for his Richard III; during the preproduction of the film version of *Doctor Zhivago*, Ralph Richardson drove the producers crazy looking for a coat and hat suitable for his character. After working with Stella, Bobby, and Olympia, I realized that the technique that would work best to help me find my character was working from the inside out. The question they taught me to ask was not "What would the character do in this situation?" but "What would *I* do if I were this person in this scene?" The payoff to personalizing my performance in this way came in one of the earliest and most visible roles of my career.

I decided not to return to Yale for my third year because I had auditioned for a small part in a new Neil Simon–Burt Bacharach–Hal David Broadway musical, *Promises, Promises* (produced by David Merrick), and gotten it. But my big break arrived in the role of Thomas Jefferson in *1776*, the hit musical about the men who invented America, which also starred William Daniels as John Adams, Howard Da Silva as Benjamin Franklin, and Betty Buckley as Martha Jefferson. Like most breaks, it was a lucky one. I had played the lead in the musical

How to Succeed in Business Without Really Trying for director Peter Hunt in the final production of the summer in Williamstown, and he insisted to the producers of *1776* that this no-name twenty-four-year-old actor, playing a bit part in *Promises, Promises,* could play the tall, thirty-three-year-old author of the Declaration of Independence. After three auditions, I got the role. And so, two weeks into the run of my Broadway debut in a hit show, I was giving my notice to David Merrick so that I could appear in my second, more experimental Broadway show of the same season. Many people thought I was crazy to leave *Promises, Promises,* but as luck would have it, *1776* would win the Tony Award for best musical and earn me some gratifying acclaim.

The role of Jefferson in *1776* is relatively slim. He kisses his wife, sings a couple of songs with Adams and Franklin, and says a few dozen lines in the entire show. Historically, Jefferson was a last-minute substitute for the Second Continental Congress in Philadelphia, filling in for his uncle and mentor Peyton Randolph, the most powerful planter-politician in his native Virginia, who decided to return home to attend to what was perceived as the more important task of drafting Virginia's state constitution. When he arrived in Philadelphia, Jefferson had spent only six years in public life as a member of the House of Burgesses, the legislature in colonial Virginia. But he had already established his radical credentials and his reputation as, in Adams's phrase, "a masterly pen" by writing "A Summary View of the Rights of British America," a paper declaring outright that "the British parliament had no right to exercise authority over us." It happened to be the same conclusion that Adams and several other radical members of the Continental Congress had come to, arguing that a full break with England was necessary. Like many members of that famous Congress, Jefferson was a talented lawyer. But unlike the ambitious Adams and the worldly Franklin, the young

Virginian was shy by nature and an indifferent public speaker. Historically, the great man didn't give even one speech during his first stint in Philadelphia before traveling back to Virginia in December 1775 to visit his wife, Martha, who was ill. But Jefferson was back in Congress by May 1776, and in the musical version of those days leading to the Declaration of Independence, the stage directions for Jefferson's entrance were: "and last to enter, unnoticed, Thomas Jefferson of Virginia, thirty-three, six feet three, with copper-colored hair, carrying several books." It was an example of the writer Peter Stone's ironic brand of humor. "Unnoticed"? I am six feet six, and the audience members were already elbowing one another and saying, "There's Jefferson, the guy with the red hair and the books has to be Jefferson." After all, the show was about the writing and ratification of the Declaration of Independence! My challenge as a young actor was to make the laconic Jefferson come to life and be anything but "unnoticed." One of the ways I accomplished this was through a very personalized acting choice—what Walter Kerr of *The New York Times* described, to my great pleasure, as "the evening's nicest bit of stage business."

It came in the scene in which Jefferson finally but reluctantly (he hasn't seen his wife in six months) sits down to the daunting task of drafting the Declaration of Independence. According to the original stage directions, Jefferson starts writing and crumpling the paper, writing and crumpling, more and more, in frustration. What I did was look at the blank parchment, think, write half a line, stop, crumple it up, and throw it on the floor. I then looked at the new piece of parchment, thought, wrote a couple of words, stopped, crumpled that up, and threw it away. Then a third time: I looked at the new parchment, thought, crumpled it up, and tossed it without having written a word. It produced a big, big laugh from the audience. My mother loved that moment because, she explained, "That was you." And she was absolutely right. I had based this little bit of stage business on my own experiences with trying to start term papers in school. It worked perfectly. The contrast between the audience's image of Jefferson and this blocked, frustrated writer in his little room was funny. It was not only my idea, it was me. And it helped make Jefferson come alive for the audience. Walter Kerr noted that my crumpling of the empty parchment showed Jefferson "meaning the gesture with his heart and soul."

Many young people are drawn to acting because they like the idea of becoming someone else. But acting is not really about losing yourself in fictional characters. Quite the contrary: Acting is bringing as much of yourself to the character as possible to make the role come alive onstage. You must personalize everything you can. This does not mean imposing your personality on the role: "Hey! Thomas Jefferson is a guy like me." No, I was a kid from Long Island who played basketball and wound up becoming a professional actor, a far cry from Thomas Jefferson. But my job was to discover what acting choices would make Jefferson seem real and accessible in a musical about the Second Continental Congress. As Jefferson, I crumpled the paper before I even wrote on it because that was me. If I had been Jefferson suffering writer's block, that is what I might have done. The audience responded to it because it was human, something they could relate to, something even they might have done.

In working with young actors, I have found that they will improve very quickly once they understand the difference between turning a character into themselves and bringing parts of themselves to the role in order to connect to a character more personally. The character is yours and will be revealed by your way of playing his actions, rather than how somebody else might do it. This revelation has led me to my own gloss on the Method:

Acting is not only what you do, *it is also what* you *do.*

IT'S ALSO WHAT GOOD SPEAKERS DO

As you prepare to meet your audience, whoever they are, you must ask, "What is the character I am playing today?" Today my role might be the guy walking into a meeting to win an audition. Tomorrow I may be the guy walking into a Ramada Inn to convince several hundred people to write a big check to an animal-rights organization that my wife and I support. Is there a big difference between my selves in my daily roles? No, but there are some differences: the audience, the room, the stakes. And to succeed, I have to take each situation into account and prepare for it.

How you prepare is a matter of personal style. When you appear before an audience as a speaker, the real you is in the room, at least from your point of view. For the audience, it depends. If you stand before a group of people without making the kinds of gestures that human beings ordinarily make when talking, the audience will see you as a robot. If you speak your words in a monotone, you will not impress anyone. Indeed, if you concentrate only on the words, you are not likely to succeed in delivering your ultimate message. During the last presidential campaign, Al Gore seemed to be reading off index cards in his head; his tone was patronizing, like that of a kindergarten teacher reading a story to the kids. But at least Gore didn't seem scared and out of place, like his opponent, George W. Bush, who had every speech coach in America wishing to get ahold of him for a day. Bush looked like he had been wound up before coming onstage; he read from the TelePrompTer as if he had never seen the speech before. "But he's really terrific one-on-one," his friends and closest associates said, though Bush continued to play the not-so-great communicator as president.

There have been some flashes of potential, and I would contend that when the president has succeeded as a speaker, he has done so because he allowed the real George W. Bush to appear in public. I have heard at least one political commentator claim that the "Bush presidency began" with the president's first visit to Ground Zero a few days after the terrorist attacks on the World Trade Center. A New York fireman helped Bush climb up on a pile of rubble, and from there the president, casually dressed, assured the assembled rescue workers shouting "USA! USA!" that the rest of the world was listening. For once Bush was away from the TelePrompTer; instead of fiddling with his notes, he was talking straight to a bunch of rescue workers with a bullhorn in one hand and what seemed a genuinely appreciative arm around the shoulder of that fireman at his side. Great stuff. Why? Because the president was acting like a real human being. Like the rest of the country, he was sad and angry and showing it. By not trying to appear presidential, he was coming off as extremely presidential.

The importance of what you *do* as a public speaker—how you act—is underrated. When you move into the public arena, you have to think carefully about what you will be doing and the consequences of your choices. Will that blue blazer tell them that you are well dressed or a square? In your circle, body piercing may be cool and sexy, but do you want to walk into a job interview with that ring in your nose? I am assuming that you want to leave people with the impression that you are an intelligent, entertaining, charming, effective person. But being impressive is not your objective. Getting the job is. The perception that you are impressive—intelligent, charming, passionate, moving, funny, or whatever else is required—will be the result of what you do. Actors choose behavior that will fit their characters. As a speaker, you have to choose to do things that fit you, the kinds of gestures and movements that would come nat-

urally to you in private and are connected to what you are saying. You do not gesture for the sake of gesturing ("I'll throw in a
fist in the air here, pound the podium there, point to the audience after that sentence"). There must be a reason for you to
gesture. George W. Bush threw his arm around that fireman not
to show what a great guy a president could be but because he
didn't want the fireman to leave. The fireman had reportedly
been instructed by Bush's people to help the president up and
then disappear. But as he went to step down from the rubble,
Bush said, "Where are you going?" and threw his arm around
the guy, mainly to make himself feel comfortable, I think. It
turned out to be a brilliant natural (and theatrical) choice. As
President Bush thanked the rescue workers and warned America's enemies that justice was in their future, he had a symbol of
heroism by his side. It was pure instinct but dramatically powerful. I felt at that moment that I finally understood what his closest friends and advisers meant when they said Bush was "great
in private." On that pile of rubble that was once the World Trade
Center towers, as he spoke to the world, Bush seemed at last to
bring his private self into the public arena.

That kind of private moment in public—what I quoted the
great American philosopher William James as calling "public
solitude"—should be the ultimate goal of every speaker. It is in
your reach, provided you put in the work. Here is something
that can help you connect what you do in public to what you
want to achieve.

Assignment #2

In the previous chapter, I suggested a one-minute introduction
of yourself. To get the hang of creating an overall purpose, I advise fooling around with my second assignment for my Harvard
course:

*Relate an incident from your life that taught you a lesson,
demonstrating it just as it happened in your experience. I
want you to get physical. Activity and abundant gestures
will help loosen you up physically, and this, in turn, will
help loosen you up mentally and emotionally. It will also
help you to connect instinctively to the questions "What am
I doing?" and "How shall I do it?" You have one minute.
Good luck!*

To jog my students' memories, I provided a list of possible topics that you might also find useful:

Tennis (hitting a serve in the final set)
Gardening (getting a sore back)
Skiing (taking a bad fall)
Golf (scoring the best or worst shot in a round)
Decorating (painting or papering a room)
Fishing (hooking the big one)
Football (acting out a great pass play you pulled off or saw)
Basketball (showing how to shoot a foul shot)
Changing a tire
Catching a bus
Slipping on a street
Jaywalking during rush hour
Diving off a cliff into the water below

As Hamlet advises the players, "Suit the action to the word,
the word to the action." If this assignment seems more like the
show-and-tell exercises you did in elementary school than performing Shakespeare, that is because it is. It is also an effective
way to begin learning how to perform in front of people. The
exercise is simple to prepare because it is familiar—not unlike a
story you might tell your family or friends. Being forced to

demonstrate something will require you to be more physical than you might be in most presentations, and you will discover that re-creating certain gestures and actions will help you to relax mentally and emotionally as well as physically. Sports coaches and psychologists advise athletes to focus on certain moves to keep their mind from wandering to thoughts of failure. Timothy Gallwey explains this technique very helpfully in his best-selling books *The Inner Game of Tennis* and *The Inner Game of Golf,* using the now well-known tasks attributed to the right and left sides of the brain. Psychologists tell us that the left side of the brain is the home of our ability to think analytically and logically; it is our inner bean counter and severest critic. The right side of the brain is our Picasso, the origin of our creative and visual urges—if allowed to get by the gloomy left side. You visualize curving a six iron to the pin 165 yards away, but a little voice inside is saying, "Be careful of that tree over there, and then there's that sand trap in front of the green that you will definitely land in, not to mention the water behind the green, that is, if you don't miss the ball entirely."

The trick, according to Gallwey, is to shut up the bothersome half of your brain by giving it something to do so you can have some fun—the objective, after all. (Parents of small children will recognize the technique immediately.) Tennis players can avoid thinking too much about what might go wrong with their swings by naming an action as it happens—saying "Bounce" when the ball bounces in their direction and then "Hit" as they strike it back. For golfers, who get more time to stare at that motionless ball and can easily get tangled up in thoughts of what can go wrong at every stage of the golf swing, Gallwey suggests saying something while executing the swing. As you take the club back, for instance, you might say "Back," and then, as in tennis, "Hit" as you make contact. I use "Back," but for the downswing, my preferred mantra is "Through" instead of "Hit" because it sounds smoother to me, the effect I want in my swing. Whatever works for you. (My father used to hum the opening of "The Blue Danube Waltz," which got him into the right swing rhythm.)

The acting equivalent of Gallwey's "Bounce, hit" is what actors choose to do onstage—the actions they use to make their characters seem real, guided by their overall purpose of serving the role and the play. In speaking terms, it is another example of having something to do. Using a pointer or dealing with the slide machine can help you put aside your fear. But even without those tasks, there are physical things you can do that contribute to your overall objective and will not only loosen you up but also make you seem more spontaneous. This assignment will convince you of that without making you agonize over choosing what to do. When your goal is to show how to change a tire, describe your best moment in sports, or report on that regrettable day when you slipped in the rain and fell in the middle of Fifth Avenue, the logic of your actions—"First I did this, then that"—will be obvious. These actions will also make it easier to remember what you have to say. (I will come back to the role of memory later.) Above all, by getting physical, you will also make it your own. While anyone can describe how he learned to ski or put oil in the engine, once you begin the story of your own experience, you will transform a general, abstract activity—the kind of thing that could be written in a how-to book or a directions manual—into something personal. Your presentation will be in your language, in the order that you have chosen, with anecdotes that are part of your life, using your own physicality. Remember the time when your father opened up the hood and got splattered with oil? All of a sudden, a demonstration on how to fix an automobile engine becomes a funny story from your own life. The details count. It all happened outside of Newark or on the Grand Corniche. How the family got to the

Grand Corniche is likely to make an interesting anecdote. Then again, it might not be worth explaining the reason for your first trip to the French Riviera, particularly if you have only a minute to talk about fixing carburetors. Your presentation will depend on what your goal is, whom your audience is, what you want them to leave with, and how much time you have. (There are other variables of communication, but let's keep it as simple as possible for the time being.) At any point in your remarks, you should be able to answer the question "How does what I am doing serve my objective?"

One of my students at Harvard was a foreigner who was very self-conscious about her heavy accent. Her audition for the class was among the least sophisticated, but I accepted her into the class on the grounds that if I could help this student—naturally shy, raised in another culture, and struggling with English (albeit her third language)—then I could probably help anyone get better at public speaking. The second assignment worried her, but as we talked, she began telling me how much comfort she got from weaving. In fact, her family was in the process of sending her loom, which she had missed so much. I saw an opportunity to help her: "Tell me about this loom." She explained how it worked, how she kept it dry, the way she prepared the different colors, how she positioned her hands. As is often the case when people are interested in what they are talking about, they become animated. Suddenly, the student's shyness was replaced by her expertise, and she came alive. When she got up before the class the following week to explain how cloth is woven on a loom, her improvement was impressive. I had simply asked her to tell me a personal story and then persuaded her to tell it to the class. Preparing a presentation filled with purposeful behavior about something she loved to do was a breakthrough moment for her as a public speaker.

Many other students went far beyond my pedestrian suggestions. They discussed landing a plane for the first time, crashing a bike, cleaning roaches out of a utility sink, waiting for the tooth fairy as a kid, playing spin the bottle in the sixth grade, even finding a place to pee in a very public space. One guy described going to his high school prom. His story began quite predictably: There was this girl he had a crush on. He finally got up the courage to ask her to the senior prom and was flabbergasted when she accepted. Next he described his delirious happiness. He then described his white tuxedo and her formal gown and the big car his father had loaned him for the big night. Then, his story got interesting. He sat down and demonstrated in detail how he drove up to the tollbooth on the bridge leading from Long Island into Manhattan. Suavely, he tossed the exact change at the basket—and missed. Not so suave. He then opened the door—again showing us exactly what happened— and leaned out of the car to pick up the coins, a move that caused his foot to press down on the accelerator, sending his father's car in the direction of the stop-go bar at the tollbooth, which he barely avoided plowing through. He looked at the line of waiting cars behind him, already tooting impatiently; he looked over at his date, who rolled her eyes. He got out of the car—here making believe he was getting out of the car—then stopped showing us what had happened and switched to a description of how he felt: "So there I was . . ."

And so were we, his audience; we were all there at the tollbooth in anticipation of what would come next. We didn't need to see him crawling around on the floor of the Harvard lecture hall, trying to retrieve the cash from under his imaginary car without getting his white dinner jacket dirty. It was funnier and even more effective to join him in looking back on this pathetic high school experience, as he reacted to his own description of his humiliation, shaking his head at the misery of it all. We all laughed, and when his two minutes were up, the class applauded wildly. So did I. An apparently shy and quiet guy, this student had shown some good performing instincts by making a choice about not acting out every humiliating moment at the tollbooth. I intended to emphasize physical economy later in the course, but he had already given me a good example of less being more. I was not surprised to discover several years later that he had become a successful producer-writer of TV situation comedies. One other thing: He was one of those four students who had originally not made the cut but had asked me to reconsider. So much for my ability as a talent scout.

Try to come up with your version of the loom or prom-date story. Just a minute's worth. If you need more time, fine, but certainly no more than two minutes. Part of the point of this exercise is to learn how to be as concise, descriptive, and physical as possible. Working on your presentation for a week will make it much easier for you to follow Hamlet's advice. The connections between what you say and what you do will come naturally, helping you to avoid consciously adding gestures to particular phrases and appearing like a puppet on a string. Again, test out your remarks in front of a friend or family member, then try them out in front of a small audience. Once you get the hang of connecting what you do to your objective, you'll be well on your way to learning how to structure any presentation—the subject of the next chapter.

3

THE SPEAKER PREPARES—

STRUCTURE AND STORYTELLING

> Tell 'em what you're gonna tell 'em, tell 'em, and then
> tell 'em what you told 'em.
> —Advice from an anonymous Irish politician
> as quoted by Dale Carnegie in *How to
> Develop Self-Confidence and Influence
> People by Public Speaking*

In early 1973 I began rehearsals for *Seesaw,* a musical based on William Gibson's play *Two for the Seesaw,* about a naive, married midwestern attorney named Jerry Ryan who falls in love with a New York Jewish girl named Gittel who dreams of being a dancer. After five weeks of rehearsal, and in spite of the great music and lyrics by Cy Coleman and Dorothy Fields, who had teamed up for the 1966 Broadway hit *Sweet Charity,* the show was not working. During the out-of-town tryout in Detroit, the producers replaced the director with Michael Bennett, who also took over the choreography, hiring the remarkable six-foot-six dancer Tommy Tune. Bennett also replaced Lainie Kazan, the original Gittel, with Michele Lee, and proceeded to restage the big numbers, cut out others, redesign the sets, and battle with the writer, Michael Stuart, to refocus the show on the relationship between Jerry Ryan and Gittel. During the day, I was working with Michael, Tommy, and Michele on the new show, while every night performing the former version with the original cast.

During previews in New York, Stuart left the show. Bennett brought in the legendary playwright Neil Simon, who had written the book for *Sweet Charity* and had a good working relationship with Coleman and Fields. In musicals, as the old saying goes, "It's the book, the book, the book." Everyone involved in the production—including the director, the choreographer, and the set and costume designers—must serve the story. Simon quickly detected that *Seesaw* had too many elements that were confusing the audience about what the real story was. With a week to go before opening night, Simon, famous for his ability to rewrite under pressure, went to work on resuscitating *Seesaw*.

In the original version Gittel's opening number was a terrific song called "Big Fat Heart," in which she confides to the audience what a softy she is. On the road, the critics had been rather harsh, partly because the zaftig beauty of talented actress-singer Lainie Kazan encased in a dancer's leotard gave the song an unintentional double meaning. After replacing her with Michele Lee, thin and shapely but with a big voice, the producers figured they had solved the problem. But Simon disagreed. Michele was adorable and a wonderful singer, but "Big Fat Heart" was the wrong way to open the show. The first song, Simon advised, should allow Gittel to explain in that sardonically self-effacing way so typical of New Yorkers that if anyone can screw up a relationship, she can. Simon had quickly cut to the juice of *Seesaw*—a story about a relationship that was bound to have its ups and downs. Forty-eight hours later, the amazing Dorothy Fields returned with a new song, "Nobody Does It Like Me," that went, "If there's a wrong way to get a guy, a right way to lose a guy / Nobody does it like me." Michele belted out this new opening in her big Broadway voice, and it delivered exactly what Simon had ordered: It was funny, straightforward, and it let the audience know precisely who Gittel was and what the story would be about.

I stayed my course, exhausted, but also exhilarated and in awe of the chaos of creativity swirling around me. Simon made more cuts, and added a few calamities in the first act to make my character more sympathetic and a show-stopping solo dance later on to do the same; he also encouraged Coleman and Fields to have Gittel sing a summary as part of her final number, a song called "I'm Way Ahead," to tie a ribbon around the show's final message. This last-minute retooling turned the production from roadkill into a hit Broadway musical. It was an amazing and welcome lesson in the importance of structure to storytelling.

Years later, when I began to think about applying acting techniques to public speaking, I realized that Simon's advice was essentially what Dale Carnegie's Irish politician offered as the recipe for an effective stump speech: "Tell 'em what you're gonna tell 'em, tell 'em, and then tell 'em what you told 'em." Musicals are more like speeches than regular plays, which tend to maintain the illusion of the "fourth wall" (the life of the play proceeds as if the audience were not there). Like speeches, musicals play to the audience. A good speech must also hammer home its message every step of the way. Anything that is off message, as the politicians say, does not belong in the speech, even if it stops the show. No matter how entertained an audience might have been, if people walk out wondering, "What was that all about?" then you will have failed, because your presentation was *pointless*. But no matter how great or clear your message is, you'd better put in the time preparing and practicing, for days, maybe weeks, depending on how big or important your presentation is. If the greatest actors on the planet spend five weeks, day and night, rehearsing a play, why should you think you can be good in public just winging it? The goal is to seem spontaneous, but to do that requires a lot of hard work. Anyone who is skilled at anything—a job, a sport, cooking, gardening, you name it—knows that the ease of a pro comes only from doing something over and over until no thought is required—until the hard stuff *becomes second nature*.

I'm sure you've heard that old joke about the tourist in New York who says, "How do I get to Carnegie Hall?" Answer: "Practice, practice, practice." Practice will help you improve as a speaker: exponentially. Pick a public person you admire, a great communicator. At the risk of dating myself, I have always found Winston Churchill an inspiring speaker. John F. Kennedy was urbane and witty. The passion and poetry of Martin Luther King, Jr., moved my generation. No one could make a State of the Union address seem like a friendly chat better than Ronald Reagan. Bill Cosby is not only one of the great stand-up comedian-storytellers, he is also one of the most popular commencement speakers in history, giving several speeches every spring. Am I promising you that a lot of practice will turn you into a Reagan or a Cosby? Of course not. As experienced a speaker and performer as I am, I am no Reagan or Cosby, not even close. But I would like to think that over the years I have had my moments of Reaganesque charm and Cosbylike hilarity. And that is my promise to you, at least a few minutes of glory every time you step into the limelight—if you do the work. I'm not asking you to win Olympic gold in the downhill or grand slalom; I'm asking you to work at learning to ski. And isn't it all relative? You can become the best speaker in your department or company, or you can just get good enough so that your friends and family will say, "That was really you up there, and you were great!" For most people, that is a huge improvement.

IT'S ABOUT STRUCTURE—AND TELLING A STORY

When you sit down to prepare a presentation, you should pin two questions on the wall: 1) What is my message and its purpose? 2) To whom am I delivering it? The answers will provide the bare armature on which to hang your remarks. Creating something from scratch is virtually impossible without some kind of structure. Once you have settled on your message—to show why your idea or product is so superior, to inspire the marketing team, to celebrate the bride and groom, to get the audience to write a check to your favorite charity or candidate, to prove that you are the person for the job, and so on—you will then have to decide what information is required to sell it. What story are you telling? Virtually every speech can be a story with a beginning, middle, and end, tied together by an overall message. How you tell that story, point by point, is called its structure. Your English teacher called it an outline. With a work of imagination, the difference between failure and success often lies in how its parts are arranged. Songs get cut or moved around in musicals, scenes get slashed or added in plays, chapters of books get dropped or rearranged, paragraphs in magazine articles get canned or reshuffled. I would even go so far as to say that creativity is less about what you put in than what you leave out. Fidel Castro may enjoy delivering three-hour tirades, but I suspect even his most passionate supporters would prefer a tighter presentation. The speeches you will be called upon to deliver are likely to be brief. The shorter the performance, the more egregious any rambling will be. The structure ensures the tightness and clarity of your message.

Every creative work depends on structure. Even those that aim for a kind of anarchy will start, proceed, and end; there will always be a method in their madness. Drama or comedy, whether stage, film, or television, can always be broken down into a story built from what is known as "the three-act structure": You meet the characters and their situation in Act One; their lives get complicated or are placed in jeopardy in Act Two; and the problem is resolved in Act Three. Classical music, from a sonata to a symphony, also uses this basic three-part structure. So does opera. In ballet, there is the introduction, which includes the theme of the entire piece; then comes the body of the work that elaborates the theme, laying out its variations; and then the coda, which summarizes what has come before: "Tell 'em what you're gonna tell them, tell 'em, tell them what you told 'em." And then it's time to go home.

Magazine stories also depend on this structure. I have grilled an old friend of mine who is a veteran magazine writer and an alumnus of *Time* magazine on how a good article is constructed, and I have concluded that the architecture of a news story probably comes the closest to the basic outline of a brief speech.

• Typically, newsmagazine stories begin with a you-are-there anecdote (known as an "action lead") that fills the first paragraph or two, transporting the reader to the scene of the story. For example: Friday night in a college-town bar, a co-ed's efforts to match the guys beer for beer turn into a screaming match with her boyfriend, ending with her putting a fist through the car window.

• The next paragraph explains why this particular anecdote merits coverage in a national newsmagazine (some editors called this summary paragraph "the billboard"): College administrators are concerned about binge drinking among female students; studies have shown that alcohol abuse among college women has risen exponentially; and schools are trying to cope.

• The next paragraphs give details about the phenomenon, including various sociological and psychological explanations, plus information about what college administrators are specifically doing to cope with the increase of drunkenness among women students.

- This kind of story will typically conclude with something
  high-minded about the issue—a quote from a student, for instance, who has scaled back her drinking after realizing that
  she had to set her own standards and stop competing with
  men. Thus the story circles back to another take on the beer-
  drinking contest of the first paragraph.

Notice how the structure of this story (based on a recent report in *Time*) might be turned into a speech that a parent or college dean might give to wise up teenage girls entering college.
The message: A fun social life is a vital part of the college experience, but trying to outdrink the guys is a dangerous way to
make friends. The dean might begin with an actual horror story
from her own campus, where a night of social drinking puts a
student in the hospital. Any story will do, so long as it illustrates
the message. The dean could then lay out the figures backing
up her message that binge drinking among women has become
a big problem on that campus and around the nation. The
speech could proceed to discuss various explanations for why
young women overdrink (to loosen up socially, to impress the
guys, to prove that women are equal to men), programs that
other colleges have tried, what the rules are at this particular in-
stitution, and how students who want to stop abusing alcohol
can get help. All of this information serves the message. The
dean might end the talk by introducing students who have been
there, done that, and are eager to explain how they turned
things around.

No matter what your message is, the structure of your speech
need be no more complicated than that of the newsmagazine
story or the dean's talk. I would advise checking out an issue
of *Time* or *Newsweek,* for example, breaking down several stories into outline form, and analyzing the narrative flow. Tight on
space, the newsmagazines are expert at summing up a week's

worth of events in a concise and entertaining way. But notice how everything has its place: The scene, the statistics, the subject's main ideas, the counterarguments from critics, and biographical information, each in its own paragraph. When my friend started writing for *Time* almost thirty years ago, an editor advised him to write his stories "as if you were telling what happened to a friend at a cocktail party."

That is good advice for delivering most speeches and presentations. Every speaker must be a storyteller. If your objective is to make a toast at a party celebrating a friend's promotion to a senior management position, you will not have to stray from the basic structure. In this case, the message is straightforward: Your friend is a wonderful, talented person with a promising future. You might start with an anecdote about why you're there—you told your friend to go to business school (or maybe you were the genius who warned him that the company would never give him the time of day; don't be afraid to have some fun). You might say something about why it worked and will continue to. And you end by toasting to his continued success. Again: "Tell 'em what you're gonna tell 'em, tell 'em, and tell 'em what you told 'em."

BUT HOW TO BEGIN?

Every artist works differently; we all have our creative quirks, including the inability to sit down and begin working. For most people, the biggest obstacle to preparing a good speech is thinking they have to sit down and write it. But notice that this chapter is not entitled "Writing a Speech." To be a brilliant speaker, you do not have to write a brilliant speech. How many of us can expect to be brilliant writers? Handling yourself in public and writing something in the quiet of your own home or office are two different skills. By now I hope that your one-minute introduction and brief how-to have proved to you that you can impress your listeners with a presentation that requires no written script. You do not write a speech; you *prepare* it. You establish your message, organize the information relevant to that message, and put it into some kind of logical order. The only writing you need to do at this stage involves outlining the main points that will help you tell your story, then fiddling around with them until you get the best effect. You begin telling that story according to the order you have chosen, first rehearsing it in your mind, then out loud, adding, subtracting, embellishing along the way. Maybe there will be a few complicated ideas or fact-laden notions you need to be precise about, so you write them down. Maybe you need to keep some names and titles straight. Write them down, too. But I guarantee that if you work on your structure, practice your speech, and test it out, those complicated facts and names that you had to write down will soon be cemented in your brain. For the kind of brief speeches, introductions, presentations, and interviews most of us do, you do not need to write out everything you want to say and memorize it word for word. You *will* have to remember what you want to say, and in the next chapter I will offer several techniques to keep you from forgetting your prepared remarks. For now, however, I ask you to remember just this:

Please do not write a speech.

As a speaker, you have no obligation to stay loyal to any text. The words are yours. If you muff one, or that catchy phrase you liked seems to have disappeared from your memory, so what? Substitute another. You want to avoid the impression of reciting a written speech, because it will immediately undercut that sense of just being up there, talking to an audience as if they were your best friends sitting in your living room. Think back on the presentations that have impressed you the most. I would bet that the speaker was neither reading the speech nor reciting it from memory, as if he had a TelePrompTer rolling in his head. Yes, we constantly hear speeches that have been carefully scripted. Some of them were great and historic, such as Franklin D. Roosevelt's "date of infamy" speech, John F. Kennedy's "ask not what your country can do for you—ask what you can do for your country" inaugural address, and the unforgettable "I have a dream" speech by Martin Luther King, Jr. These are beautifully written speeches. But I would argue that while each had a memorable phrase or two, they were great because of why and how they were delivered and who was delivering them. Each man brought a lifetime of experience to those words, not to mention the passion of the moment that enlivened what they read. Let me quickly add that a good actor can take those same words and make them as powerful as when they were first said (or, to put it another way, make them seem as if they're being said for the first time). The actor, however, can be convincing as FDR, JFK, and Martin Luther King, Jr., only if he plays the actions and meets the objective of being each one of those men. Although the actor might like to light his matches with a flip of his thumbnail, the audience would never accept such behavior from his FDR. It's not just about the words. Good actors can bring inner life to even the silliest soap-opera speeches, or presence and power to the simplest voiceovers. (James Earl Jones's dramatic "This is CNN" comes to mind.) This is what actors are supposed to do. We create a character and a whole world of thoughts and feelings that turn someone else's words into our own.

How do we do it? It is called *preparation*. But I will be the first to concede that beginning is not always easy. I find that if I have some specific tasks to fulfill, I'm more likely to get to work and make some progress. One of the biggest obstacles to creativity, even for professional artists and writers, is the sense of being overwhelmed by the task ahead. "My God, I have to produce a three-hundred-page book!" (or a symphony or a play or a long article or even a short public presentation). A friend of mine who has written many books explains that he overcomes the daunting prospect of spending a year or more on a single project by persuading himself that "It's like laying bricks. You do it one brick at a time." You don't have to think all the time about the cathedral you're building or even the barbecue in the backyard. Just get to work one brick at a time. By the end of the day, you will have accomplished plenty. The following day, you grab the next brick, see where it fits in your blueprint, then add another brick, and so on, until you have built a structure for your presentation. And then you will examine it, rearrange it, add and subtract from it, until you think it is finally the speech you want to give.

No one I know has ever prepared an instant great speech. I remember my wife looking in on me one afternoon while I prepared for a speech and saying, "Nobody will ever know how hard you work to make it look so easy." The reason I work so hard on my presentations is that I have gone onstage in the past, thinking I've mastered a speech, and found to my chagrin that I wasn't as prepared as I thought. You not only want to avoid humiliation up there, you also want to be able to have a good time and be at your most natural. You enjoy yourself as a speaker only if you have really done your homework. Without the proper preparation and practice, you will be stepping off a cliff.

You must give yourself time to get your message straight and marshal the research to back it up. Then you will have to decide the order in which to deliver it. The speech should take days to get right. Here is a preliminary checklist of the bricks needed to prepare any presentation:

The Purpose. Most communication experts would agree that every speech should accomplish at least one of three things: 1) entertain, 2) inform, or 3) persuade people to take action. Overlapping is allowed. An informative speech is likely to be persuasive. If you are skilled at informing and moving people to action, you are likely to be entertaining, at least to the extent of impressing your audience. But no speech is likely to accomplish any of these goals unless you are clear about what you want to communicate.

The Message. Beware of trying to say too many things. Generally, it is better to have one simple point to get across. For example: It is time to go to war. Racism is evil. This is the reason you should vote for me. This is the product for you. I am the person you want to hire. Let's celebrate their marriage. Let us remember what a wonderful person this was. Let me tell you why you should contribute to this cause. The first question you must always ask yourself as you begin to prepare is: What am I trying to communicate? A good measure of that is the answer to another series of questions: What do you hope to have achieved when your presentation is over? What is the juice? What are you trying to get the audience to do? The answers to those questions will shape what you say from beginning to end. If you try to accomplish too much, or even back up your point with too many facts and figures, you risk leaving your audience wondering what you were talking about. Another danger is pushing a message so hard that your audience will overreact. If, for instance, you do not want your listeners to storm the ramparts, then you'll have to strike a delicate balance between being persuasive and not generating too much passion. In the "I have a dream" speech, Martin Luther King, Jr., was quite candid about the injustice African-Americans were up against in 1963. He warned that "it would be fatal for the nation to overlook the urgency of the moment and to underestimate the determination of the Negro." Their "legitimate discontent," he said, would not disappear. King warned that "the whirlwinds of revolt will continue." Pretty strong language. But with his very next words, King made it clear to his African-American listeners that he was sticking to his policy of nonviolence: "Let us not seek to satisfy our thirst for freedom by drinking from the cup of bitterness and hatred." King deftly sent a message to white America without sending his people into the streets.

The Editor. Once you have determined the purpose, you will move section by section through the speech, making sure that everything serves your overall purpose. Thus, your message becomes your editor or the filter for everything that goes in or out. Anything that does not serve the main purpose will have to go. That does not mean you are doomed to some dry, logical performance. A marvelous digression might fit perfectly into your overall plan, and so will humor or a touching anecdote, as long as each variable serves you. My original sin as a speaker is an inclination to digress (as you may have noticed). I like to tell stories, so as I prepare my talks, I have to keep reminding myself of my purpose and that I am not there just to entertain the audience. A funny story might derail certain speeches; as the laughter dies down, it can be hard to get the audience back to the subject. So remember William Faulkner's advice to writers: "We have to learn to kill our darlings." No matter how poetic the sentence might be or hilarious the story, if it doesn't contribute to your objective, kill it.

The Story. No one has come to hear you recite a laundry list. Even if you have a series of talking points that you want to cover—boss's orders—you must find some way to make them come alive. The simplest and most effective way to communicate a message is by telling a story. One of the great storyteller public speakers of all time was Ronald Reagan, who had the uncanny ability to make a State of the Union address sound as if he were just jawing with the crew on the set at Warner Bros. Reagan loved to tell Hollywood stories to Oval Office visitors, but he was that rare politician who could transfer his charm from a fireside chat to a major speech to a nation (or world) full of strangers.

Where to get the story to build your speech around? From your own life. With almost no exception, a good speech will come from the thoughts and feelings of personal experience. Every point can be related to something from your own life or career. If you are trying to sell your company's products or services, you can relate them to your own career as a salesman. If you are celebrating a friend's marriage, you can tell stories from your friendship. If you are speaking to the nation about creating a better life for the young and the poor, you can explain how your policies have helped particular people's lives. A few years ago, I attended a speech by a friend of mine on the controversial subject of affirmative action. The audience numbered a few hundred people, and it is is fair to say that most of them were not supporters. But my friend knew as much when he was preparing his speech, so he decided to confront that obstacle right away. He began his remarks by declaring that he was a fan, then immediately threw his critics off balance by explaining that he himself was an "affirmative action baby." Although neither African-American nor female, he'd been accepted to college in the 1960s, when prestigious schools were looking to diversify their student bodies from the traditional eastern WASP, prep school clientele. As the son of a working-class Irish-Catholic family who also happened to be an excellent baseball player with a talent for Latin and Greek, he was just what the admissions office was looking for—even though there might have been other high school students with more impressive grades and College Board scores. By giving his audience a piece of his autobiography, he had also cleverly served up an example that did not fit their stereotype of the usual beneficiary of reverse discrimination. His personal story had not only summed up his message, it also moved beyond the presumption that only women and people of color benefit from affirmative action.

Personal experience is not limited to things you have actually done; your experience also includes books you have read, movies you have seen, other speeches you have heard —all the things we vacuum into our minds throughout our lives. By experiencing those things, we make them part of our own biographies. We all accumulate stories. It just takes some work to dredge them up, then some preparation and practice to deliver them.

The Picture. Try to tell your story as vividly as possible, creating pictures that stick in people's minds. If people leave your presence with a strong image that encapsulates your message, you will have been successful. For example: Abraham Lincoln's "house divided" to symbolize a nation in the middle of a civil war; John F. Kennedy's "torch . . . passed to a new generation"; Winston Churchill's "iron curtain" that the communists had placed across Europe. If you were raising money for poor children in the third world, you would be well advised to describe their thin, hungry bodies, the hopelessness in their eyes, and the garbage strewn on the unpaved roads that lead to their infested and disease-ridden cardboard shanties where large, extended families live without electricity or running water. You want your audience to leave saying, "I can't get that picture out of my head."

The Take-Home Line. The communicator who delivers a vivid, straightforward message has achieved much. But even the best speakers need something to reach for. Include a line or phrase in your presentation that not only encapsulates your speech but also has an afterlife. Following the Japanese attack on Pearl Harbor on December 7, 1941, President Roosevelt, eager to inspire the nation to enter World War II, described the day as "a date that will live in infamy." At the center of President Kennedy's famous inaugural speech was the notion that a new generation was taking over and the nation was embarking on "a new frontier." Martin Luther King, Jr., famously declared, "I have a dream." The less historic but no less effective motivational speaker is trying to get his audience to "seize the day"—a phrase as old as ancient Rome. Business leaders call it "the marching song"—a phrase with which they inspire their employees over the next few years. (For General Electric it was "Quality," for IBM it was "Think," for Avis it was "We try harder.") Ideally, that phrase will be so memorable that it will become the name of the speech, as with King's "I have a dream speech" or Roosevelt's "date of infamy speech."

Reserve Power. You are not likely to dry up in public if you are filled to the brim with information. As a speaker, I am always overprepared. For a twenty-minute presentation, I have forty minutes' worth of stuff to go to. If, for some reason, you lose a train of thought or an anecdote vanishes from your brain, you will have all sorts of alternatives. Five minutes into my friend's affirmative action speech, a woman in the audience was already so annoyed by his message that she could not resist leaping to her feet to criticize him. The audience, most of them well over fifty and bourgeois, were stunned by her rudeness. I was more concerned that the interruption would derail my friend. But he kept his cool and reminded the woman that he was the invited speaker and had barely introduced his remarks; he also added that there would be a question-and-answer period after he finished. The woman stood her ground, but he simply waited for a few seconds, allowing the stares of the rest of the crowd to convince her that it might be a good idea to sit down and shut up, which she did. He returned to his prepared remarks without missing a beat. He knew his subject too well for a bit of heckling to make him lose the thread of his argument.

If you are an expert on an issue, or you have a certain job or hobby, you probably know as much as anyone in the room. What sports nut, passionate fly fisherman, skilled home decorator, adventurous chef, or opera fanatic ever runs out of things to say? When preparing a presentation, you must make yourself the expert, and when you stand before your audience brimming with that information, you are not likely to go to Cleveland if something unforeseen happens.

THERE'S A REASON IT'S CALLED
PUBLIC SPEAKING: WINNING YOUR AUDIENCE

Neil Simon did not begin restructuring *Seesaw* until he'd sat in the audience and watched the show—and watched the rest of the audience watching the show, noting how his fellow audience members were responding to every scene and song. When Gittel and Jerry first get together, they dance, to the delight of the audience; later in the show they dance in a big ensemble number that wows the audience. But when the moment came for Jerry and Gittel, madly in love, to dance together again while I, as Jerry, sang my big number, "We've Got It," the audience response was restrained.

In the original production, Gittel is in the hospital after surgery for a chronic ulcer that has been exacerbated by her new romance. Jerry visits her, they're in love, he sings a song, pulls her out of bed, and they do a big dance number. What is wrong with this picture? Simon put his finger on the problem immediately: "The audience is worried about the stitches tearing." He explained that while an audience is willing to suspend disbelief on many matters, watching a woman who has just had surgery dance in her hospital room was asking too much. Too many people were thinking, "What about the stitches?"

How to fix it? "Have him dance for her," Simon advised, adding that we should play up the fact that Jerry is doing it to cheer her up and make her laugh. As Jerry, I was required to dance like a guy who'd never had a dance lesson in his life and was winging it. This was hardly a stretch for me. Michael Bennett and Tommy Tune managed to teach me a whole dance number using every step I'd ever learned in summer stock and every move I could make that resembled something out of an old movie musical. After I sang the first part of the song to Michele, I sat her back in her hospital bed and danced around the room on my own, at one point cracking, "Don't look so surprised . . . Fred Astaire came from Omaha, ya know!" It worked. With the same lyrics, the same set, and the same actors, Neil Simon—by taking into account the audience's concern and changing the scene slightly—had prompted a dance number that went from eliciting polite applause in Detroit to stopping the show on Broadway.

Speakers, too, must try to see a performance from the audience's point of view. This is another one of those principles that seems obvious; yet the creators of *Seesaw* did not see what seemed obvious to Neil Simon and the rest of the audience. Too often the people mounting a big production get so caught up in their vision and passion that they lose sight of whether it is really any good. How often have you sat through a show or movie (or sermon, lecture, speech, or presentation, for that matter) and thought, "Surely they knew this was bad and boring!" More than likely, they thought it was great. It is not easy to step outside your own work and cast a cold eye on it. But every speaker must try to see both the message and its delivery. The audience is always asking the question "What are you *really* telling us, and why?" You have to keep asking yourself, "What are they *really* thinking, and why?" If you intend to communicate, you must understand whom you are trying to reach.

For more than twenty years, my friend Tom Sullivan has been one of the most successful motivational speakers in America; he gives more than eighty speeches a year to corporations. Tom is not only an articulate, well-organized speaker, he is funny and can move the toughest audience to tears. He attributes his longevity on the lecture circuit to being committed every time to winning the audience, or, as he puts it, "taming the beast." I attribute it to the fact that Tom is an experienced entertainer and a natural actor who understands that to make a performance look easy, you have to work extremely hard. Tom has been blind since birth, but no one connects with an audience better. He is particularly astonishing at responding to the mood of an audience he cannot even see. With his incredibly developed sense of hearing, he seems to be able to tune directly in to the hearts and minds of the people. "You have to want to connect to your audience as a speaker and as a human being," Tom has told me during our conversations about what it takes to be a successful communicator. "If you treat them like a workforce, you're dead." Tom never gives a speech without knowing exactly who his audience is and what their expectations are. Before every corporate speech, he does extensive research on the company and its competition, so he can tailor his message and actions to make a personal connection with the audience. Above all, like any good actor, Tom gives them what they want most:

A real person.

THE POWER OF PERSONAL STORYTELLING

Actors, as we saw in the previous chapter, come alive onstage by making choices that personalize their performance. For a speaker, that same kind of spontaneity can be achieved by preparing a presentation in such a way that when you finally deliver it, it is part of your experience, a piece of your biography. The easiest way to make that happen is to convey your message with some real-life stories.

Great speakers like Tom Sullivan tend to be natural storytellers. They seem able to relate everything they say to a story from their own lives—"something that you can pull right out from inside you," as Tom puts it. He has a lot to draw on. In spite of his blindness, he wrestled competitively in high school, rowed crew for Harvard, has run marathons, loves to ski, and plays golf every chance he gets. He is also a first-rate entertainer who plays the piano, writes music, and sings beautifully (his rendition of "Danny Boy" never fails to knock 'em dead). He has been married to Patti forever and has two grown kids. He wrote an early autobiography called *If You Could See What I Hear* that was made into a successful movie for television.

Tom Sullivan is often asked to address business audiences on the topic of dealing with adversity. He is hardly the only motivational speaker to tackle this issue, but I assure you no one on the lecture circuit can bring as much personal experience to it. Tom brings his own life experience to every speech he gives, and the effect is always masterful and moving.

Even if you are the sort of person who has trouble digging inside, you will have personalized your presentation simply by preparing it. Someone else trying to accomplish the same thing—win financing, give away the bride, sell more widgets—will have come up with a different set of things to say. You choose to make your case in your way, or, in acting terms, to make it your own. To act natural up there, you have to be you—the best possible you, to be sure, but still no one other than you. This effort to personalize your message is a crucial step to appearing real. And remember: It is this sense of reality that grabs the audience. So as you prepare your presentation, you must try to make every detail you include part of your own biography, even information you have just learned. Before I spent my first summer at the Williamstown Theatre Festival, Nikos Psacharopoulos thought it would be useful for me to "go down [to New York] and talk to Gadg." Gadg was Elia Kazan, who, among his long list of accomplishments in the American theater, had directed the original productions of Arthur Miller's *Death of a Salesman,* starring Lee J. Cobb, and Tennessee Williams's *A Streetcar Named Desire,* starring the twenty-three-year-old Marlon Brando. Kazan had been nicknamed Gadget, which friends shortened to Gadg, because he liked to tinker with things (and people). What young actor would not be delighted to be invited to meet with such a living legend? I put on a suit and took the train to Manhattan, expecting Kazan to give me a few minutes of his time. We spent two hours together. I found out later that this was pure Kazan, who was known to audition actors for a part by asking them to talk about who they were and where they came from.

A former actor who had also been a member of the Group Theatre and the Actors Studio, Kazan was particularly curious about Yale School of Drama. He asked me how I liked it there, and after I gave him my take, he asked, "What did you do for your audition to get in?" I told him I had done Jamie Tyrone's speech, in which he talks about the hooker named Fat Violet in *Long Day's Journey into Night,* and Macbeth's "Tomorrow and tomorrow and tomorrow" soliloquy. Kazan seemed impressed and wondered if I had spent some time on these roles in an acting class. I told him I had done both in college productions. "Perfect," said Kazan, who then launched into a discussion about the difference between getting up in front of a cold room with a speech you've learned for an audition, and a role you've performed onstage. When you've done the role, you see in your mind the other characters, the lights, the audience, the pause that held here, the laugh you got there, the applause afterward. The people auditioning you see an empty stage or room. You are seeing a whole show under way—indeed, reliving an unforgettable series of moments in your life—and it cannot help but affect your audition positively. (This is assuming you were any good in the first place.) That original performance is as much a part of your life as your first kiss, your high school graduation, your marriage.

Kazan was making the same point to a young actor that I am making to the speaker eager to improve: If your listeners think they are hearing your talk for the first time, but you have done it many times before, you are bound to be more impressive. How do you make a single speech part of your biography? By practicing it. You can make any presentation your own or second nature through extensive preparation and practice, including test-driving it in front of friends or family. When you finally appear in front of your real audience, in your mind, it will not be the first time you delivered the speech. Preparation of this kind should do wonders for your self-confidence as a speaker. A couple of years ago, I was asked to perform live and on-camera at a big bicoastal extravaganza called *Stage Blue,* celebrating Yale's contribution to the dramatic arts over the past century. The producer, Richard Maltby, Jr., wondered if I would consider doing a medley from *Man of La Mancha.* "No problem," I said. My quick commitment seemed to surprise him. An experienced director, Maltby knew how much work it would take me to get several songs up to speed, and I suspect he thought my response a little on the cocky side until I told him that I had played the role of Don Quixote at the Pasadena Civic Auditorium in 1990. Not that I wouldn't have to put in some rehearsal time, but refreshing your memory of songs you've already performed in front of large audiences is a lot easier than preparing from scratch. It was another twist on Kazan's advice to go with something that is already part of your biography. As Kazan also told me, "It's amazing how, no matter what you do as a director, writer, or actor in the theater, the real work begins once the audience starts looking at it. Not just comedy. Tragedy, too. It starts to take on a whole new life with an audience."

But the audience is a fickle beast. Once you have won them over, you cannot rest on that triumph. You must hold their attention to the very end. Over the years, I have learned how quickly and easily you can lose them.

DANGER SIGNS:
RESPECTING YOUR AUDIENCE

Like any construction site, presentations and speeches in the works ought to have some danger signs. Here are some to watch out for:

Don't try to say too much. Creating a speech from scratch is a hurdle for every speaker. Worse still can be learning how to put on the brakes once you get rolling. While you test yourself as a speaker, I would advise keeping your remarks brief. I think I have already shown how much you can say in a minute. Keep it focused. Even in a half-hour presentation, there is usually an idea or two you want to get across, and that's it. A journalist friend of mine once explained that the recipe for a good editorial, column, or op-ed piece is to have one point and then make sure everything else in the article serves it. Grab a pile of recent newspapers and read the editorials. If a reader finishes an opinion piece without understanding what it was getting at, then the writer has failed. The speaker has the same obligation: to make the point of the speech crystal-clear to even the dimmest member of the audience. So stick to one major idea and several paragraphs, making them come alive with stories and images.

Don't try to be too memorable. The effect you are looking for is conversational, and when you're talking to friends, your language is not likely to be too flowery. A nice phrase for effect can be useful, and a take-home line would be great. But if you pile on the poetry, you risk burying your audience rather than impressing them. I thought President George W. Bush's inaugural speech was quite good for him—a very good professional politician but an amateur speaker. He seemed more comfortable than usual and much better prepared. Clearly, someone had worked with him. The downside of the speech, at least for me, was that it was overwritten. There were so many nice phrases that I ended up not remembering any of them.

Don't try to be too original. When I asked my students to tell me how they would approach the podium, they were inclined to say the following: "You head directly for it, stand there, relax, wait for things to get quiet, get a fix on your own presence, and don't rush." Yes, but not necessarily. Somebody might begin talking on the way to the lectern. I'd prefer not to be dogmatic and say such a beginning is a big mistake. I would have to see it first. But my students' conservative instincts are probably right for the beginner. Even though you might be ready to start speaking as soon as you get to the podium, your audience might not be ready to listen. It will be a shame if you have a great opening and only twelve people in the front row hear it, while the rest are spending the next thirty seconds asking one another, "What did he say?" Or worse: "If only I were up front in the expensive seats, I would have heard that." You want to impress your audience, not tick them off, particularly with your first sentence. You can make sure your audience is ready by taking the time to look directly at them for a moment or two. See who's there. It will help settle them. It will help you, too. If you pay attention to them, they will pay attention to you.

Don't risk losing your audience before you even say a word. Audiences have their preconceptions. Whether you like it or not, your listeners will be building their own prejudices about you even before you show your face. When you do step into the room or up to the podium, keep in mind that your performance has already begun. And while you may think that your clothes or hairstyle or tattoos are nobody's business, members of the audience will take all of the above very personally. If you are eager to impress, then avoid distractions. "It's the message that counts," advised Dale Carnegie. "Think of yourself as a Western Union boy instructed to deliver it." He told students to "pay slight attention to the boy, it is the telegram that we want." I agree. Your primary aim is to stay focused on the message, know it cold, and deliver it with feeling and determination. But I would add that if the messenger is delivering a serious point, he'd better not be wearing a silly hat, and he should leave the neon tie in the closet. Anything else that deters the audience from your message should not accompany you into the room. When I prepare for an audition, the question "What are they expecting?" is paramount in my mind. By the time I drive into the parking lot, I'm already the character I think they want. I know that to have any chance of getting the part, I have to satisfy the buyer. Does that mean that if I'm auditioning for the role of a scary bad guy, a murderous driver is loose on the freeways? No. If my first audience on the way to work is a state trooper, I will be meek and very polite indeed. Everything I am doing as an actor is coming from within me. The rest of the world does not have to know that I'm on my way to an audition, any more than they will know that I'm heading to buy groceries for dinner.

Don't get too cocky. I recall a certain student with some talent for public speaking who, after one triumph, decided it wasn't so hard after all. The next time up he proceeded to wing it— and fell apart. He discredited in his mind the work he had done the first time around but soon discovered that to avoid embarrassing himself, he had to prepare extensively.

Don't forget that most accidents happen close to home. Just as you must be careful about the first impression you make on your audience, you do not want to blow all the goodwill you've built up during the presentation by not knowing when to stop. Studies show that most accidents happen close to home, and it has been my experience that the same is true of speaking disasters. A speaker often gets a little too cocky in the last few minutes of the presentation. The audience has responded well, the speaker knows he's on his way home, a sense of relief overtakes him, and he lets his guard down. That's usually the moment when he makes an unwarranted crack, decides to tell another story, or forgets to say something important.

DON'T FORGET THE MOST IMPORTANT STEP IN PREPARING A SPEECH:

PRACTICE, PRACTICE, PRACTICE— IN FRONT OF OTHERS

I often told my students that the best way to prepare a little story or joke, or even an entire speech, was to try it out on some friends. "No way!" was their reaction. It was as if I'd asked them to undress in public. "I would be too uncomfortable, too self-conscious," they typically answered. My counterargument went something like this: "It's a lot easier to try out what you're going to say before friends or family than a roomful of three hundred strangers."

I understand the resistance. You don't want anybody to see you—not even your closest, kindest friend, and definitely not your immediate family—until you have it just right. But you will never get your speech perfect without taking it out for a test drive. Comedians are great at this. They try out their jokes and stories in conversation, then before friends, then in a small theater. No experienced comedian (with the exception of Robin Williams) tries out a joke for the first time on *The Tonight Show*. To be great under pressure, you have to get used to it. After all, it is *public* speaking. You are already good at talking to yourself, and probably adequate at shooting the breeze with your friends.

At some point, you have to go public, the sooner, the better. Extensive practice and rehearsing in front of a friendly audience will not only make your words seem second nature—part of your biography—they will also build up your self-confidence.

If there is a weakness in your presentation, the quickest way to flush it out is to go public. And you want to know about all your weaknesses. If you stumble now, when you're fooling around, there's a reason for it, and you'd better get to the bottom of it immediately. Otherwise, under pressure, you will arrive at that problem spot and go to Cleveland. I promise you. Your inability to get past that stumbling block will also become part of your biography.

WORKING ON YOUR WEAKNESSES

The assignment that got the biggest groan in my class at Harvard Law School was preparing to sing a song in public. Most of those kids had no problem singing in private, in the car or in the shower, even with friends at a party. Singing alone in front of an audience was quite a different story—but quite similar to giving a speech. I cotaught the course with Charlie Nesson, one of Harvard Law School's legendary teachers. With more than twenty years' experience lecturing to some of the brightest young legal minds in the nation, Professor Nesson did not need any help with speaking in public. But he decided to prepare a song for the class because, as he confessed to me, "I am so horrified by the prospect that it must be valuable."

I had advised the class to get up there and sing a song they loved. Charlie picked the classic golden oldie "Earth Angel," which was pretty funny coming from an eminent law professor known for tackling First Amendment issues and teaching criminal evidence. But he sang it, and while there was no chance that

he would be abandoning the law for Broadway (or even wedding gigs), the students seemed touched by his effort to express
solidarity with them in their suffering. Afterward, Nesson admitted to being "a little bit in shock," but a few days later he explained to me what he had learned from the experience: "Most
people go with their strengths all the time, never attacking their
own weaknesses." In his lectures, he taught how to expose the
weaknesses in one's own case by trying to make the strongest
case possible for the other side and then countering it. My
singing exercise had given him another analogy: Find your
weakness and fix it, thus depriving the opposition of a way to
undercut your case.

Taking the cue from Nesson, I worked a lot more efficiently
with the law students by ignoring the things they were good at
as communicators and concentrating on what needed work. Be
clearer about your message, I told them, add some gestures,
speak louder, hold the lectern to keep that hand from shaking,
and so on. After preparing an oral argument and working on the
weaknesses I had pointed out, they would perform in front of
their classmates. The next time they stood up in class, they
would realize that they had become exponentially better as
public speakers, having improved practically overnight.

So . . . what are your weaknesses? A common problem is
speaking too softly or too slowly. Actors can suffer from both of
these defects. An old friend of mine with a lot of classical acting
credits, whose terrific voice made him a nice living in TV com-
mercials, went to the Ahmanson Theater in Los Angeles to see
Charlton Heston play *Macbeth*. Heston in a great Shakespearean
role was a risky night out for starters, but my friend was a
Shakespeare lover, and he, like many other Hollywood actors,
was curious about what Ben Hur would do to Macbeth. *Macbeth* is a very long play, so when Charlton Heston's aspiring
king made his entrance and launched into a stentorian and ex-

tremely slow version of "So foul and fair a day I have not seen," massaging every word for all it was worth, my friend said, "I'm outta here. If he's going to make a meal of that speech, we'll never get home."

Deliver your remarks in as conversational a tone and pace as possible. If you are speaking in a large room, don't practice in a small one; no one will hear you. And if you have never used a microphone, try a run-through in front of a microphone. I always find it distracting when a speaker leans in to the microphone, as if worried that it won't pick up his voice from the normal speaking position. Some speakers are great in certain circumstances, a small group versus a large auditorium; others may be great in pitches or company speeches but feel out of place in a formal situation. Just because you're in black tie or wearing a cap and gown doesn't mean you can't be yourself. Your old school may have invited you to give the commencement address, but why should you be as boring as most of the graduation speakers you've heard? With each of the several graduation speeches Bill Cosby gives each year, he begins formally, acknowledging the college president and the esteemed faculty, but manages to fill the rest of his time with humor. Cosby is careful not to deliver a pure stand-up routine; he has a message to convey to the graduates and their families about how their investment in higher education is a wonderful thing. Informative and even serious does not necessarily mean boring.

If you are still not sure what your weaknesses are, prepare the following assignment, try it out in front of a pickup audience, then ask for a candid appraisal. And remember: Your goal is not to be Ronald Reagan or Bill Cosby. For the moment, you are looking only to get better than you are, and even a few minutes of your best possible self is likely to be a huge improvement. The quickest way to improve your performance, as any actor will tell you, is to put in as much rehearsal time as possible.

Assignment #3

Prepare a presentation of an experience from your own life that taught you a lesson.

Feel free to embellish this biographical incident, even if it means taking some poetic license. The point of the exercise is not to tell the unvarnished truth but to get the feel for structuring a speech that will help you come alive before an audience. We all have a story that we like to tell. It can be funny or sad, but it should be instructive. Such a presentation should almost structure itself: You know the story, then you hammer home its point. But find a story that belongs to you. You do not need to go searching for something new and original. It can be a favorite anecdote from school or your career; it can be a story your grandmother used to tell you. It can be from a book you've read or a movie or play you've seen or a speech you heard someone else give. All this information is stored in your memory bank and is therefore part of who you are.

Before you start racking your brain for stories with a moral, keep in mind that once you know what lesson you want to convey—your message—the story will be a lot easier to come up with; you can even tailor a favorite chestnut. I do it all the time. For example: From the first paragraph of this chapter, I have been telling you a series of anecdotes from my own career that serve my overall objective: to help you learn how to prepare a brief presentation. Each anecdote has also helped me make a particular point. I began with the story of a Broadway show that was in big trouble on the road and needed revision. In this way, I established the chapter's theme: the importance of structure to delivering a clear message. I then described Neil Simon's constructive advice. The purpose of that story: the importance of an explanation in your opening of what your speech is all about.

And thus the connection between my Broadway anecdote and public speaking: Speeches, like musicals, are about something, and exactly what they are about must be clear; so tell 'em what you're gonna tell 'em, and don't let the rest of the speech confuse your audience or divert them from your main message.

That brings me to the second big point of this chapter: A good speaker must win over his audience. To do that, you have to anticipate their expectations. I illustrated this point with my story about Neil Simon's observation that the audience was worried about the leading lady's stitches.

Frankly, I have told these stories many times before, for all sorts of different purposes: to explain what a great script doctor Neil Simon was, to show the kind of pressures an actor is up against in a new show on the road, to show how a few key changes can turn a struggling production into a hit. My Neil Simon stories are part of my own biography. But this is the first time I've used them to demonstrate the importance of structure in public speaking. What focuses each of my tellings is the message I want to make. (Notice how the previous two paragraphs again repeat the overall objective of this chapter: Figure out the point you want to make in your speech and why, then structure the rest of what you say around that basic message. Let the message be your guide and editor.)

There is, however, another important reason why I want you to tell a story that you are very familiar with: I want this exercise to be as easy as possible. I do not want you agonizing over whether you can remember it under pressure. Recall the story, refresh your memory with its details, then be sure it is making your point. Tell it once and then again. Keep improving it, embellishing it, making it more dramatic, funnier, more touching. Make it as good as you can. And then gather a small group around and tell 'em what you want to tell 'em, tell 'em, and tell 'em what you've told 'em. *And do it all without notes.*

Without notes? Why not? It's your story about your life. You've told it before, prepared it, practiced it. Do you need notes to tell your friends about that day you went fishing with your father and caught a huge fish? Do you need to write down the story about how your date to the junior prom showed up at your place, met your father, and lost his voice? This exercise should include an anecdote that is equally familiar, so you will give yourself the best chance to be relaxed and natural before your audience. It is virtually impossible for most people to act natural when they are reading a speech or reciting it verbatim.

Give yourself several days with Assignment #3. If you put in the work, you will take your public-speaking ability to a new level. In the process, you will discover something amazing about your potential as a communicator: You have a photographic memory! We all do, and in the next chapter, I will help you develop it. But first do this assignment, and when you are ready to move on, let me tell you another story.

4

DISCOVERING YOUR

"PHOTOGRAPHIC MEMORY"

In the spring of 1999, I delivered the commencement address at Kent State University's advanced-degrees ceremony, where I was also getting a Master of Fine Arts. You know the scene: a large gymnasium lined with banners of the Kent State basketball team (the Golden Flashes), graduates in their caps and gowns, proud parents, a couple thousand people staring at the university administration, faculty, and me sitting on the dais in my cap and gown. The president of the university, Carol Cartwright, welcomed the audience, awarded a special medal to an English professor who had served Kent State for most of his long life, then introduced the featured speaker, me. It was a formal occasion, so I began formally: "President Cartwright, Dean Sullivan, members of the platform party, members of the faculty, fellow graduates, graduate and undergraduate students, friends and family, honored guests . . ."

But I did not want to be too formal. I continued: "I am honored to stand before you as the geriatric member of the graduat-

ing class of the Master of Fine Arts program at the College of
Fine and Professional Arts here at Kent State University."

That got a nice laugh. The audience was now comfortable. To
make sure I had won them over, I let them know that in spite of
my showbiz credentials, we had much in common:

> It seemed to me not altogether inappropriate to share with you
> today the story of how my being here came to pass. Or, more
> specifically, to answer the question that was posed to me
> rather succinctly a little more than a year ago by the proprietor
> of Palcho's Donut Shop, a place I frequented often on my way
> to class. He looked at me and said, "What the hell are *you*
> doing *here?*"

Just mentioning Palcho's got a laugh because most of the people
in the audience knew the place and its crusty owner. His question got an even bigger laugh.

The answer to that question became the theme of my commencement address—why, thirty years after leaving Yale to take
a small part in a Broadway musical, I had returned to this particular university to finish my M.F.A. degree. I told them how, a few
years before, I had been invited by Kent State to the ceremony
presenting the Robert Lewis Award for Exceptional Contribution
in the Teaching of Dramatic Arts, named in honor of one of my
favorite teachers at Yale. I accepted gladly, mainly because it
would be an opportunity for me to see Bobby Lewis, who was
in frail health. I told them it was with Bobby's blessing that I
took the small part in *Promises, Promises* rather than returning
for my final year and my M.F.A. degree, when many others at
Yale were telling me I was making a big mistake. "But something
in my heart and dreams told me to seize this opportunity, and I
did." Bobby Lewis had encouraged me, and the rest was hardly
history, but it did turn out to be my career: *1776,* great reviews,

a multimovie deal with Otto Preminger—all within a year of leaving Yale. Kent State was honoring Bobby, and I wanted to be part of it.

The town of Kent, Ohio, was founded as part of the Western Reserve for settlers from New England. I told my audience how, on my first visit to their town, Kent's clapboard houses and tree-lined streets reminded me of my own college days in the colonial Massachusetts town of Amherst, where I first began thinking about an acting career. The connections between Kent and Amherst and Bobby Lewis and the unusual path of a career in theater, I explained, had also brought back a memory of Robert Frost on a porch in Amherst reciting one of his most memorable poems, which I then recited for my audience, ending with Frost's famous lines

> I shall be telling this with a sigh
> Somewhere ages and ages hence:
> Two roads diverged in a wood, and I—
> I took the one less traveled by,
> And that has made all the difference.

I told my audience that though my career has had its ups and downs, I have always been thankful for the encouragement from teachers like Bobby Lewis to take the road less traveled by. I thanked my teachers at Kent State and the administration for their flexibility in setting up a program that would allow a working actor to meet the academic requirements for an M.F.A. Finally, I wished my fellow graduates Godspeed on their own journeys down different paths toward their dreams.

And I did it without notes. Many members of the faculty seemed quite surprised that I would get up there to speak for twenty minutes without even an index card to refer to. One of the things nonactors always ask actors is "How do you memorize all those lines?" For most actors, getting the lines straight is the least of it. I have always been blessed with a good memory. By age fourteen, I realized that I had a photographic memory when I was reviewing the information for a history exam in my head and saw a smudge on the upper right-hand corner of that mental page—the same smudge my notes had. Frankly, learning my lines quickly used to be my way of showing off on the job. But all actors manage to learn their lines eventually. I would venture to say that not everyone who has played Hamlet, Macbeth, or any other of the famously long roles in the history of theater has been blessed with a camera for a memory. Someone once asked the great Laurence Olivier, who had played, well, everything, how he got all that dialogue into his head. "I close myself in my office with my script and a bottle of Scotch," said Olivier, "and I don't come out until I've got it." That is pretty much it, with or without the Scotch. For most actors, mastering the script is a slow, lengthy process. It is one part of the preparation for any role, which always requires, as I stressed in the previous chapter, practice, practice, practice.

But as I have also stressed, you as a speaker do not have to deliver the words verbatim. If you fluff a phrase, so what? It is likely to make you seem a lot more real up there. That must always be your primary goal. It is the actor's goal, too. When you are playing one of William Shakespeare's great characters, or one of Tennessee Williams's, you never want your audience to say, "Isn't it great what Shakespeare [or Tennessee] is saying"; you want them to think that Hamlet or Stanley Kowalski is inventing those words on the spot. Any actor who looks to be reciting the playwright's words will not be successful, and any speaker who reads a speech, even if it is off of an imaginary cue card, will not impress the audience. (Note that skilled communicators manage to seem like they're just talking to the audience even when they're reading their speeches.) The goal is to get out there and remember what you prepared to say. The primary cause of performance anxiety is the nagging feeling that you might forget what you want to say. A reliable memory is essential for public speaking. It not only does wonders for your confidence but will also allow you to spend more time practicing all the other things that will make you seem real and spontaneous in public. Anyone can develop reliable recall. There is a computer inside your head with remarkable storage and retrieval capacities—if you know how to load it, turn it on, and trust it.

WHAT MAKES A MEMORY PHOTOGRAPHIC

As I get older and cementing things in my mind takes longer, I have become more sympathetic to people who are insecure about their memories. My solution has been more time in preparation and practice. Yes, on the face of it, an actor's ability to master the number of lines to play Hamlet is a wonder. But when you consider that actors get five weeks of rehearsal to prepare for a Broadway play, is it really so amazing? Doing a play is not about a quick grasp of the material—what I have heard some soap-opera actors, who are required to learn a new script every day, call "shallow memory" (enough to get through a scene or to the point where the camera can pick up where you left off from another camera angle). Learning a role becomes a full-time job that has an actor's mind working day and night.

If you put in even a fraction of that kind of hard work, you will not forget the remarks you want to make. I can't tell you how many times I have heard people say, "I've got to get to work on a speech I'm giving in a couple of days." My usual reply: "How brave of you!" They are surprised when I inform them that I am inclined to spend a couple of weeks preparing a speech. (I worked on the Kent State talk for at least that.) It is work that pays huge dividends. Few of you will ever be called on to prepare a two-hour presentation, but even pulling off a one-minute introduction requires the same kind of focus and intensity. If you do the work and give it time to settle in your memory, what you learned will be there when it comes time to roll the tape. I have watched this phenomenon happen again and again with students. With proper preparation, they knew they wouldn't get lost, and that self-confidence freed them up to adjust according to the audience and the moment. When the presentation was over, they realized they had done it almost verbatim, even though they weren't trying to; it didn't even seem difficult. There is a reason why athletes work on their moves and swings constantly, or why astronauts train in simulators, or why soldiers in special operations forces spend most of their time in various war games. That, after all, is the point of rehearsal and practice: You want to work so much on the skills you need that they become second nature and will be there under pressure. Good athletes are not thinking about fundamentals during the game. As the skier hurtles down the slalom course, she is not thinking about the edges of her skis or the positioning of her poles; she's looking for the next gate, she's thinking only "faster" or "slower," "higher" or "lower," and "get to the bottom." You, too, must put yourself under the gun and test out your remarks before a few friends or family; by the time you get before your scheduled audience, everything you want to say will be there. Your success will have nothing to do with remembering something word for word. With the right kind of practice, you won't have to worry about the details and can react to the situation at hand.

One of the reasons it was relatively easy for me to give the speech without notes at Kent State is that I was telling the twenty-minute version of how I came to be an actor. As we saw in the last chapter, a story is built around a message with information and the images that serve it. Such a speech-story will have an internal logic, and once you have that clear in your mind, you will easily be able to move from one idea and image to the next, relying on the structure of what you are saying. At Kent State, I went to the podium with an outline in my head, a kind of mental map to follow: the guy in the donut shop, what brought me to Kent, Ohio, how that reminded me of my own college days at Amherst, where I learned the value of taking the road less traveled, decided to take an acting fellowship at Yale, bucked the conventional wisdom, once again with a teacher's encouragement, went to New York and launched my acting career, and thirty years later was back at another university advising acting students to follow their dreams. I did not have to memorize that trajectory. It was my life. How many times had I told my story about deciding to take a chance and go to drama school and then to Broadway? To turn it into a commencement speech, all I had to do was modify the story according to the question I got in Palcho's. Sure, I had to get the names of the university president and the dean straight, and the order of the acknowledgments, plus the local term "platform party" for those on the dais. Anyone could memorize that by reading the lines several times and including them in rehearsals at home.

What about the Frost poem? I had to memorize those words verbatim. But I had done that decades before as an English major. For my Kent State speech, I had only to review the poem to make sure I hadn't modified it in my mind over the years and then practice it a few times. Truth in advertisement: During my recitation, I actually flubbed a line. It happens. I backed up, restated the line, and continued as if nothing had happened. I suspect many in the audience did not even realize I had made a mistake. But notice how even that poem from my college days was also part of my biography—and my memory.

Photographic memory is not remembering every single word.

It is about setting the entire map of what you are saying clearly in your mind. By structuring your remarks in one way rather than another, you have already imposed a logic on them. That logic should help you remember the main points you intend to stop at on your mental map—donut shop, first trip to Kent State, associations with Amherst, drama school, Bobby Lewis, and so on, one bit following the other. The way you create that map is through three simple techniques that are crucial to memorizing just about anything:

Impression, association, and REPETITION.

You have probably used these memory techniques many times without realizing it, particularly in learning people's names. It is definitely one of my secrets for learning names quickly. By the second class of my Harvard course, for example, I was able to call on the students by name—all sixty-four of them. I had their names so nailed that when I fumbled once, the class laughed and applauded.

Here's how I did it: I asked all the students who auditioned for the class to give me index cards with their name, hometown, class year, and major. As each student auditioned, I watched and listened, making notes on their cards about how they did, something they said, what they looked like, or any other detail that stuck out: "roly-poly—cookies and milk," for example, a reference to a student who told a funny anecdote about his mother keeping track of his late-night intake of cookies and milk; or "high C," the talented singer who hit that note after using the speaker's cliché "on another note." To recollect a name, I have to give myself something to hang my memory on, like a jacket on a hook with a student's name on it. Auditioning more than a hundred kids at a minute apiece took a few classes, and after each session, with faces and performances still fresh in my mind, I would spend time looking over the index cards, associating the names and my notes with the faces. I actually had a little home movie in my head of each student speaking in front of the class.

Isn't this how you often remember the events of your day? You revisit them and see them happening in your mind's eye, hear the voices in your mind's ear, as if they were characters in a movie you have just seen. We all have our own instant-replay camera. Once you've replayed the events, how hard is it to break down what happened into an outline and remember that breakdown for days afterward? The combination of the information on the index card and a full minute of each kid made it pretty easy for me to form a clear imprint in my mind of their faces, names, and something striking about their individual personas. At the next class, with my sixty-four select students before me, I made sure to refer to various members of this audience by name as I asked questions or referred to their auditions. My memory trick had the desired dramatic effect. The students were first surprised that I knew a couple of names. This surprise quickly turned to astonishment as I referred to several more people by name. As I continued through the hour using more names, the appreciation— "Hey, that is really impressive; he already knows who we are"—quickly turned to quiet horror: "Oh my God, there's no way to cut this class without this guy knowing I'm missing!" I enjoyed the moment, but by showing off, I had also suggested how impressive such a small thing as knowing someone's name could be outside the classroom, in the world of business and careers, where so many of my students would be heading with big ambitions.

I had learned their names via the age-old memory techniques of impression, association, and repetition. I studied each person so I could keep a picture in my mind as I said his or her name (impression). I noted a trait ("roly-poly") or reference ("high C") that would also punch up the student's picture and name (association). Later, looking over the index cards and running the movie of their auditions in my head, I worked at matching the names to the pictures. In my mind, I would see the student again, say the name, and I had it. By then it was as if the name were superimposed on the face, spelled correctly (I always made sure I had the correct spelling of a name on the index card). After a few repetitions of this simple process and a quick review the following day, then again the next day before class, I knew who was who.

And those names stuck. Fifteen years later, I can still roll that movie in my head and recall at least half the names. I suspect you could do the same if you pulled out one of your old class pictures, the older the better. Do you remember the name of every kid in your eighth-grade class? Probably not. But you're likely to remember the name of the teacher and several of the kids. Why? Because teachers make a big impression on kids, and so do some classmates—the girl you had a crush on, the kid who stole your lunch money, the guy who accidentally hit you with a baseball bat, the girl who used to dance all by herself in the schoolyard. You do not forget such things. I would also bet that just seeing those faces and recalling those names will ignite a series of memories you hadn't thought about for decades. Our photographic memories are like that.

MEMORIZING A HUGE PART—BIT BY BIT

If you've ever memorized even a short poem, you will already have a sense of how an actor learns a big part. The main difference is time and work. The Broadway plays usually budget four or five weeks of rehearsal time, during which actors work through their roles, trying to understand their characters' motivations and behavior by discovering exactly what the writer's words mean. Many actors I've worked with do not try to learn the words at home. They tend to show up at rehearsal, script in hand, and go over the lines again and again until the point where, usually several weeks into rehearsal, they don't have to refer to the script anymore. Only then are they ready to "go off-book." I have done that; but for lead roles, if I haven't done most of my work at home, I risk slowing down the whole process of rehearsal. For films and TV, the memory process is a lot easier, because the actors are required to learn the dialogue for only a few scenes each day; also, if they screw up, they can reshoot it. But even with that kind of safety net, I like to show up on the set knowing my lines. Getting off-book as soon as possible is the way I like to work, but it also frees me up to begin making the role my own. Here's how I go about learning dialogue:

If a car sideswipes you and then speeds away, what do you do to remember the license number, 391J052, until you can get to a piece of paper and write it down? First, you have the image of the plate and the number in your mind's eye: 391J052. Second, you immediately start repeating the number out loud "391J052" (perhaps under your breath, but audibly), until you can write it down. "391J052, 391J052 . . ." The repetition of the numbers on either side of the letter "J" takes on a rhythm or beat, like music—bum, bum, bum, J, bum, bum, bum; or it becomes another rhythm that suits the memory pattern you are developing for yourself—bum, bum . . . bum, J, bum . . . bum, bum. Whatever works. Finally, you can write the numbers down. 3-9-1-J-0-5-2. You look at the numbers again to make sure they're right. A pattern will emerge that makes some kind of sense of the sequence 391J052 as you keep looking at it and repeating it aloud. (Some patterns will be more obvious than others—repeated numbers, for example; I purposefully chose a number that was more difficult.) Now you can look away and see the sequence in your mind as you say it again. Now say the sequence one more time. "391J052." You've got it.

Impression and repetition. You have an image of the numbers in your mind and now on paper. But having repeated the numbers so much, you will also have an aural impression that is likely to stick. After you phone in the license number of the hit-and-run driver, you can go about your business. But I suspect that at dinner, when you report what happened to your family, you will still be able to remember that license number. I use variations of this repetition-writing-seeing-hearing drill when I'm learning lines. Sometimes I write down the dialogue without any capitalization or punctuation, saying the words and hearing them while seeing them as I form their letters. As with the license number, you will see the words and get a picture of them lodged in your mind. I purposely leave out the capitals and punctuation, because the natural rhythm of speech expressing thought—where the pauses are—often differs greatly from the way language is structured to be read.

You can do the same thing with visual images you want to remember, including faces. Few things are more memorable than a strong visual image. Sounds, too, can be memorable, so I rehearse my lines out loud. Even when I think I've got them down, I find it particularly useful to run them out loud the night before I go in front of cameras. The day I film the scene, I will be saying the dialogue to myself and moving around as the character, right up to the moment I am called from my trailer to the set to begin shooting. Dale Carnegie enjoyed pointing out that Abraham Lincoln practiced his speeches out loud to get them locked into his memory bank. You get the words straight because you've actually heard them said correctly—by yourself. What was that license number again? Have you got it? Good! If not, go back and look again. Say it out loud. 391J052! Eventually, it will stick. I promise. It has to.

When an actor prepares for a big role, the dialogue can seem endless. But a play is a series of small stories, one scene moving into the next one. The actor conquers the dialogue line by line, speech by speech, scene by scene. A large play is a series of smaller stories all interconnected. Learning five hundred lines is a daunting prospect. But once you know you can learn a ten-line poem, for example, it becomes at least conceivable to do that fifty more times over the next five weeks. If you can plant two rows of peas, you can do an acre. Once you figure out how to put in one spark plug, you can do a thousand. I believe the same holds true for learning words: just a matter of time. By the time you step before your audience, it is a question of getting the tape rolling. When I performed the lead role in *Equus,* a massive undertaking, I worked out a little routine that became a running joke during the production. Every night before the play began, I would stand offstage with my English cigarettes in one hand and my lighter in the other. I have never been a smoker, but Dr. Martin Dysart, the lead character in *Equus,* is a chain-smoker, so I stood ready to fire up my first of many cigarettes when I stepped onstage as Dysart—but not before the stage manager fed me the first line of the play: "With one particular horse called Nugget, he embraces . . ." With that line in my mind, I could make my entrance in the dark and let the audio-tape in my head begin.

I cannot emphasize enough that by the time you have to perform, the language must be second nature. Even though you, as a public speaker, aren't responsible for uttering a writer's every word, after settling on your structure and telling your story in a particular order over and over, eventually you will be repeating your remarks almost verbatim. Certain ways of telling an anecdote work better than others; the statistics and data line up in a particular way; this conclusion will be more effective than that one; and you will stick with it. That is the way our memories work. Nothing should distract you from the words you have prepared. One of Robert Redford's favorite acting stories makes this point wonderfully: An inexperienced actor gets his first speaking role in a big production. It's just one line—"Hark, I hear the cannon roar!" The actor practices it, goes to the Actors Studio in New York, and works on the inner life of his character and the subtext of the line. He takes lessons in diction and breath control to help him perfectly deliver "Hark, I hear the cannon roar!" Finally, he's ready. Opening night arrives; he's in his makeup and tunic; the stage manager says, "You're on." He hustles out onstage, and no sooner does he get to his mark than there is a huge explosion: KABOOM! The surprised actor ducks reflexively, then turns to the audience and says, "What the fuck was that?"

In a live performance, all sorts of things can happen that might distract the actors: the air-conditioning fails, a light explodes, a member of the audience gets ill, another actor screws up, a prop breaks. The danger is that the actor is so intent on not forgetting the next line that he doesn't respond to what has happened. The audience can't ignore the elephant in the room, and neither should you, as an actor or speaker. If the last two rows of seats collapse with a crash, you have to acknowledge that or risk appearing very weird. One night during the production of *Child's Play,* my costars Pat Hingle and Fritz Weaver were in the middle of a scene when Hingle accidentally spilled coffee all over his papers. "I hate when that happens," Hingle ad-libbed, and spent the rest of the scene drying his desk, rearranging the papers, and saying his lines. Most of the audience probably thought the coffee spill was part of the play. Hingle's recovery was a wonderful piece of acting. But he wouldn't have been able to pull it off without a clear understanding of what he was doing in the scene, or without his lines securely stored in his inner computer. When my friend was heckled during his speech on affirmative action, he could hardly proceed as if that woman were not standing up in the middle of the audience, criticizing his position. He handled the situation and went back to his argument, which, since it was a well-considered personal conviction that he had written about and discussed for years, he was not about to forget, no matter the interruptions.

ACTIONS HELP THE MEMORY, TOO

In my experience, Shakespeare is the most difficult to learn . . . at first. Not only is the language complex and not always easily understandable, but actors often find themselves required to recite dialogue in which the subtext is spoken and most aspects of contemporary physical behavior must be avoided. Typically, in a regular play or film, the actor will be doing something while speaking—filling a pipe, loading a gun, putting away the dishes, driving a car, or embracing a lover. But if you are Hamlet, facing the audience and launching into the soliloquy "To be or not to be: that is the question," what do you do? Well, one thing you soon come to find when required to recite Shakespeare is that, although initially daunting, it is easier to memorize and deliver than damn near anything. It is written to be spoken, in blank verse, with words that seem so right for the ideas they express and so beautifully and rhythmically tied that they will stick in your mind forever. I can call up any number of Shakespearean speeches that are part of my permanent memory bank. You will be able to do the same.

But in most roles, what you are doing onstage provides a series of benchmarks for what you are saying: You light your pipe or pour the coffee as you say this line. If you've been taking my assignments seriously, you've already experienced how this correspondence between doing and saying helps you deliver a talk. At the end of Chapter Two, I asked you to prepare a how-to presentation. My primary goal there was to show you how actions and gestures would help you seem more spontaneous in public. But that kind of demonstration should also be easier to remember. Explaining how to fix a carburetor or showing how to swing a golf club has its own logic—first you do this, then you do this—that makes what you must say easier to remember.

The secret in any presentation is to outline the main points you want to cover and make sure they are connected, in the right order, in your mind. I like to create a series of pictures in my mind, the kind of mental map I used in my Kent State speech. Another analogy that might help you is a scrapbook, with each image that provides the basic structure of your remarks on its own page. Not long ago, I delivered a eulogy at a memorial for my mother-in-law, structured around several pictures in our family scrapbook. Linda's mother, Lorene, took pleasure in her final years, and she particularly liked to dance. To remind her mourners of that exuberance, I had a sequence of pictures in my mind, highlights of my relationship with Lorene as well as examples of her dancing spirit: dancing with her at our wedding; dancing together like Fred and Ginger to "The Way You Look Tonight" during her first trip to New York, outside in the snow under the lights of Central Park's Tavern on the Green; and the pleasure she took in her first visit to California's wondrous Monterey Peninsula. Those pictures were in chronological sequence, and I had plenty to say about each one that conjured up Lorene for her friends and family. Most of you will seldom be covering more than five or six points. How hard is it to keep that many issues straight, particularly after days of practice?

MEMORY TRICKS

There are all sorts of books on memory, and no shortage of memory gurus armed with an arsenal of tricks to help people remember numbers, faces, lists, and other information. Their mnemonic techniques, however, are as old as the ancient Greeks (*mnemosune* is the Greek word for "memory"). Before the invention of writing and then the widespread availability of books, poets, storytellers, and professional speakers had to train themselves to remember vast tracts of words as long as Homer's *Iliad* and *Odyssey* (15,693 and 12,109 lines). The central subject in the education of young Greeks—and then Romans, who, after Rome conquered Greece, were mad for Greek culture— was rhetoric, the study of speaking. How to remember what you had to say was essential, and memorization how-tos were the stock-in-trade of local teachers.

They were teaching techniques compiled from people who had formidable natural talents for recall. From my reading of the memory teachers, contemporary and ancient, I learned that most mnemonic devices are variations of organizing what you want to recall into pictures that will stick in your mind. One trick favored by the ancients was putting each item in its own "locus," the Latin for "place." The modern variation is to create a mental picture of a familiar room in your home, such as the kitchen or living room, and move around the room picking out several pieces of furniture—the sofa, then the table next to it, and the lamp next to that, and then the mantelpiece, the TV, and so on. With this image locked in his mind, the noteless shopper can place one thing on his mental list on each piece of furniture: milk on the sofa, eggs on the table, chicken on the lamp, two bottles of wine on the mantel, a box of pasta on the TV, and so on. To recall the list, all he has to do is picture the room in his mind and walk through it, noting the items on each piece of furniture. The key is to use a room in your house where the furniture arrangement is already locked in your memory.

Another popular technique for remembering lists or other bits of information is to create a series of bizarre but interconnected images in your mind. If, for example, you want to remember that Napoleon attacked Egypt in 1798, fighting the Battle of the Pyramids, you can easily imagine the classic portrait of Napoleon with his tricornered hat, his right hand half inside his tunic, astride a horse positioned atop one of the three famous pyramids of Giza—with a huge neon sign flickering "1798." Similarly, you can recall Napoleon's famous 1812 retreat from Russia with a mental picture of him running through the snow, chased by the Russian bear, creating a bird's-eye view of "1812" with his tracks. If what you have to remember is merely the list of clients you have to visit this morning, you can imagine the skinny guy sitting on the lap of the fat guy who is being pushed in a large stroller by the female sales director of your last stop.

I use this "silly picture" trick all the time to prepare speeches, particularly when I'm just getting started. Usually, whatever memory methods I use will fade away as I get a firm hold on the words and their sequence and meaning for my purposes. These days I work in a kind of memory shorthand that is all my own. If you memorize enough material, you'll undoubtedly find ways to use your own personal bag of tricks. But however you proceed, your memory process will always depend on *impression, association,* and *repetition.*

Assignment #4

Recall your day, from breakfast until dinner. The goal is to tell a story about what happened to you and the people you had to deal with.

Everyone has this story to tell. Begin by reviewing the day—literally *re-viewing* what happened by running the movie of the day in your mind. What could be simpler? You already have a photographic memory of your day.

You can also pick and choose moments. Get the structure of the day clear chronologically. If it was a particularly busy day, you might want to rearrange your story into a kind of "highlight reel" of best or most important moments. If it was an unusually bad day, you could focus on that. Play around with these variations in your head. If today was unusually uneventful, who's to know if you embellish it here and there? Remember, it is your story. If you want to drive a new Porsche today, go for it. How about an intellectual or creative breakthrough? Add it. Do you see an opportunity to be funny at the expense of someone else or, even better, yourself? Be my guest. Already you can see how a comedian might take a day's worth of events—a series of setbacks, for example, or upsetting personal interactions—and turn them into a hilarious or self-deprecating story about "my day in hell."

Consider breaking up the day into headings or topics: breakfast, driving to work, conversations with colleagues, the big meeting, lunch, a doctor's appointment or a few errands, the afternoon's work, getting to the Little League game or driving the kids to music lessons, shopping for dinner. Put a number next to each, and you have the bare outline of your day—and the outline for a story. Notice, too, once you have this outline, how easy it is to select certain things and knock out others. You don't have to include every single thing you saw on your drive to work. You will have to settle on various criteria for what you keep and what you cut out: degree of importance in your day, for instance. But if the story you want to tell is what a nothing kind of day you had, then the measure of what you include might be how trivial something was.

Warning: This is a movie, but it is definitely not a documentary of you going through your day. You are the camera. The story is about what you did, whom you talked to, what you saw. It is told from your point of view. Select which parts you want in your story, rehearse it in your mind, and tell it to someone else.

By now you will have realized that there is no need to write down the story of your day. Even to think about it is to remember it; it is already cemented in your memory. You just have to tell it. If your story has gotten so rich and complicated that you're afraid of leaving out a moment in its sequence—say, the ridiculous sweater one of your colleagues was wearing—all you have to do is connect it to another moment in your memory chain. As you recall exiting your car and locking it, you will see the image of your colleague sitting on top of the car, smiling at you, wearing his goofy sweater. You will not forget it. As you continue telling this story, what you are likely to forget is that you originally needed a mnemonic device to remember the sweater. After a while, the language of the story takes on its own reality.

Once you have your story straight and have told it several times, these events will be like a tape in your head. You can then slow down this recall tape, or stop it any time so that you can reinterpret or embellish your story as you are going along, without ever getting lost. What are you waiting for? Tell a story about your day. From memory, and without notes.

Assignment #4a

During my first year in drama school, Sir John Gielgud and Irene Worth came to Yale to perform in *Men and Women of Shakespeare,* a kind of concert performance of Shakespeare's memorable couples: Romeo and Juliet, Antony and Cleopatra, Hamlet and Gertrude, Troilus and Cressida, Macbeth and Lady Macbeth, along with various other characters from the comedies. Without costumes, props, choreography, music, or any lighting tricks, these two extraordinary actors took control of packed houses every night with only their minds, hearts, and voices. Dressed in formal attire and standing behind two lecterns that were angled toward each other, Gielgud and Worth did have scripts that they glanced at occasionally, but neither ever seemed to be reading. There were occasional gestures, a step or two toward or away from each other, as the stage filled with Shakespeare's people, young and old, of all sizes, beautiful and not so, more real than the person sitting next to you. It was an amazing display of what great actors can do.

During their run at the Yale Repertory, Gielgud and Worth spent some time with our acting class. Most memorable for me were Gielgud's two sessions on Shakespeare's sonnets. He had played his first Hamlet in 1930 at the age of twenty-six and gone on to become one of the greatest interpreters of Shakespeare in any century. John Gielgud had amazing technique, particularly in his breath control. With impeccable diction and a voice that the London critic Kenneth Tynan once described as having "the range of a violin, a Stradivarius controlled by a master," he was able to convey the sound and sense of a Shakespearean sonnet as if delivering it on one long stream of air. I watched carefully and saw him subtly catch whatever breath he needed in a pause here or there that seemed only to benefit the text and not his lungs. There was no mouthing of the words; he seemed able to say everything without any effort, his diction not insisting on pronunciation as much as simply serving the English language at its most sublime. Gielgud's speeches, as Hamlet advised the players, were "pronounced . . . trippingly on the tongue." But this was not just a bravura recitation. At times what he was saying seemed to come not from his lips but from his heart, and his eyes shone with tears. No wonder the critic Kenneth Tynan, who was a big fan of Laurence Olivier, Gielgud's main competition for great English actor of the day, still referred to Gielgud as "not an actor, but *the* actor."

Gielgud noted that one of the best ways for us young actors to test our abilities in diction, phrasing, and breath control was to study, memorize, and deliver the sonnets, particularly those that touched us in some way. I immediately began working on a sonnet, and over the years, I have often returned to my favorite sonnets as a way to give my speaking technique a regular tune-up. I discovered that this work allowed me to focus the more technical aspects, diction and breathing, on a specific task; namely, attempting to deliver the sonnet with Gielgudian efficiency and force. Learning how to manage the correct articulation of the words while conveying their meaning helped me to become a better actor. I also used the sonnets with my Harvard students to help them work on vocal technique.

Learning a sonnet is also a good exercise for improving your memory. Sonnets are not long: by definition, a mere fourteen lines. But the Shakespearean variety provides a worthy challenge, with built-in complexity and unfamiliar bits of Elizabethan language and elisions, which require some work to memorize. I gave my students a week or two to commit a sonnet to memory. I began the class with some Shakespeare I had memorized. It was one of the few times I performed for my class as an actor. (Playing the role of Harvard lecturer, I was onstage in that room three times a week, sweating it out.) I took a few strides away from the podium, raised my arms in the manner of a formal, welcoming greeting, and delivered the following:

Two households, both alike in dignity,
  In fair Verona, where we lay our scene,
From ancient grudge break to new mutiny,
  Where civil blood makes civil hands unclean.
From forth the fatal loins of these two foes
  A pair of star-cross'd lovers take their life;
Whose misadventur'd piteous overthrows
  Do with their death bury their parents' strife.
The fearful passage of their death mark'd love,
  And the continuance of their parents' rage,
Which, but their children's end, nought could remove,
  Is now the two hours' traffick of our stage;
The which if you with patient ears attend,
What here shall miss, our toil shall strive to mend.

I had chosen the prologue to *Romeo and Juliet*, which is a sonnet, though not ordinarily thought of as that—fourteen lines of iambic pentameter (140 syllables) with the rhyme scheme ABAB CDCD EFEF GG. Shakespeare was literature's most brilliant practitioner of the sonnet form, having written 154 sonnets, most of them of such high quality that it boggles the mind. When I finished, I pointed out to the class that I had not tried to sound like an Elizabethan, nor did I affect a British accent. I was just trying to speak Shakespeare's words succinctly and clearly and tell the story embodied in the 140 syllables I had uttered. I asked them to pick one of Shakespeare's sonnets and do the same.

I advise you to try it, too, because it is a great way to exercise your memory. (It is also a useful way to prove to yourself that you still have a memory.) Don't try to learn the entire sonnet in one go. You might be able to pull it off if you were writing it out. But to speak fourteen lines of rhymed verse clearly and smoothly, with feeling, takes more than one practice session. Pick a sonnet you already like. If you're not familiar with Shakespeare's sonnets, read some; see which one speaks to you or is easiest for you to understand (some of them are filled with lines that are extremely opaque to a modern reader) and read it several times to make sure you know what it's about. Then read it aloud in an effort to match how you say it with its meaning. Staring into space and reading it from your photographic memory in a computerized voice is not what we're after. You will have to work on your breathing and your negotiation of some Elizabethan words (doth, hath) and elisions (shouldst, mayst) that are no longer part of spoken English, all the while trying to serve the music of the language as well as its meaning. And, oh yes, you must get every word right. No paraphrasing! You do not wing it with Shakespeare.

Enter the fear factor. The difficulty and unfamiliarity of Shakespeare's poetry can pose a formidable obstacle to even the best memories. You might find that a few lines come easily, then suddenly, you have gone to Cleveland. You may have repeated the lines twenty times, but you get to a certain place and the only thing that comes to mind is "What comes next?" You can solve this problem only by working on your recitation, over and over. Here's how to do it:

1. Read the sonnet again and again, first to yourself, then aloud.

2. Learn the first two lines, then the first stanza. Go about your day.

3. A little later, try it again from memory—out loud. Work on the spots where you err or go blank, try to figure out why, then sleep on it.

4. The next day connect what you learned the day before to the second stanza, working on that in the same way. Then sleep on the first two stanzas.

5. And so forth. Just devote ten or fifteen minutes to it for a few days, for as long as it's fun, day by day working your way through the entire sonnet, slowly committing it to memory.

Do these steps in your mind, then rehearse it all out loud, while washing the dishes or exercising or commuting to work. Teaching the tongue and teeth to wrap themselves around difficult words and phrases will require saying them. Work on your diction and your breathing, figuring out where to catch a breath before you run out of air at the wrong time. Also be careful about being so focused on your breathing that you end up grabbing more breaths than you need, thus disrupting the poem's flow of thought.

A Shakespearean sonnet is meant to be spoken. By saying the words aloud you will find their music, which, in turn, will help you to memorize them. One of the most provocative results of memorizing a poem is that bits of it you didn't understand or maybe only thought you did become clearer as the poem becomes part of you. Friends have told me that years after they learned a poem, they have recited it from memory, and a part of it became clear in a way that had never occurred to them before.

Practice it, but be patient. Give the process a day or two. Often I will be trying to master a particular scene, and as I work through it, trying to think of what I will do as I say certain things, very little seems to stick—even after I have worked on it for several hours. I'll know certain bits and pieces but I definitely won't be ready to stand in front of a producer or director and do the scene without a script. But the next morning I get out of bed and I have it. My grasp may not be perfect, but by the end of the second day, I have brought the scene to a whole different level—I can run it through while brushing my teeth and with Mick Jagger wailing in the background. The scene is now emblazoned in my memory. You will actually be able to see and hear the words in your mind. Within a few days, you'll be able to speak these fourteen lines aloud with a certain spontaneity. You will have made Shakespeare's sonnet your own.

Two thirds of my class did quite well with this exercise. Some played their sonnets straight and seriously, while others had some fun sending up their Shakespeare. One guy spoke the lines in an accentuated version of his Tennessee Mountains accent; another wore black with a touch of a white ruffled collar and acted the part of Will Shakespeare, speaking in an English accent flutier than the queen's. A fresh-faced girl from out west glowed with rapture as she breathlessly intoned her lines in the manner of an old-fashioned, melodramatic movie star. Virtually all the students who blew it had waited too long to absorb the material. They had committed their sonnets to that "shallow memory" favored by hardworking soap-opera actors. More preparation is necessary to lock in any speech to a live audience, particularly your first Shakespearean sonnet before an audience of sixty-three fellow students who have worked hard to do the same thing. But failing once due to lack of preparation means that you are unlikely to do it a second time. The only defense is to make sure you've done a perfect cement job the next time around.

A USEFUL ACTOR'S SELF-TEST:
"THE ITALIAN RUN-THROUGH"

Before I dare to say any lines in public, I know them so cold that I can say them at high speed and even in a crazy accent. Actors call this the Italian run-through. The idea is to speak it as fast as you can, even in a foreign accent, without sacrificing phrasing or meaning. I have practiced entire plays in this way near the end of the rehearsal period, doing the dialogue as well as the actions as fast as possible. (It is just like speeding up the videotape of a movie. The actual performance is there, only on fast-forward.) Nothing will expose the areas where you don't quite have it—where you have to think for a second of what comes next—faster than the Italian run-through. If you stumble or go dry at certain transitions in a speedy rehearsal, you will definitely head for Cleveland in the same spots when you give the speech in public.

Believe it or not, committing poetry to memory can be a lot of fun. To make sure you have no excuses—"I don't have a copy of Shakespeare's sonnets"—I offer one of Shakespeare's most famous sonnets, XVIII, for your reading and memorizing pleasure:

> Shall I compare thee to a summer's day?
> Thou art more lovely and more temperate:
> Rough winds do shake the darling buds of May,
> And summer's lease hath all too short a date;
> Sometime too hot the eye of heaven shines,
> And often is his gold complexion dimm'd,

And every fair from fair sometime declines,
By chance or nature's changing course untrimm'd;
But thy eternal summer shall not fade,
Nor lose possession of that fair thou ow'st,
Nor shall Death brag thou wand'rest in his shade,
When in eternal lines to time thou grow'st.
   So long as men can breathe or eyes can see,
   So long lives this, and this gives life to thee.

Confession: I like assigning one of Shakespeare's sonnets because none of them is easy to learn. Therefore, if you can memorize just one, I think you will have proved to yourself that you can memorize anything. Here is another sonnet from Shakespeare, XXIII, that should strike several chords for you:

As an unperfect actor on the stage,
Who with his fear is put besides his part,
Or some fierce thing replete with too much rage,
Whose strength's abundance weakens his own heart,
So I, for fear of trust, forget to say
The perfect ceremony of love's [rite],
And in mine own love's strength seem to decay,
O'ercharged with burthen of mine own love's might.
O, let my books be then the eloquence
And dumb presagers of my speaking breast,
Who plead for love, and look for recompense,
More than that tongue that more hath more express'd.
   O, learn to read what silent love hath writ:
   To hear with eyes belongs to love's fine wit.

My goal is to get you to master a batch of words so well that you can actually watch yourself reciting them. If the sonnet seems too daunting for starters, then try something more modern with an internal music and rhyme that make it easier to remember.

Robert Frost, for example. "The Road Not Taken," the poem I used in my Kent State speech, is one of his most famous. Whenever you want to inspire your listeners to be more creative or original or daring, what better way than quoting some Frost? Here is the complete poem:

> Two roads diverged in a yellow wood,
> And sorry I could not travel both
> And be one traveler, long I stood
> And looked down one as far as I could
> To where it bent in the undergrowth;
>
> Then took the other, as just as fair,
> And having perhaps the better claim,
> Because it was grassy and wanted wear;
> Though as for that, the passing there
> Had worn them really about the same,
>
> And both that morning equally lay
> In leaves no step had trodden black.
> Oh, I kept the first for another day!
> Yet knowing how way leads on to way,
> I doubted if I should ever come back.
>
> I shall be telling this with a sigh
> Somewhere ages and ages hence;
> Two roads diverged in a wood, and I—
> I took the one less traveled by,
> And that has made all the difference.

The Irish poet William Butler Yeats, who won the Nobel Prize for literature in 1923, is famous for the musical quality of his poems, some of which he actually called songs. Several have been set to music, and I cannot resist offering one of my favorite Yeats poems, recently recorded by Judy Collins:

> "THE SONG OF WANDERING AENGUS"
> I went out to the hazel wood,
> Because a fire was in my head,
> And cut and peeled a hazel wand,
> And hooked a berry to a thread;
> And when white moths were on the wing,
> And moth-like stars were flickering out,
> I dropped the berry in a stream
> And caught a little silver trout.
>
> When I laid it on the floor
> I went to blow the fire aflame,
> But something rustled on the floor,
> And some one called me by my name:
> It had become a glimmering girl
> With apple blossom in her hair
> Who called me by my name and ran
> And faded through the brightening air.
>
> Though I am old with wandering
> Through hollow lands and hilly lands,
> I will find out where she has gone,
> And kiss her lips and take her hands;
> And walk among long dappled grass,
> And pluck till time and times are done
> The silver apples of the moon,
> The golden apples of the sun.

Simply by reading this poem aloud, you will feel the music of the words. Like speeches, poems are made to be heard. Notice, too, how this Yeats poem is filled with vibrant images: a trip into the woods, a homemade fishing rod, the night, the moths, the stars, the stream, not just a trout but a little silver trout, a girl with apple blossoms in her hair who runs away. Such images also make the poem easier to memorize.

If you are like most people, you already know many songs by heart. Did you sit down with paper and pen to memorize them? I doubt it. I'll bet you don't even have any memory of trying to learn them. You liked a song's words and the tune, you kept hearing it, singing along, and before you know it, it's thirty years later and you're staring out the window and singing that same old song. Popular songs, like sonnets, are often about love or regret or some kind of loss. Much of their success depends on the words bringing up a lot of feeling, and that is a lot more likely when they're attached to a memorable tune and meant to be sung or spoken aloud, shared with others. This is another reason you remember them. I have heard the Yeats poem sung a cappella at two different memorial services, and both times everyone was fighting back tears.

There is no better way to connect to an audience than through a shared emotion. The language you use and the images it conveys will touch an audience if it represents something that has touched you. By calling upon your emotional memory in the right way, you will discover a great source of power that, if used correctly, will always win over your audience.

5

GETTING REAL—

THE POWER OF EMOTION

How does a poem or song or play or movie or even a speech move us to tears? Everyone has experienced such an emotional exchange and knows how powerful it can be. Surely such feelings are among life's most worthwhile moments. Great art moves us, and so do great speakers. Conveying emotions is a big part of what communicating in public is all about. If you want to inform people, entertain them, inspire them, get them to work for your cause, if you really want to impress people in public, you have to connect with them on a personal and emotional level. The American playwright Arthur Miller (*Death of a Salesman, The Crucible*) has said, "People wouldn't watch a play if they couldn't find themselves in it." Success in public speaking also comes when the audience begins to see and feel themselves in what the speaker is saying.

Nothing, however, is more misunderstood than this emotional component of performing. In my experience, producers, writers, even directors often have no idea how an actor displays emotions on cue. It is almost as if they are afraid to find out, as if the knowledge will force them to look deeper into their own emotional life than they'd like. And when you tell a business-man, a politician, an academic, or an experienced journalist that to be effective on their feet they must connect emotionally to their audience, they are inclined to recoil with horror. Emotional display and the rest of that touchy-feely stuff may be okay for actors, but hardheaded professionals want to stick with the facts, the figures, and the ideas that got them the speaking invi-tation in the first place, thank you very much.

And they will never be any good as public speakers. Many of my students resisted my urging to bring some emotion to their presentations—until they saw how much more effective their more emotional classmates were as speakers. Effective speeches not only brim with feeling, they ignite similar feelings in the au-dience. A skilled communicator can do this every time—without the audience ever sensing that they are in the presence of false or manufactured emotion. And that is because a good speaker is trading on the real thing. During World War II, Winston Chur-chill delivered many of his greatest speeches over the radio, but his patriotism and passionate resistance to the Nazis rang through every sentence, inspiring his fellow Britons to support a long and deadly war in which more than sixty thousand civilians were killed by German bombs. At certain crucial times during the war, Churchill gave memorable speeches week after week. No one ever suggested he was faking his unique combination of pride, arrogance, courage, and humor in the face of Hitler's bombs. Ronald Reagan brought his own laid-back California style to the art of political persuasion, invigorating a nation whose self-esteem had been damaged by the humiliations of Vietnam, Watergate, and Americans held hostage in Iran. Even his critics conceded that his ability to stand before a television camera and convey his vision for a stronger America, destined to triumph over the Soviet Union's Evil Empire, made him the Great Communicator. Bill Clinton, too, seemed able to connect emotionally with almost any audience; after such disasters as Hurricane Hugo, the bombing of the federal building in Oklahoma, and the shootings at Columbine High School, he could walk among the victims and their families and console them with a kind of genuine compassion that even his detractors could not help admiring. As different as all these leaders were, they had one thing in common: They were talented performers. And I would argue that a good bit of that talent stemmed from their ability to share a piece of their emotional lives with their audiences.

At a more mundane but no less moving level was a speech that some of you might have caught on television during the 2001 Golden Globe Awards, which honored Al Pacino for his career as an actor. Acceptance speeches can be deadly, but Pacino showed how well a good actor can play the role of speaker. In front of a large live audience and millions of TV viewers, he managed to express his gratitude in a way that never sounded like a formal speech. We had all seen Pacino before; the icy young Mafia don in *The Godfather,* the nutty but sympathetic bank robber in *Dog Day Afternoon,* the tough undercover cop in *Serpico* who could also cry, and the screaming drug dealer on drugs in *Scarface,* to name just a few of his most famous movie roles. (Pacino has also done much memorable stage work.) At the Golden Globes, we saw a different Pacino— subdued, humble, and magnanimous. But his performance as Al Pacino was no less riveting than any of his movie roles. His message was simple: how he got from being a street-smart New York kid, with a dream of becoming an actor, to being honored for his career. He began by announcing that he was a big fan of teachers because they changed people's lives. Then, in a relaxed, conversational style, without notes or a TelePrompTer,

Pacino began to tell the story about the New York City public school drama teacher who had noticed and encouraged his talent. He brought his audience back to his childhood, into the apartment he shared with his grandmother, where we stood with him at the kitchen door. For it was there that the young Pacino, unnoticed, watched his favorite teacher sitting at his grandmother's kitchen table, persuading that old-school Italian woman to let Al pursue his crazy dream of being an actor. As Pacino told the story, the TV cameras cut back and forth between him and the live audience, populated mainly by fellow actors. Most of them looked to be in tears. I know that this actor sitting at home was moved, and friends of mine who aren't actors confessed that Pacino had gotten to them, too.

Why were we so emotionally involved in Pacino's story? Because he had led us to a common emotional ground. Most of us had someone in our own past who had changed our lives, and anyone who didn't wished they did. For me, this speech was almost perfect: It had a straightforward message, and it was both personal and universal. Pacino's emotional involvement was evident, but he was in control as he recalled this important moment in his childhood, which was bound to move his audience. More impressively, he was not reading or reciting his speech but delivering it in a conversational style, as though he made it up as he went along. But this was no surprise award. The Pacino speech was a scheduled part of the show, and clearly, he had prepared what he was going to say—but in such a way that it seemed to have just occurred to him that his audience might be interested in learning how a guy like him became an actor.

How do you do that? How can you bring emotions to your speech as if on command? Where do these feelings come from? What makes them real? Your emotions must come from you—from your past—and when emotions are really yours, they will appear real to your audience. You will be emotional, and they will feel that so deeply that they, too, will become emotional. Emotions are what connect us to other people at a deep and strong level. A performer connecting to the audience emotionally is an extremely creative experience. I think it is the closest we ordinary folk get to being poets. Like a poet, you have to create feelings by putting together words and images that are moving, first to you and then to your audience. To pull that off in the course of a presentation, you have to experience that feeling and display it, then and there—in the moment. When you can share a feeling with others in public, the result is magic. It is the kind of magic that everyone can do. But first you have to understand how actors actually create *real* emotions in their roles. I am talking not about sticking an onion in your eyes to cry but about revisiting your own past to re-create the feelings of being sad, angry, delighted, or in love. Actors call this process "sense memory." Anyone can do it. All it requires is some imagination and practice. And if you insist that you don't have the imagination to summon such strong, deep, and real feelings, I can prove you wrong with two words: sexual fantasy.

But before I can teach you how to use your own emotional experiences to become a more effective speaker, you must understand clearly what I mean by "emotional."

SHOWING EMOTION HAS NOTHING TO DO WITH EMOTING

Let's first get our terms straight. Here are some definitions from my *American Heritage Dictionary:*

- emote *intr. v.* To express emotion, especially in an excessive or theatrical manner.

- emotion *n.* 1.a. A complex and usually strong subjective response, as love or fear. b. Such a response involving physiological changes as a preparation for action. 2. A state of agitation or disturbance: *controlled her emotions with effort.* 3. The part of the consciousness that involves feeling or sensibility: *a choice determined by emotion rather than reason.*

- emotional *adj.* 1. Of or pertaining to emotion. 2. Readily affected with or stirred by emotion. 3. Capable of stirring the emotions. 4. Marked by or exhibiting emotion; agitated.

- emotionalism *n.* 1. An inclination to rely on or place too much value on emotion. 2. Undue display of emotion.

When I say "emotion," I never mean the kind of emotionalism that comes from emoting. But I certainly understand the confusion. Gushing or indulging feeling for its own sake is as common as horse manure at a rodeo in television dramas, movies, and various other forms of public display, with the accent on "display." Sentimentality is always easier to show than genuine feeling, and melodrama much easier to write than drama. I have acted in some of the best series currently on television (including such recent Emmy winners as *The West Wing* and *The Practice*), and the writing was terrific. But I have also appeared in plays by Aeschylus, William Shakespeare, Anton Chekhov, Eugene O'Neill, and Tennessee Williams, and the difference has to do with more than the size of the ideas involved. Great writers reveal the human heart, and no actor will ever get close to that with the kind of emotionalism we are used to getting from most TV dramas. Here I am echoing my acting teacher Bobby Lewis, who spent a lot of time helping his students put Stella Adler's acting theories into practice. As Stella's explicator, Lewis brought common sense to the teaching of acting. He was neither pro-

Method nor anti-Method. He did not seem to favor one technique over another. To him, it was all a matter of jargon. He constantly stressed to us that the Stanislavski system was literally "a method," just another approach to acting, a technique, not a dogma. The real test for the actor was, said Lewis, "just getting up there and doing it, one way or another."

One thing "it" was not, according to Lewis, was getting caught up in your own emotions. After a young actress had opened all the gates of her heart as Juliet, nose running, tears streaming down her face, barely managing to choke out Shakespeare's blank verse between her sobs, Bobby comforted her. "There, there, sweetie. We can all see how much feeling you've invested in this, and we do appweciate that," he said, drifting into his Elmer Fudd delivery, "but you must always wemember—'IF CWYING WERE ACTING, MY AUNT WIFKA WOULD HAVE BEEN THE DUSE!'" (Pronounced "dooza!" Eleanora Duse was the great nineteenth-century Italian actress more able to move the audiences of her day than any other performer, thus earning her onstage fame as "The Duse.")

"Cwying" has little to do with showing genuine emotion or effective communicating. Really touching people's hearts is not about weeping and pounding the podium. When was the last time you heard a favorite singer sobbing during her performance? Those poems you learned in the last chapter will have no emotional effect on an audience if you are too choked up to say them clearly. Great actors move their audience, not themselves. To be an effective speaker, you must arrive filled with the appropriate emotion, keep it under control, and inspire similar feelings among your listeners. You want to *convey* your feelings, not drown in them. People who experience strong feelings in public often are trying to fight back their tears. Both Reagan and Clinton, for instance, were known to mist up or maybe even bite their lips, but I can think of no instance where either president wept. I believe it is this effort to maintain composure that moves people most. No matter how sympathetic the audience is, they will not enjoy watching a speaker lose it in public. Jacob Adler once said, "If you come to the theater and feel one hundred percent, show them eighty percent. If you feel sixty percent, show them forty percent, but if you only feel forty percent, put the understudy on."

Most actors have to work to keep a lid on their emotions. By nature, we actors are inclined to live with our feelings too close to the surface. I think this is what attracts many of us to acting; it becomes an acceptable outlet for all these pent-up feelings. This emotional sensitivity is sometimes all a young actor brings to the job. Looking back on my own career, I suspect that some of my early success had a lot to do with how easy it was for me to access my emotions. I can remember directors saying to me, "Whoa! That's a bit too much." And I remember thinking, "Really? If it wasn't too much for the family dinner table, surely it can work in this scene, where the stakes are a hell of a lot higher."

The goal is to be brimming with feeling and to keep it under control, with a whip and a chair if necessary. The result will be that the emotion is always under the surface, straining to let loose. Suddenly, it will get away, and you will have to chase it back into its cage. The audience, however, is bound to notice that the feelings are there, and they will recognize them as true. My younger brother died a few years ago, and I spoke at a memorial service for him. I prepared my remarks very carefully and even wrote out the speech in full. I also broke my no-notes rule and read what I had written. My only brother had died much too young, and the danger of my emotions overtaking me while I talked about our relationship was too large. The time for my grieving was not during the eulogy. For that performance, my main objective was to keep it together. All through my remarks,

I kept saying to myself, "Hang on, hang on, gotta get back to my seat in one piece." The audience knew exactly what I was doing, and I am certain that my eulogy for my brother was more effective (and more affecting) because I did not allow my own grief to take over the proceedings.

REAL EMOTIONS TEND
TO BE MIXED EMOTIONS

At the climax of the movie *A Man for All Seasons* (based on the successful play), Sir Thomas More, Henry VIII's lord chancellor, refuses to accept the king's break with the Roman Catholic Church and is condemned to death. His wife and daughter come to visit him in prison, carrying food. More, played by the superb English actor Paul Scofield, assures his family in a moving speech that he is fine and "with God." Full of intellectual calm and the certainty that he will go straight to heaven, More ends up comforting his wife and daughter. By this point in the movie, we know how close he is to his family, particularly his daughter, whom he has taught to read Latin and Greek, the kind of education unavailable to young girls of the time. The women are upset, but More is the model of courage. To change the subject, he turns to eat what they have brought. But as soon as he tries to do this very normal and necessary human thing, he breaks down. It is as if this simple meal stands for everything that he will lose; the man who has stood up to a king and accepted martyrdom for his religious beliefs crumbles at the taste of his wife's homemade pie. It is an extraordinary moment of writing, acting, and directing, and it knocks the audience over every time. Why? Because we are also trying to keep our emotions in check as the saintly More puts on a brave face for his family. His speech ends, More seems strong, and we are relieved. And then he tries to eat and can't, dropping the fork, his hand waving them away and covering his face in a gesture that speaks volumes. Like More, we can no longer resist our grief.

Was Scofield "just acting"? Yes and no. He was playing a historical character in a movie. But he was not faking the misery that informed this physical response. That is how real feelings are exposed, unpredictably and often at the wrong time. Sometimes people are so sad that they weep uncontrollably; other times they are so sad that they cannot cry anymore; sometimes, like Thomas More, they try to soldier on, and their grief breaks out in full force when they sit down to eat a piece of homemade pie. They might even be so sad that they end up laughing. The actor Christopher Walken has said that he realized what an amazing actor Laurence Olivier was when he saw him play Dr. Astrov in Chekhov's *Uncle Vanya,* a role that Walken himself has played. There's a moment in the play when the doctor enters, and it is clear that he is distracted, but you are not sure why. Another character asks him what's wrong, and Astrov answers, "A patient died on my operating table this morning." When Olivier said this, according to Walken, he laughed a little at the tragic absurdity of it all. Olivier's choice as an actor seemed bold to Walken, who had realized as soon as he saw it how much more powerful that laugh made the scene. Does laughter seem an appropriate response to a patient's death? No. Is it real for a doctor to express his frustration in this way? Of course. In that laugh is the career of a talented doctor committed to saving lives, who must also live with the tragic fact that some patients will die no matter what he does.

The success of an actor's choices is determined by one set of judges only—the audience. Even the least sophisticated theatergoer is able to detect the difference between presenting an emotion—"Look at me, I'm sad"—and *doing something that is naturally accompanied by emotion.* The audiences watching

Scofield and Olivier had no doubt that these men, as characters and actors, were in misery. Where does such genuine feeling come from? How does an actor turn it on, as if reaching into his pocket for a spigot marked "real feelings"?

SENSE MEMORY

In the course of every performance, actors are called upon to create a range of feelings, from love to hate, joy to depression. It is here that a major part of the art of acting takes place. To generate real feeling, to fill themselves with emotion that they can draw on, modern actors trained in the Method will often use what is called "sense memory." Few things are more misunderstood. In discussions with fellow actors, I have often been surprised when they define sense memory as creating emotion —anger, sadness, dread, longing, delight, you name it—by remembering how they felt at some moment in the past. Wrong. Conveying feelings through the use of sense memory has nothing do with saying to yourself, "Okay, now I'm going to act sad," then trying to remember what it felt like the last time you were genuinely sad.

Memory of the past is crucial, but it is not the feeling the actor should try to remember but the situation, the setting, the moment-to-moment details that provoked his five senses at the time. The French writer Marcel Proust begins his famous novel *In Search of Lost Time* (also known as *Remembrance of Things Past*) with an account of how the taste of a madeleine, a kind of butter cookie the narrator liked as a child, abruptly filled him with the sensations of his childhood. The return of those feelings unleashed a series of memories that Proust spun into the several volumes that became one of the indisputably greatest novels of the twentieth century. This is a classic example of sense memory. It has nothing to do with Proust recalling what the joy of his childhood was like way back then; rather, it re-creates a situation, provoking a feeling *now* that is every bit as strong and real as the first time around. This happens to Proust through the sense of taste. (He similarly employs the other four senses throughout the novel to retrieve emotional states: the sight of a church steeple, the musty smell in a public lavatory, the touch of a napkin against his mouth, hearing the noise of a spoon against a plate.)

Proust's emotional memories were involuntary, sparked by a current sensation. An actor or speaker cannot wait around for this kind of emotional experience to happen. Let me follow Stanislavski and advise that to access genuine feelings and share them with an audience, you must "forget about your feelings." He counsels the actor to look to his own experience, research the character and his times, then add the power of imagination to demonstrate real life. "When the inner conditions are pre-pared and right," explains Stanislavski, "feelings will come to the surface on their own accord." It is this imaginative effort that the public speaker can learn and benefit from

Since the early twentieth century, psychologists have been in-trigued with the memory's ability to retrieve past emotions that seem as real today as they were then, and acting teachers were quick to recognize the advantages of such a technique. Stella Adler believed that the writer-director-actor Richard Boleslav-sky, who was quite a famous figure in Adler's youth, was one of the best explicators of how emotional recall works. According to Boleslavsky, the more engaged all the five senses are, the more likely genuine feeling is to follow. He told a story about how a young man had proposed to the woman he loved one summer evening as they were strolling through a cucumber patch. "Being nervous," Boleslavsky writes in his book *Acting: The First Six Lessons,* "they would stop occasionally, pick a cucumber and eat it, enjoying very much its aroma, taste and the freshness and richness of the sun's warmth upon it. They made the happiest decision of their lives between two mouthfuls of cucumbers, so to speak."

A month later they married. During the wedding supper, a dish of cucumbers appeared on the table, and the couple laughed at the coincidence. They made a life for themselves, children came, there were struggles and quarrels, sometimes they didn't even speak to each other, but their youngest daughter noticed that if she put a dish of cucumbers on the table, peace would be declared. She concluded that her parents simply shared a love for cucumbers, until her mother told her the story of their courtship twenty-five years before in the cucumber patch.

To work on the emotional content of a role requires an actor to discover his or her own cucumber patch. The elderly married couple, comforted by the memory of their engagement, were not recalling how wonderful they felt at that moment in the cucumber patch. Boleslavsky was quick to point out that it was unlikely that this simple Russian couple ever analyzed their feelings. That engagement day had been full of sensations—the aroma of the cucumber patch, the warmth of each cucumber, and the taste, not to mention the mixture of anxiety, excitement, and love they felt that day. All it took was the sight of a cucumber to trigger the feelings they had felt decades ago.

MY CUCUMBER PATCH

Like many actors, I make a point of keeping this kind of working technique to myself. Secrets are a big part of acting, and I believe that the more secret weapons you have, the better you will be. I have also noticed that my tricks tend to run their course. One day in rehearsal, you return to the cucumber patch and find it scorched by the sun and useless. Frankly, my fear is that by talking about how I bring back various emotions, I will dry them up before their time has come. But in the interest of helping you benefit from sense memory, I will risk a reliable sense memory that fills me with emotion in a flash.

One of the most emotional experiences of my childhood was the day I lost my new tricycle. I was an uncommonly big toddler, visiting my great-grandmother in North Carolina, and had ridden to the local schoolyard to play. I left my new tricycle on the other side of a nearby gravel road I had been forbidden to cross. A big truck came along and ran over my tricycle as I watched in horror. The driver actually got out, saw the mangled tricycle, and looked around to make sure he hadn't hit a child. I hid where he would not see me. When I returned to the scene of the accident, the tricycle was gone. I knew I had done something terribly wrong. When my great-grandmother asked me where the tricycle was, I lied, claiming it had been stolen. But I was very young and my guilt very big, so I soon admitted the awful truth to my great-grandmother. I began to cry. She embraced and comforted me, but her compassion only made me cry harder.

As an actor, I use this autobiographical moment all the time. But to make it work the first time, I had to recall how all my senses had been engaged that miserable day so long ago. It is incredible how much you can retrieve from memory once you set your mind to the past. One image sparks another until, like Proust, you are back in your childhood looking around and feeling the same way you felt that day. I asked myself a series of questions. The answers filled me with emotion and still do:

- What did I see? There was a red-and-white-checked tablecloth on the clothesline out back that I could see rustling in the wind from where I was sitting on the back porch swing. My great-grandmother was sitting in her green wicker chair with a metal bowl in her lap, shelling peas. Her favorite shawl was draped over her lap because the sun was close to setting, and she was starting to "feel a bit o' chill." Bright yellow flowers were on the table next to me.

- What did I hear? A gentle wind playing the wind chimes near the utility shed and flapping the checked tablecloth.

- What did I smell? That old house smelled of a mixture of musty furniture, jasmine, and Toll House cookies. I loved that smell. Something always seemed to be cooking. I don't remember what was on the stove that particular day, but my great-grandmother's special fried chicken was a big favorite of mine, so I will add that smell in my present memory.

- What did I taste? Dr Pepper. I do not remember if I had one that day, but it was my drink of choice when I visited, so a bottle of Dr Pepper is also in my memory.

- What did I feel? It was late afternoon, warm and humid. My skin always felt sticky by the end of one of those summer days in North Carolina. When Great-Grandma said to me, as I was crying, "Come on over here, sugar," and pulled me close to her, I could feel her wool shawl next to my knees and arms. Hot tears on my face, a cooling summer breeze, and that scratchy shawl of hers against me as she said to me, "Let it go, sugar. That's all right. Let it go."

As I write this, I'm already back on that porch in North Carolina. Perhaps you are, too. What exactly is the feeling that this particular sense memory brings to the surface? It is hard to say, exactly, because there seems to be a mixture: fear, loss, shame, guilt, love, safety, and relief, to name the ones that come immediately to mind. But the important thing is, thinking about that day so long ago ignites a feeling in me right now that is undeniable, strong, personal, and true. Experienced actors usually are able to use one part of a particular sense memory to retrieve the entire set of feelings. When I prepare for a scene that might benefit from my tricycle emotion, just thinking of the feel of my great-grandmother's wool shawl will get me there. How an actor controls such feelings and chooses to reveal them is quite another matter, not to mention another big part of the art of acting.

Pulling this kind of real emotion from the well of sense memories is also a big part of what good writers do. As I was considering how to write about this memory, I came across an interview in the Writers Guild magazine, *Written By,* with the young screenwriter Stephen Gaghan, who wrote the screenplay for *Traffic,* a very strong movie about the international drug war, starring Michael Douglas. Gaghan, a high school dropout who received a college course on Proust from a friend as a gift, talked about how important sense memory had been to his evolution as a writer. He realized that we all had "memory touchstones," like Proust tasting the madeleine. Gaghan's touchstone involved the death of his own father from cancer when the screenwriter was only fifteen. Here's how he described it to an interviewer:

> The way he told me he was dying was by saying, "I want you to have my camera." It was in the afternoon, and he was in the hospital bed that we'd set up in our study. I just started crying, and he didn't know what to do. After a while, he said, "You've probably heard I'm dying, right?" "Okay, Dad, I heard."

Decades later, all Gaghan has to do is hear the sound of a camera shutter: "Kuchick, kuchick, and I go right there, and I can write out of that emotional feeling," he explained. Does he have to be writing about the death of his father, or even death in general? No. But you can bet that if Gaghan has to write a scene filled with sadness or longing, he will be returning to his father's bedside. Gaghan added that as a writer, "you have to hoard those memories." Every good actor I know would agree.

And you as a speaker will have to plumb your memories for similar emotions, because getting the audience to share your feelings is pretty much the whole ball game.

APPLYING THE SENSE-MEMORY
TECHNIQUE TO PUBLIC SPEAKING

Speakers can learn from both actors and writers. Like an actor, a speaker stands before the audience and must move them. The speaker is also playing a role—his or her best possible self—and must prepare for the performance, making sure the appropriate emotions will be available. Unlike the actor, however, the speaker is not handed certain emotions to perform. Speakers have to figure out what emotions fit the message and the audience—like the dramatic writer, who must find an emotional place to write from by accessing a sense memory. The speaker, too, must prepare his remarks using real feelings, bring them before his listeners, then help them find similar feelings inside themselves.

This, as I suspect you have already guessed, brings us back to Al Pacino's speech. While I have no inside knowledge on how Pacino prepared for this performance, the source of its emotional power seems clear to me. In the speech, he stated flat out that he was a big fan of teachers because they change people's lives. But notice that he didn't just say, "And I want to thank my public school drama teacher for making me an actor." Where's the emotional punch in that? Instead, Pacino told a story about the day his life was changed; more important, he painted a picture of that wonderful teacher sitting at the kitchen table with his grandmother, making the case for why she should allow her grandson to pursue his dream to be an actor. Finally, the audience did not witness only Pacino's picture; they also saw their own lives flash before them, marked by a similar moment or its absence. In Arthur Miller's terms, that Golden Globe audience was not unlike the theatergoers who "wouldn't watch a play if they didn't see themselves in it." Surely we all saw ourselves in the little drama that Pacino created, and we were moved, just as he knew we would be. (Sappy guy that I am, I find the story so effective that I am moved merely by its repetition.)

WHY DOES THE AUDIENCE RESPOND?

Mainly because they want to. You must never forget that your audience, large or small, is a living, breathing entity, responding to everything you do and say. Audiences are inclined to endow performers with what they themselves are thinking and feeling. People sitting together in a room also influence one another's responses; feelings become contagious. Audiences tend to be so eager to understand and connect to you that sometimes they will be ahead of you in terms of feeling. Watching Greta Garbo and Humphrey Bogart stare into space, we think we know exactly what they are thinking: Bogart's Rick must be thinking about Ilsa (Ingrid Bergman), Paris, or the Nazi threat, because if we were in his shoes, those would be the issues distracting us. According to *Casablanca* lore, Bogart stood on the second floor and stared down across Rick's Place because the director had asked him to, just in case they needed a soundless shot of him to cut to when it came time to edit the film. Bogart gave the director what he wanted, but in the process, he also gave the audience a moment to be moved by all the feelings that he had filled Rick with until then. During that famous take, Bogart, for all we know, may have been counting to ten, in much the same way Greta Garbo claimed to have done during her famous screen silences. Marlon Brando never ceased to be amazed by how audiences facilitated his job. The actor, Brando explained in his autobiography, must keep in mind that the audience is "a pivotal part of the process." According to Brando, "every theatrical event, from those taking place in the Stone Age to Punch-and-Judy shows and Broadway plays, can produce an emotional participation from the audience, who become the actors in the drama."

The smart speaker will capitalize on this emotional neediness in his audience. Even if you're a novice speaker or just shy about expressing emotions, if you've done your work, you can count on the audience to meet you at least halfway, filling in the blanks as much as they can, wanting to be won over. They have come to hear your message, and even a skeptical audience will give you the benefit of the doubt—up until the moment you start speaking. From then on, it is up to you not to lose them. They have shown up to hear you, they are giving up some of their own work or free time, and they expect to be compensated. But no matter how important your message and how perfectly you have structured and prepared its presentation, unless you appear passionate and committed to what you are saying—positively pumped—you will not succeed. Every talented speaker I know exhibits a kind of incandescence that attracts the audience. The by-now-clichéd metaphors that a speaker was magnetic or mesmerizing have their source in the intensity, the élan, the zing that good speakers bring to the podium. When business books talk about "leadership presence," it is this ability to fill the room with personality that they are describing; when headhunters talk about how the most talented managers exhibit passion for their ideas and business strategies, they are pointing to the way that extraordinary business leaders make their convictions contagious. The best communicators arrive not just with a well-prepared and strong message, they also show up in public with a glow.

When I discussed how to prepare a speech in Chapter Three, I advised trying to view your message from the audience's point of view. Now let me add another touch: The more you can identify with your listeners, the more they will embrace you. While most professional motivational speakers, for instance, are giving essentially the same speech to every audience, the best ones tailor each performance to the people in the room. As I said, for every one of the eighty or so corporate speeches he gives a year, my friend Tom Sullivan does extensive research on each company and its competition so there is no doubt among his listeners that his message can work for them. By joking about their competition or pointing to some good or bad deals, he makes it immediately clear that he has studied the company, thus assuring the audience that listening is worth their time. His respect for what they do translates into their willingness to give him a hearing. It is then up to him to build on that goodwill. By the end of the session, a skilled speaker like Tom Sullivan will have that audience on their feet. Such success lies in the speaker's ability to convince the audience that he knows that what they think is important.

Politicians are trying to make this kind of emotional attachment with voters when they tell stories of how their grandparents arrived at Ellis Island, how their parents sacrificed to educate their children, how they learned the value of hard work on Granddaddy's farm; and, if the audience is Hispanic, "Hola, mis amigos . . ." What better way to win over an audience than to speak their language, either literally or figuratively? One of the most famous—and shameless—uses of this device was President Kennedy's 1963 speech before more than a million people in Berlin, a city divided in half between the Allies and the Soviets after World War II. It was a short speech but one of Kennedy's most emotionally charged. "There are many people in the world who really don't understand . . . what is the great issue between the free world and the Communist world. Let them come to Berlin." Kennedy turned that divided city into a metaphor for the worldwide struggle between totalitarianism and freedom. "Let them come to Berlin," he said, using a line that tens of thousands in his audience had probably uttered themselves; to increase their sense of recognition, the American president actually repeated the phrase in German, "*Lass' sie nach Berlin kommen.*" Kennedy memorably wrapped up his message with the line "All free men, wherever they may lie, are citizens of Berlin, and, therefore, as a free man, I take pride in the words *Ich bin ein Berliner.*" The roar of the crowd was heard all the way to Moscow as a million Berliners cheered the American who declared, "I am a citizen of Berlin."

Warning: While it is easy to say that you are one of them, convincing an audience that it is true is another matter. No audience wants to be manipulated. When President George Bush—son of a Wall Street investment banker and U.S. senator from Connecticut, graduate of Andover and Yale, former congressman, ambassador to the United Nations, director of the CIA, and vice president—claimed that his favorite game was horseshoes and that he loved crispy bacon rinds, eyebrows shot up throughout the very American heartland the president sought to identify with. But his son the president has had little trouble selling himself as "just folks"; his Texas twang, experience in the oil fields, career in professional baseball, delight in bestowing nicknames on Washington heavies, and even his tendency to malapropism have won over many Americans tired of slick politicians. No matter his failings (or his family and educational background), the latest President Bush seems like a regular guy.

Except when he speaks in formal public situations, particularly in front of the cameras. During his campaign and early days in office, George W. Bush looked plain scared in public. As he settled into the job, his fear gave way to simple discomfort. But then, as I noted earlier, history nudged his real self into the spotlight.

FROM LOUSY SPEAKER TO REAL LEADER— THE REQUIRED INGREDIENT IS FEELING

I return to the president's difficulties as a public speaker not because I want to pick on him but because he is a very visible example of a poor public speaker who has the potential to be a good one. Bush has two qualities in particular that can make for an effective communicator: genuine charm and deep feelings. The president's problem is that he cannot seem to bring either with him to the podium. He could certainly learn about presidential performance by studying videotapes of Ronald Reagan and Bill Clinton. But he could also learn plenty from his own best performances.

Bush himself repeatedly revealed how feelings can inject life into even the stiffest speaker after the terrorist attacks of September 11, 2001. A day and a half after the attacks, during a standard photo op of the president on the phone to world leaders, a reporter asked him to describe his present level of emotion. "I don't think about myself right now," Bush said. "I think about the families, the children . . ." As soon as he said "children," he was filled with feeling and almost lost it. But he didn't. He rode on this real emotion, blinking back tears. "I'm a loving guy," he continued, with resolve replacing his tears. "I am also someone, however, who's got a job to do, and I intend to do it." Some in the press and in official Washington saw this impromptu display of emotion as unpresidential. For me, it was the first time Bush had appeared real and spontaneous and truly presidential. If there was ever a time to display emotion, it was within a few days of that attack. If Bush had broken down and wept uncontrollably, that would have been unpresidential. But to fight back grief and layer it with angry resolve made a strong connection to the American people, who recognized the authenticity of Bush's feelings because they were feeling equally emotional and enraged.

Six months later, Bush had another emotional public moment, this time during a speech in Florida discussing his commitment to the fight against worldwide terror, even during the worst week of U.S. casualties in Afghanistan. Among his audience was the family of one of those soldiers. The president said: "My fellow Americans must understand that—that we will be relentless and determined to do what is right. And we will take loss of life, and I'm sad for loss of life, and today we've got the mom and dad of a brave soldier who has lost his life, and his brother . . ."

As soon as Bush said "mom and dad," another wave of strong feelings caught him unaware. He managed to get to the end of the sentence mainly by biting his lip. Nevertheless, he stayed in the moment and spoke directly to the family in the audience: "I know your heart aches, but your son and brother died for a noble and just cause." As the crowd applauded, Bush wiped away a tear. His emotional moment was all over the news that night, but this time no one said anything about his behavior being unpresidential. On the contrary, the consensus was that such a strong response was appropriate to the times and the situation. One network anchor noted that politicians must always walk a fine line between "looking human and looking like a leader." The implication was that Bush had done both. Another commentator said that the nation wanted a president who "understood the risks of sending young men into battle," and added that in the president's Florida speech, "we saw the real George W. Bush."

Bush's on-camera emotions were classic examples of sense memory, involuntary ones, to be sure. The mention of "children" or "mom and dad" set Bush off, not unlike the taste of the madeleine for Proust. (My Harvard students would have enjoyed that one: George W. Bush and Marcel Proust in the same sentence.) His feelings could not have been more genuine. No one needed to be coached to respond with horror, anger, and sadness to September 11, and most of us would have been similarly moved in the presence of a family of a fallen soldier. But if the president's moments in the Oval Office and Florida were evidence of the real George W. Bush and true leadership in a post–September 11 world, then surely any politician (and his advisers) will want to figure out how to repeat them. The president is faced with all sorts of events that require an emotional answer, and the more effectively he can express his true emotions in public, the better a leader he will be.

American leaders are required to be men of the people, regular guys. Aloof, elitist, and arrogant do not score votes, and any U.S. politician who affected a Churchillian haughtiness would be risking his political future. From the beginning, Bush's strong suit has been his common touch. Growing up in and politicking in Texas taught him the advantages of being one of the guys. When that regular guy suddenly appeared on a pile of rubble at Ground Zero with a bullhorn in his hand and his arm around a fireman, this new Bush, in the eyes of many Americans, morphed into a leader.

Bush must now strive to bring these parts of himself into the public arena on a regular basis. In spite of reports that the president puts in a great deal of rehearsal time on his addresses to Congress, Bush is still a work in progress as a public speaker. He is still too stiff in front of the TelePrompTer, reading rather than speaking. If the White House called me (sorry, I'm unlisted), I would advise that the president work at bringing his off-the-cuff persona to the podium. By making his feelings and humor part of his preparations, he could improve this sense of spontaneity. Even when rehearsing speeches from a TelePrompTer, Bush could experiment with putting his emotions on display. He could add the kind of funny remark he makes in a meeting or press conference—and then, instead of reading it, practice telling it. Certainly whatever ignited his emotional responses to the words "children" or "mom and dad" is worth exploring and using. My bet is that not only would audiences and voters love the more human Bush, the president might also find himself being compared more often, in a favorable way, to Ronald Reagan.

ISN'T THIS SENSE-MEMORY STUFF ABOUT FAKING IT?

No. But I certainly understand the concern of a businessman, politician, teacher, community volunteer, or social activist that he might look to be putting one over on the audience. Using a moment from our past that caused anger or grief or passion to express a feeling in a meeting or during a speech is a technique. But there's nothing fake about the results. Audiences, as I have noted, can spot a phony emotion from the back seats. I am not asking you to fake emotions or mimic some kind of classic emotional response. As I stressed at the outset, I dread public displays of emotionalism.

What I am advising is quite the opposite: bringing in real feelings that not only fit the moment but are *in* the moment—you are experiencing them right now. But haven't you prepared these feelings? What's spontaneous about that? Isn't this perfect speaker *manufacturing* feelings for his performance? First of all, there is nothing spontaneous about a public-speaking assignment. You have prepared what you will say, and to be any good, you should have rehearsed for days. A speech is not an extemporaneous conversation.

> **But a good speech will appear**
> **like a spontaneous conversation.**

Actors impress us because they appear to be conversing with others onstage, even though their remarks were written and everyone in the theater knows it. Effective speakers must also seem to be talking to you in your kitchen, one-on-one. That is your role as a speaker—to play your best self before an audience. If your message needs to be passionate or touching or funny, you have to show that you are all of those things. To pull that off, you'll control your anxiety by being so well prepared that you can use the inevitable adrenaline to look alive rather than like a frightened animal. You also have to do things that fit your message, and one of the most effective things to do is to re-create the right emotions.

I realize that this notion suggests something shady. We are inclined to think that real feelings are, by definition, spontaneous responses. The idea that a feeling may be *voluntary,* that we could choose to feel a certain way, seems strange. Yet consider the person who walks into a meeting or an interview or makes a speech on an issue he cares about more than anything in the world, but he's so nervous that he comes off like a robot. It happens all the time. To observe that a speaker must exude intensity is so obvious that one hesitates to say it, yet most speakers cannot show their passion.

Enter the technique of sense memory. Sense memory produces real feelings for a particular moment, and it allows you to find those feelings repeatedly. Communicating in public is a craft, sometimes even an art. Craftsmanship—and even great art—can be done again and again. Picasso knocked off a lot of great Picassos, Mozart and Beethoven kept writing extraordinary music on commission, and Yeats and Frost churned out great poems. But none of these artists was repeating or mimicking himself; each was making art that moved people. It could be said that, in a sense, every effort to get some kind of rise out of other people is manufactured; that all art is, in fact, a hoax. The poet W. H. Auden once described a poem as a "contraption." There are rules of meter, rhyme, syntax, and form that make up every good poem. But Auden also added that such contraptions "have a guy inside." Someone makes the poem, just as someone puts words on a page that turns into a play. The person playing Oedipus did not really tear out his eyes, and Laurence Olivier is not really an old king gone mad. They are actors in man-made contraptions. But this stuff really works. Such plays and roles inspire and move people, generation after generation. When they do, audiences seem to forget that they are enjoying a well-made contraption. And while there are all sorts of explanations and arguments for why great art is great (which I will leave to the philosophers and literary theorists), the artists, composers, writers, and performers who make it happen know that one common denominator is its emotional force.

Great communication is no different. Churchill stood in Parliament week after week during World War II without a note in his hand, delivering many of history's most quoted speeches. His son later wrote that no one worked harder to make his speeches seem extemporaneous. Martin Luther King, Jr., galvanized audiences every time. Ronald Reagan's success on the lecture trail convinced leaders of the California Republican Party that this out-of-work actor had a political future. By all accounts, Reagan was a charming guy in person and a great storyteller. He managed to bring both talents to the podium. These men were all supremely talented communicators who almost never gave a bad speech. It was not just that they were experienced speakers; they were also able to summon the appropriate passion and conviction for that moment in front of that audience. I would argue that every professional speaker is terrific virtually every time out. That kind of consistency is within everyone's grasp— provided you prepare properly and figure out how to get your real feelings into your performance.

If you want to move other people—and believe me, no matter what the subject of your presentation or speech, you do — there is one question you have to pose as you prepare your presentation:

"WHAT MOVES ME?"

You need to find a memory that brings up feelings—all kinds of feelings. If you can move yourself—choke up a bit or get angry or laugh out loud—you're halfway to touching your listeners. Playwrights and screenwriters devote a lot of time to making themselves laugh and cry. How do you write a scene in which the main character is ticked off, or crippled by depression, or has to fire up his troops to take on an enemy who has them outgunned? The writer must find such feelings in himself to get in the right mood for writing the scene, and then he tackles the equally difficult challenge of finding the words, images, and stories that will spark the right response in the audience. Like the writer, you have to search for the right feelings. Even if you use a sense memory from your childhood, you will have made the feeling a part of your recent biography in preparing it. You are now in a position to bring that world to your audience. Like Pacino's in his Golden Globe speech, your feelings will be there; you do not have to sell that. The audience will sense that you have invested yourself in this emotion, and they will accept what you display as the real thing, because it will be. But as Pacino did, you have to set the scene. You already know that what you have to say is moving, since it moved you as you prepared it. But unlike the original emotional experience, the sense memory is under your control, and by reexperiencing it, you give it an emotional truth different from the original feeling. The day I lost my tricycle, when my great-grandmother embraced me, I gave in to my shame and wept uncontrollably. When I use that sense memory as an actor, I rein in those feelings. The only evidence that I am upset might be a brief constriction of my voice or a pause to keep from losing it. The audience senses my feelings, and they are moved.

I have been concentrating on strong emotions to make the idea of sense memory easier to understand. But most speakers spend their time trying to inform or persuade colleagues; the kind of public speaking that we do in business meetings or conferences or even pitches to small groups is more about filling people in or getting them to buy your message than reducing them to tears. Still, your bare-boned case, no matter how strong or logical, is often not enough. Successful managers and certainly top CEOs are known for their ability to convey passion, every time out. That requires you to line up your feelings and bring them to the meeting. If you want to excite the troops at work, or make it clear that they have screwed up, there is no need to pound the table or shout. My instinct would be to analyze most cases of anger. Typically, there are obstacles or some kind of conflict that provokes them. You have a purpose, and stupid, wrong, unethical, or irresponsible behavior is keeping you from doing the right thing. That causes the anger. A good director would say, "You're just trying to get this done, and I'll put so many obstacles in your way that you'll have to fight through a lot of emotions to get past them and do the responsible thing." If you are a top manager in a company eager to inspire employees to go out and beat the competition, all you have to do is list the things they have done to take away your customers. You will get ticked off by saying them, and your audience will get equally miffed by hearing the list of grievances and watching you get angry before their very eyes. Creating this kind of anger in politics is a snap. Each side hates something about the other: They're lying about our record; they're stealing votes; if they get in power, they will raise your taxes, ruin your family, destroy your children's chances of getting a decent education. Do you have to shout about that? All you have to do is bring your passion and lay out your case in details so vivid that the audience will become as fired up as you are.

Please don't think that you need a sense memory that correlates exactly with the feeling you want to convey in your presentation. Actors have to play emotional scenes involving events that have never occurred in their own personal experience: marriage, for example, or dealing with a surly teenager, or having a child, or losing a child. How do we do it? We come up with sense memories of similar feelings; it's called "substitution." If the part calls for dealing with the joy of childbirth, an actress might go back to the time in her life when she was a little kid and got an amazing gift; if she wants to feel the joy plus the anxiety of motherhood, she might think back to being accepted into college or getting her first full-time job (elation) and wondering if she could deal with being away from home or working in a corporation (anxiety). My tricycle has filled in for many scenes involving loss, shame, embarrassment, longing, and tears.

Can the loss of a tricycle substitute for a more momentous emotional moment—losing a job, for example, or even a parent? Absolutely. Stella Adler used to warn us about creating a hierarchy of emotions. Her contention was that no emotional experience is less worthy than any other, so long as it gets the job done. As anyone who has explored his or her feelings knows, often it is those childhood feelings that are the most powerful, no matter how relatively trivial the events that caused them might seem in hindsight.

(SENSE) MEMORY AIDS

Many of my students were self-conscious about their emotions or inexperienced at analyzing them. A good place to start is with popular songs and movies that provoke an emotional response in you. TV and movie writers often find inspiration in their favorite films. Struggling for the next plot move or the right emotional tone, collaborators will point to a movie with a scene that was trying to accomplish the same thing: "Remember what Brando did in *On the Waterfront* to hold Eva Marie Saint's attention?" (She dropped her glove, and he picked it up and started putting it on as he talked, making it impossible for her to walk away.) "Let's go for the kind of emotional mix at the end of *Casablanca*, where Ingrid Bergman and Humphrey Bogart say good-bye with her husband standing by." "We need a moment where we know his world has been smashed—like the scene in *The English Patient* where the guy sits in a taxi getting drunk on the champagne he brought his wife as a gift to celebrate his return home, while she spends the evening with her lover." And so on. Sometimes, writers will take an old movie cliché, or what they call the "TV way" or "the bad version," and search for a new spin.

Don't be afraid to borrow from what has already worked on you, no matter how cheesy. Noel Coward once famously noted "how potent cheap sentiment can be"! All you're looking for is some inspiration to help you wander down sense-memory lane. The sentimental stuff may help you find the most powerful emotional moments of your own life. During one of my own conversations about what inspires feelings among audiences, the late Broadway director Robert Moore (*The Boys in the Band; They're Playing Our Song; Promises, Promises; Deathtrap; Woman of the Year*) suggested, half seriously, that you could break down the charged moments in movies into three classic types:

1. "The Running Reunion." Moore's favorite example was from a Civil War movie called *So Big* with Jane Wyman. By the end of the film, she's working in the fields and suddenly sees a faraway figure heading her way. She squints into the distance and realizes what the audience already knows: Her son, whom everyone thought was dead, has returned, injured but very much alive. He sees her and starts heading her way, and she starts walking toward him, the rake still in her hand. He begins moving as fast as he can on his crutches—I said this was classic! subtle it is not—and she starts to run. The music begins to swell. The wind is blowing; she drops the rake as the music hits its crescendo and begins running as he hobbles toward her. "I defy anyone to sit through this movie and not lose it," Moore used to say.

2. "The Superhuman Effort." This is Gary Cooper at *High Noon*. It's Sylvester Stallone in *Rocky*. It's Brando in *On the Waterfront,* having been helped up off the ground after a savage

beating ("Am I on my feet?") and managing to make the walk, half conscious, back to the loading dock—as the other longshoremen finally decide to join him in the fight. No matter how many times I see the climactic scenes of these movies, I am moved.

3. "The Cagney Moment." This was Bob Moore's favorite, that genre of movies in which the star (not always Jimmy Cagney), in spite of being struck blind, beaten to a pulp, or mortally wounded, says to his companion, "Don't worry about me, kid, you make a break for it, and I'll be fine." A version of this tale of the ultimate sacrifice has been a storytelling staple since at least Homer's *Iliad*.

These classic movie moments pull us into an emotional situation where we cannot help but share the characters' feelings. That is how we hope we would act.

Often our most powerful sense memories are feelings that we share as a nation, such as the sight of President Kennedy's beautiful young widow standing with her daughter and son as the caisson carrying their murdered father's body passed, accompanied by a horse without a rider. The courageous mother whispered in the little boy's ear, and he dutifully stepped forward to salute his dead father. More recently, the image of those New York firemen charging up the stairs of the World Trade towers as civilians ran down has provided us with another common sense-memory. For many New Yorkers, just the word "fireman" provokes a series of images that moves them to tears. A shared memory, however, can also be a deliriously happy moment: The U.S. amateur hockey team beats the Russian pros in the 1980 winter Olympics. Gymnast Mary Lou Retton vaults to a perfect ten. Your favorite team wins the World Series or the Super Bowl. Back then your feelings were strong. Putting yourself into that moment can generate the same elation, in all its intensity. This has nothing to do with faking it. The tears that flow when you see that little boy saluting or the elation you feel when you take yourself back to the sights, sounds, and smells of that sporting event are all very real.

Compile your own list of moments from films and history that have moved you to tears of sadness or joy. I guarantee that they will generate many more similar moments from your own autobiography.

MOVING PEOPLE TO LAUGHTER

I have focused on sense memories that lead to tears, but let's not forget that humor is another way for speakers to warm up the room. Laughing and crying are emotional responses that are uncannily close: "She was crying with happiness." "They were laughing and crying at the same time." "I laughed so hard that I cried." Laughing and crying seem to pour out of us involuntarily. Neither is so much an emotion as the result of an emotion. "A lot of comedy comes through fear," the comedian Robin Williams said in a *Time* interview. "It's having a take on things that people are maybe thinking but not expressing. That's when you get the huge 'wow' laugh, because you spoke the unspeakable." We all have memories that make us smile or laugh out loud. What better way to win over the audience than with a real smile on your face or the glow that can come from telling a funny story?

I do advise against beginning a presentation with a joke, particularly one unrelated to your topic. What about a great related joke? Still risky. The main danger is that if the joke is a sidesplitter, the rest of what you have to say might not measure up. You don't want to spend the rest of your time disappointing listeners who are now waiting for another great joke. Unless you are extremely funny—and I mean the Billy Crystal kind of knock-'em-in-the-aisles-holding-their-stomachs-with-laughter funny—then I would avoid a lot of jokes.

I myself have trouble remembering jokes. But I do like stories with a punch line, and these can be very effective. They not only win over or relax an audience with laughter, they also require the kind of conversational, one-on-one style that you ought to strive for in nearly every speech. We all know people who have a talent for making people laugh. If you are one of these lucky people, then by all means take advantage of your gift. If you know funny people, study how they make others laugh. Funny people have an intuitive way of telling a good story. The most talented raconteurs I know set the scene with the skill of a professional writer, layering in every detail to bring you inside their story; good storytellers also seem blessed with the kind of charm and conversational style that take some actors years to master.

But be funny with a purpose. Make sure your laughs are related to your message. Even in a serious speech, humor can be useful, if not imperative. Television has compartmentalized humor too much; to make you laugh, they serve up situation comedies, and to move you or thrill you, there are the hour-long dramas, as if never the twain shall meet. There is now a new term used in television for when the twain do meet—"dramedy"! Can you imagine? Shakespeare's tragedies are loaded with wit, and Chekhov's comedies are full of heartbreak and loss. Peter Shaffer's *Equus* is a harrowing story about a boy who blinds horses, but there are many very funny moments in it. Neil Simon's plays are full of touching and tender moments, and all he asks of his actors is that they play their characters truthfully and seriously, letting the laughter come where it will. Some of the most moving funeral services I have been to were filled with humor. At my own father's memorial service, I was determined to bring laughter into the church. My father died after a long bout with Alzheimer's disease, and for a man known for his fine mind and sharp wit, it was a particularly tragic way to go. Dad was a popular guy in the community, the deputy mayor, a deacon in the church, a member of the choir. I wanted to remind his friends of the man they knew. I decided to tell a story I had told often over the years to describe what a funny guy my father was.

In 1968 my parents and brother came to see me in the Boston tryout of my first Broadway show, *Promise, Promises*. Afterward I introduced them to the girl I was dating, a dazzling dancer named Donna McKechnie. We all went out to a place called the Tiki Hut to have rum drinks with those little umbrellas in them. By the time of my father's memorial service in 1995, many in the audience knew Donna's name from her huge success—and Tony Award—in the Broadway phenomenon *A Chorus Line*. But in 1968 Donna was the lead dancer in a big chorus number at the end of the first act in *Promises, Promises*. After the show, she still had on her stage makeup, with bright lipstick and big eyelashes. With her red-tinted showgirl hair, short skirt, high heels, and a fox stole draped around her shoulders, she was fetching in a way seldom, if ever, seen on the campuses of Amherst and Yale, or in the social circles my parents traveled in. We had our drinks, my mother, my father, Donna—being as nice as a midwestern girl could be—and my sixteen-year-old brother, who didn't miss a thing. My family had to get back to Long Island, and Donna and I had our own postshow plans. We said our good-byes and off we went, arm in arm. My brother could not wait to inform me that when my family was back in the car and heading out of Boston, my mother, who is called Carey, turned to my father and said: "She seems like a perfectly nice young lady, but I must confess I'm not sure exactly what Ken sees in her." My father, never taking his eyes off the road, responded, "Really, Carey. Well, it's not lost on me."

The congregation burst into laughter and applause. They roared. That was the man they all knew: the deft use of language, the tongue-in-cheek, dry delivery. It may have been a memorial service, but this funny story worked beautifully because its point was to bring back the man everyone in that church had experienced, the person we all loved and respected.

Assignment #5

Create a sense memory from your own life that makes you tearful.

The goal here is to get the feel for moving yourself on purpose. Let your memory guide you back to some moment in your past: the further back the memory, the more brimming with emotion it tends to be. Use every example I have offered to help remind you of similar feelings in your own autobiography. One memory will spark another. But remember: To build a powerful emotional memory, you must recall events according to your five senses, asking the same questions I did to travel back to that emotional day I lost my tricycle. Try to set the whole scene as if you were the screenwriter of your memoirs. Like Al Pacino at the Golden Globe Awards, try to create a picture that an audience can see and thus feel.

How will you know you're going about it correctly? If you find yourself choking up a bit, you have found the right story. If it touches you, it is likely to touch others. Work on it in the same way you prepared the story about your day: Get the message clear, then build your story around that message, section by section, getting all the images, sounds, smells, tastes, and touches straight and vivid. Take as long as you need to tell it, though I doubt you'll need more than two minutes. But don't feel restricted by time. Whatever it takes to move people, get it in—then see if you've succeeded by telling someone else the story. If you have the right story, I suspect that you'll need to keep yourself from losing it. But hold it together. Emotional restraint, as we have seen, has a powerful effect on audiences. I would recommend spending a few days on this assignment.

Assignment #5a

Work on telling a funny story with a punch line.

Ideally, the story should be one from your own life that also makes a point. In certain circumstances, this kind of story can be a brief speech in itself, or an amusing introduction for another speaker or colleague or client visiting your headquarters. If coming up with a personal story proves a burden, try a funny story that you've heard and liked. (That you've remembered it at all indicates how much it tickled you.) Any story that you've liked and remembered is already part of your life.

Prepare this story and hone it the same way you did your sense memory. Be sure there are plenty of strong images; work to draw them vividly. Set the scene by adding more details to the story. Make it conversational, as if you were telling it to a friend, and then tell it to a few friends to see if they find it as funny as you do. Notice how you are inclined to change the telling somewhat to make it better. In the retelling of any story, what worked best last time is likely to stay. (Notice, too, how easily you remembered the good parts.) Make sure your language serves the purpose of the story. Shaggy-dog stories can be very entertaining, but if you get bogged down in too much detail, you risk confusing your audience.

To help you work on building your funny story that makes a

point, I offer one of my favorites. You might want to fiddle with it to get yourself in the mood, or maybe even tell it to a friend as a way to practice being funny. It is not a personal tale. But my father told it to me when I was in high school, to teach me a lesson about the accidental nature of good fortune. I took it to heart and now consider the story a part of my own life. My father's version was centered upon the image of a dime. In the interest of inflation, I have made it a quarter.

A guy is in Las Vegas. He's been gambling all his life. In fact, he's a compulsive gambler. His luck runs cold this trip, and he loses all his money, and I mean all of it. All he has left is his airline shuttle pass and return ticket. He decides to head for the airport. But first he has to use the bathroom. He walks into the john and suddenly realizes that the place is fitted with pay toilets. They cost a quarter, but all of his pockets are empty. He's so broke he doesn't have even a quarter to his name. He walks out of the men's room, sees a guy, and says, "Can I borrow a quarter for the men's room?" What's a quarter in Vegas? The guy tosses our friend the necessary quarter. He heads back into the men's room and goes to put the quarter into a slot—but before he can, the stall door swings open. The last person left the door ajar. He doesn't need to use the quarter.

As he's leaving the casino, he passes by a slot machine. The guy's a compulsive gambler, right? He still has the quarter, which he drops into the slot machine and pulls the lever—and all hell breaks loose. He's hit the million-dollar jackpot! He falls on his knees as quarters keep pouring out of the damned thing, stupefied at his good fortune. It changes his life. He invests all the money he won, parlaying it into a bigger and bigger fortune.

Years later our zillionaire is giving a speech to some group, telling his story about that time in Vegas when he was so broke he had to borrow a quarter to go to the john. He ends the speech by noting how strange life can be. "One man was the key to my whole future," he says. "One man changed my life. If it weren't for him, I wouldn't be standing before you here today."

A guy jumps up in the back of the room and says, "That was me! I swear to God! That was me in Vegas!" The speaker says, "That was you?" "Yeah," says the guy, "I'm the one who gave you the quarter—the one who changed your life." "No, no, not you," says the zillionaire. "The guy who left the door ajar!"

To make this story work, you have to keep mentioning the quarter. If the audience forgets the quarter part, they are not going to laugh at the punch line. So you set the image of the quarter in the audience's mind, and to do that, you have to throw in some mentions of the quarter in the windup of the story. You also have to set up the phrase "left the door ajar" to repeat it at the end in the same way as you build to the punch line.

A real comedian-storyteller, such as Bill Cosby, George Carlin, or Jan Murray, would embellish the setup to score laughs at every stage—when the guy loses his money, when he goes into the bathroom and finds out it's pay toilets, when he comes outside and has to bum a quarter. By the time the punch line comes, you would be so convulsed with laughter that the story's final message would be almost beside the point. Try it out on a couple of friends, playing with what works best and what doesn't. Notice again how the logic and built-in structure of the story make it easy to remember. Also notice the improvement you are making when you speak in front of other people.

Assignment #5b

Use one of your sense memories to invigorate a brief speech or presentation.

Easier said than done. But now that you have figured out how to move yourself to tears or laughter, you should be ready to apply the technique of sense memory to any kind of speech. Try adapting one of the brief presentations you have already prepared. You've practiced those a number of times and should be comfortable enough with the words and message to add some feeling. For example, prepare that one-minute introduction from Chapter One in such a way that you will have a big smile on your face and seem happy to be there, ready to have a good time. Maybe you can adapt your funny story to an introduction for yourself or someone else.

Then prepare your talk so that you're on the verge of tears—as if you were appearing at a memorial service and had to explain why you were chosen to speak. Remember that report I asked you to prepare about your day? That, too, could be infused with sadness or hilarity. Pick the mood you'd prefer to be in, and work on re-creating the appropriate emotions. Don't forget to paint a detailed picture, building in all the details you can. No image is too trivial if it helped you find those feelings. Review the examples I offered earlier: Pacino's teacher sitting in his grandmother's kitchen; my tricycle story, run through the memory of each of my five senses—with a Dr Pepper added just in case. The same images that helped you find your own feelings will also serve to move your audience. You were moved because you went back in time; bring the audience with you.

Once you have touched them, it will be a whole lot easier to sell your message.

6

PERSUADING THEM

I spent most of the summer of 1987 in London, rehearsing and performing a television production of Eugene O'Neill's *Strange Interlude* for Showtime. I played the boorish but well-meaning husband to the leading lady, who was played by Glenda Jackson, the talented English actress (and now a member of Parliament) who had recently starred in critically acclaimed productions of this play in London's West End and on Broadway. David Dukes had joined the TV version as her lover, and José Ferrer was playing her father, who appears only in the first scene but sets the tone of everything that follows. In the rehearsal of the play's first scene, it quickly became apparent that the director would be following Glenda's insistence that the new actors abide by some of the choices assigned to their predecessors in the London and New York productions. My character did not appear until later in the play, but I watched in amazement as Glenda and the director advised José Ferrer, who had more than fifty years of experience on the stage, how he was to play his part: "Walk to the window after you say this, turn back when she says that; now drink the sherry, and say this line more quickly so that you are done by the time she arrives at the door."

Ferrer listened and took a pause—brief but pregnant with his annoyance at being treated like an acting student—yet said nothing. He glanced my way a few times before proceeding, as if to say, "Do you believe this?" I had worked with him in a couple of TV films, and we'd had several long conversations, all of them memorable. José Ferrer had achieved Broadway stardom not long after graduating from Princeton in 1933 and had gone on to a big movie career that included an Academy Award for his Cyrano de Bergerac. "Call me Joe," he had said, and I did in our private conversations, but in public I always referred to him as "Mr. Ferrer," or occasionally "Monsieur de Bergerac." Joe Ferrer was a great raconteur, with a bag of funny stories full of the stuff of Hollywood and Broadway legend, but that day he was not amused. Later, during the tea break, a British theater ritual that I came to enjoy, Joe referred to the director as "her ladyship's puppeteer." A few minutes later he simply shook his head and murmured to me, "I don't need this."

"Uh-oh," I thought. "He's going to walk." I had no trouble agreeing that an actor as good as José Ferrer didn't need this kind of irritation for a one-scene appearance in a production on cable TV. But we definitely needed him. At the end of the rehearsal, Joe slipped into his Burberry trench coat, cocked his tweed fedora at a rakish angle, smiled, and said to the stage manager, "We'll be in touch." Before the perplexed stage manager could gain clarification, Ferrer was on his way out the door, with me after him, grabbing an umbrella on the way: "Want to share a cab, Joe?" He replied, "I thought I'd walk." It was raining lightly, and he hadn't opened his umbrella. "Mind if I join you?" He sighed and looked at me for a beat. Then he chuckled and said, "Oh, all right, all right." Off we went in the rain, umbrellas closed, toward the elegant Connaught Hotel, where he was staying. We went along in silence for a while, and then he started talking about how he liked to walk briskly, preferring to be by himself unless someone was willing to keep up with him. In my case, this was clearly not a problem. At my height and age—a few decades younger—I was taking one stride for every two of his. But I told him that I, too, loved to walk for hours in big cities like New York, Paris, Rome, and, of course, London. For the next hour, as we walked to the Connaught, he told a series of hilarious stories about various film locations he'd been on, and directors and actors he had worked with, including one about introducing Gary Cooper to a beautiful Parisian showgirl. "Coop" applied his considerable charm to the woman and then escorted her from the room with a wink over his shoulder to Ferrer, who was watching with considerable glee. As he told the story, Joe laughed at the image of Cooper returning red-faced to chase him down the street. Ferrer continued to laugh as he imitated Gary Cooper's graphic description of the scene in his hotel room when the handsome movie star discovered that the woman was the most famous transvestite in Paris.

Ferrer seemed surprised by how much I knew about his own career. I kept reminding him how important it was to me to know and work with performers of his experience and stature; that kind of continuity from one generation to the next had become increasingly rare in our profession. He asked me questions about my training and career. I also told him about the course I was preparing to teach at Harvard. I knew Ferrer had excelled in rhetoric and debate at Princeton, and maybe he could help me clarify some of the connections I wanted to make between acting and public speaking. It was a wonderful walk. But Joe Ferrer knew exactly what I was doing, which was absolutely everything I could think of to make him change his mind about quitting: flattering him, teasing him, laughing at his stories, trying to make him feel guilty about letting down his young friend and devoted admirer. I even begged him to stay.

As we neared his hotel, I played my wild card. Joe had once told me that after he won his Oscar, the studio didn't know how to cast him. "They thought my nose was too big, thought I looked too Jewish. I'm not Jewish, but that mattered little to the people who ran the studios, who actually were Jewish. They treated actors like puppets, and they held the strings." I put my hand on José Ferrer's shoulder and told him how much I had enjoyed our talk and hoped I would see him the next morning at rehearsal. "And please remember," I added, quoting Cyrano, " 'a great nose indicates a great man—genial, courteous, intellectual, virile, courageous.' " He said, "Ah yes, ah yes," and turned slightly to reveal his profile, albeit without the extended proboscis, against a small flourish of his right hand that was pure Cyrano. He then gave me a look that was both warm and sad. "I do believe, my young friend, that if you put your mind to it, you could sell ice to an Eskimo."

I figured I had at least sold *Strange Interlude* to José Ferrer. Though he didn't actually make a promise, I was almost positive that when I turned up the next morning for rehearsal, Joe would be there. As I headed off to my hotel I kept thinking about what had just transpired. At its most simple level, I had taken a walk in the rain in London with a great actor, two guys having a spontaneous conversation. But that trip was also a performance. I joined José Ferrer with one goal in mind—to keep him from quitting the play—and everything I did and said was in the service of that objective. I'd had little time to prepare, and my audience was one person. But it was as demanding an audience as I'd ever faced; the stakes were high; and for an hour's walk through London, I was using virtually everything I knew as an actor to keep José Ferrer from quitting. I realized that this particular London performance contained all the ingredients of what I wanted to teach in "The Self and the Role": Like an actor, the effective communicator has to have an overall objective (to keep Joe in the production) and then play the actions to fulfill that objective (flatter and befriend him so that quitting would seem like letting down a friend). Above all, the good communicator also has to impress his audience and hold their attention. To do that, he must appear spontaneous and real. (If Joe had thought I was faking even a moment's interest in him or his career, even though I intended no such thing, I was dead.) The more any public presentation is like a spontaneous one-on-one conversation, the better it is. As an actor, I knew that the best performers were those who never seemed to be acting, and every talented speaker, lecturer, and raconteur I had ever encountered displayed this same kind of private ease in public.

What hadn't occurred to me until that London walk was how similar effective communication was to a sales job. I could hardly explain to the dean at Harvard that I was going to teach a course in salesmanship, but much of performing comes down to that: selling the play, selling the message, selling yourself. At every level—in politics, diplomacy, law, education, business, social relations—effective communication is about winning people's attention, impressing them, then getting them to do what you believe they ought to do: buy the product, beat the competition, hire you, give your company a loan, accept your reading of history or literature, celebrate these newlyweds, remember your late friend or relative, write a check to this charity, vote for your candidate, end AIDS, stamp out world poverty, fight global terrorism, save the world.

To communicate is to build a winning case that persuades your listeners to step on your bandwagon. We do this kind of selling day in and day out, from getting our kids to do their homework, to persuading our spouses to buy in to the next big purchase or career move, to encouraging our friends to join a particular community group, church, or charity. Those are audiences most of us are very comfortable with, but they are still audiences, and we play the roles according to the audience. My challenge, I realized that day in London, was to show my students how they could carry their everyday acting, along with their natural skills as communicators and salespeople, into more formalized situations. In a sense, every speech or presentation you give is about persuading your listeners to see things from your point of view.

ALL IN TWO MINUTES

I have been advising brevity, and I think I have made my point that much can be said in a short time, given preparation, the right words and images, and that essential emotional connection that opens an audience to your message. But two minutes to make a case for ending AIDS and world poverty? When I first proposed to my students that they prepare a presentation that would last under two minutes, they protested that 120 seconds did not seem adequate. The next class, I appeared in the lecture hall, walked toward the podium, and stopped beside it, standing in front of my students with my hands folded in front of me. The room turned silent. Something was up. I then spoke the following words:

Fourscore and seven years ago our fathers brought forth on this continent a new nation, conceived in Liberty, and dedicated to the proposition that all men are created equal.

Now we are engaged in a great civil war, testing whether that nation or any nation so conceived and so dedicated can long endure. We are met on a great battlefield of that war. We have come to dedicate a portion of that field, as a final resting place for those who here gave their lives that the nation might live. It is altogether fitting and proper that we should do this.

But, in a larger sense, we cannot dedicate—we cannot consecrate—we cannot hallow—this ground. The brave men, living and dead, who struggled here, have consecrated it far above our poor power to add or detract. The world will little note nor long remember what we say here, but it can never forget what they did here. It is for us, the living, rather to be dedicated here to the unfinished work which they who fought here have thus far so nobly advanced. It is rather for us to be here dedicated to the great task remaining before us—that from these honored dead we take increased devotion to that cause for which they gave the last full measure of devotion; that we here highly resolve that these dead shall not have died in vain; that this nation, under God, shall have a new birth of freedom; and that government of the people, by the people, for the people, shall not perish from the earth.

When I finished the speech—Abraham Lincoln's Gettysburg Address—the room erupted in applause that seemed quite heartfelt. I know they were impressed by my ability to perform in this way, speaking from memory. But what I said, along with the tone I said it in, had also grabbed them. They had no idea that I'd played Lincoln in a production of *Abe Lincoln in Illinois,* in which I gave his famous "house divided" speech. So I had already worked on the difference between Lincoln's tone in private conversation and how he might speak in public, particularly at the dedication of a Gettysburg cemetery four months after a Civil War battle in which twenty-three thousand Union soldiers and twenty-eight thousand Confederates were killed or wounded. Emotions must have run high on that day in 1863 as Lincoln stood at the Civil War's "Ground Zero," in the middle of a war that would last for two more years. For my rendition, I made sure I was emotionally full though controlled. My class became the audience listening to a war president at Gettysburg. Because I was at Gettysburg, I was able to bring my audience there, too, and move them. But what had really seized them was Lincoln's speech, the full, emotional power of his words. It was not the messenger but the message that brought my class to their feet.

Once they settled down, I thanked them, and a voice from the room piped up: "I got you at one minute forty-nine seconds." I laughed, and so did the other students. "Two minutes is more than enough," I noted. "I rest my case." Of course, I came with my case nailed in advance. The day after the dedication of the cemetery at Gettysburg, Lincoln's fellow speaker Edward Everett, a famous orator of the day (and president of Harvard), wrote to the president, "I shall be glad if I could flatter myself that I came as near to the central idea of the occasion in two hours as you did in two minutes." Others have described it as the best short speech since the Sermon on the Mount. And thus two points central to my own method for public speaking: 1) Keep the message clear—"the central idea," as Everett put it; and 2) Keep it brief—257 words, to be exact, packed with images of birth ("conceived in liberty," "brought forth," "created equal"), death ("final resting place," "who gave their lives," "these honored dead"), and resurrection or rebirth ("a new birth of freedom," "shall not perish from the earth").

Lincoln had also come to Gettysburg to sell his audience, and the nation (the speech was reprinted in every newspaper in the land), on a new vision of America. As many, particularly his critics, knew well, this speech was an effort to move the nation away from its obsession with the Constitution, which had, in effect, sanctioned slavery. In 1857 the Supreme Court had affirmed an American's right to own another human being in the notorious Dred Scott decision. At Gettysburg Lincoln was using the emotional response to a Civil War catastrophe to inspire his fellow Americans to rededicate themselves to that other sacred founding document, the Declaration of Independence, in which "all men are created equal."

The president had turned a eulogy for a battle's fallen heroes into a visionary call for action—and had allotted himself a mere ten sentences to pull it off. It was a speech teacher's dream. I told my class a bit about Lincoln's methods of preparation, how he was known for scribbling down thoughts and phrases on scraps of paper and keeping them inside the band of his stovepipe hat. Lincoln had also admitted to what he called "brooding" over what he intended to say. Even as he walked over the battlefield before his speech, he recalled going over it "again and again and again" to "give it another lick." Above all, he took full advantage of the moment's emotion: Gettysburg was a cemetery, on a battlefield, in the middle of a civil war. Lincoln set out to prove that the war was worth fighting to preserve "a government of the people, by the people, for the people," and he was telling his audience that they must continue fighting.

There was much more I might have told my class about the ideological battles over the Constitution and slavery, or the ancient Greek tradition of funeral oratory, or the then contemporary rural cemetery movement that sought to bury loved ones not in the dank confines of church property but in a beautiful spot like the Gettysburg farmland, which family members might enjoy visiting. I might have gone into all this if I had the time—and if Garry Wills's Pulitzer Prize–winning book *Lincoln at Gettysburg: The Words That Remade America* had been published. But I was lecturing five years before Wills's book came out, and my students had to be satisfied with my simple but hardly simplistic point that even one of the most revered speeches in American history was not only delivered in about two minutes but was also a brilliant sales job.

THE STRUCTURE OF NATURAL ELOQUENCE

Since none of us is Abraham Lincoln, and few of us will be in a position to exhort our fellow Americans to rededicate themselves to the idea of America, let me show you how to construct a presentation that would get an audience to take up a more mundane cause: seat belts. Here's something a friend of mine recently saw on television in Ireland:

Cool red car on a two-lane highway, sun glinting off the paint job. Inside are two couples, early twenties, beautiful, well dressed, exuding success and a promising future. Rock-and-roll music. In the backseat, she steals a kiss from him; he pulls the soda straw out of his mouth. They laugh. The camera cuts to a scene outside the car, a normal, pleasant day on the road. And just as you expect an announcer's smooth voice to try to sell you a car that will make your life as fun and sexy as the lives of its passengers, you see up ahead on the highway a truck coming our way—and then a car passes that truck, which is suddenly in the lane of our car, which swerves off the road and flips over. Now we're all back inside the car, where the action goes into slow motion: That cute boy in the backseat smashes into his pretty girlfriend, knocking her head back violently. Her boyfriend is jerked backward, as if to gather force to drive him forward again, this time into a collision with the person in the passenger seat. We have just watched the kid's head collide with two other heads like a flying boulder. In slow motion. Very upsetting. The screen goes black, and then there's a time cut to several minutes later, outside the wrecked car, where police and emergency workers go about their grim tasks. One of the paramedics says to the camera: "It was the one not wearing the seat belt who did all the damage."

This was a public-service spot encouraging people to wear seat belts in Ireland, where the recent rise in the standard of living has doubled the number of cars in the past few years, with no visible increase in driver skill or safety. The friend who told me about this spot is an experienced journalist, not unfamiliar with public tragedy, who confessed to his own uneasiness during such a graphic dramatization of a fatal accident in the middle of an evening of ordinary television watching. "My wife had to turn her head away from the violence and horror of it," he said, adding that his two teenage daughters, both licensed drivers, were suitably moved and chastened. Apparently a very persuasive public-service commercial—all in sixty seconds.

With this picture in mind, here's how I would prepare a pro-seat-belt presentation that would be strong and stirring—not more than a couple of minutes long.

- *Preliminaries.* From the start, I know that my presentation can be powerful and moving because the images from the Irish public-service spot are so powerful and moving. What was on TV already has a built-in narrative and dramatic structure, which will make it easier to remember: the red car on the two-lane highway, the great-looking kids inside, full of fun and life, and so on.

- *Playing the actions.* I will remind myself what my ultimate objective is by asking the question "What am I doing from moment to moment, and is that serving my overall purpose?" The answer is simple enough: Everything I am doing is to assure that when people leave the room, they will never question the good sense of fastening the seat belt the next time they sit in a car.

- *Setting the scene.* Pastoral—a car on a country road. Happy— nice kids enjoying themselves. Promising—this car trip is only the beginning of a long journey into their future. I want to tell a story that puts my audience right there, with the passengers of the car.

- *Creating emotion.* I also want my audience to sense what the kids in the car are sensing. I will structure the story according to the five senses: 1) You see the car, the two-lane highway, the kids, the fun they're having, their prospects, the truck, the passing car, the results. 2) You hear the music, the sounds of the road, the screech of brakes. 3) You feel the touch of the leather seats in the car, maybe the wind from a partly open window or the air-conditioning; the girl steals a kiss from the boy—the quick touch of her lips on his cheek. 4) What do you smell? The leather seats, perhaps. It's a beautiful day; the air is fresh. There's also the perfume the girl in the backseat is wearing, or the smell of her shampoo when she leans in to kiss her boyfriend. 5) The boy can literally taste her perfume mingling with the plastic taste of the straw in his mouth.

- *Creating drama.* Once I've set this glamorous scene, under- scoring its calm with the tone of my voice, gentle and reas- suring (just as the producers of the public-service spot worked hard to create the expectation that this was just an- other car commercial), I will then shatter its beauty—with my language, tone, and gestures. I want to get us all into that car, in slow motion, then accelerate what happens as my gestures show how the kid without the seat belt slams into his girl- friend, his head hitting hers like a hammer, and we see him thrown back—and then forward into a passenger in the front seat. One of my hands slams another; I throw my own head back to give a sense of the force of the first blow, and then I send my head forward for the second. My goal is to show the violence, to shock my listeners, to allow this story to kick them in the stomach.

- *Being real.* As I describe all of the above, I am already there, in the moment. Simply thinking about what will happen in the story will change my behavior. Talking about a fresh-faced, beautiful, laughing girl affects how I say those words, just as my switch to describing the accident will cause a change in my tone and gestures. The aftermath of the accident will require another change in tone as I try to share the sadness and the shock when I quote the emergency worker.

- *Tell 'em what you told 'em.* I would go for a summary that quickly illustrates my message· "It could have all been avoided if that kid had just done this"—and I would then demonstrate the simple act of fastening one end of the seat belt into the other: "Click." I might also recall something a friend once said to me years ago, when I myself was stupidly resisting seat belts: "Just do it intentionally for a week. Grab it, pull it across yourself, and click it in—with one motion—and after a week, you will have the habit." I took his advice, and I got the habit, thus supplying myself with a possible conclud-ing (and maybe takeaway) line for my presentation: "Finally, a habit that might actually save your life."

The message is strong, the images are vivid, and the emotion is real. Head and heart: That combination is the very definition of natural eloquence, and the effect should be persuasive. I would wager that every public presentation that has grabbed you has contained those variables. Sometimes the message, the moment, the audience, and the passion are all there sponta-

neously, and you find yourself moving and winning your audience, the phrases and feelings coming out effortlessly. You know
what you're talking about and you say it, amazing even yourself
with your eloquence. We often see this on television, during a
natural disaster or a big accident. Ordinary people go on-camera
and say the most extraordinary things.

But the perfect moment and subject rarely coincide, so it is
necessary for the speaker to make this natural eloquence happen.

BACK TO THE BASICS

The desire to get your message across is the sine qua non of
being an effective communicator. When I say that to people,
they are inclined to wonder why I am stating the obvious. But
professional performers, whether they are actors, entertainers,
or athletes, know how quickly the obvious vanishes when
you're operating under pressure. Frankly, it is one reason why
athletes, coaches, and even actors often sound so banal when
they are interviewed. "I was in the moment," says the actor. (I
now hear athletes using that line to describe how focused they
were on their performance.) The golfer tells the cameras, "I had
only one swing thought: Bring it back slow." (Apparently, all
athletes were out of school the day adverbs were taught.) The
basketball coach explains to the interviewer, "I kept reminding
them to 'take it to the hoop.'" Surely everyone who has ever
played basketball knows that! And yet why is that guy dribbling
the ball around the court, forty feet from the basket, when his
team is down five points with two minutes to play? It is the pressure. In the heat of battle, even seasoned professionals forget
what is most fundamental, and that is why coaches and athletes
(and armies) concentrate so much time on basic training. I

would even argue that the best athletes (and soldiers) are those who always make their actions look simple under pressure.

No speaker has to be told of the debilitating effects of pressure. How many speeches have you heard from people whose passion for one issue or another is not in doubt but whose speeches on these issues are exceedingly dull? We all have to be reminded that the most important swing thoughts for a speaker are "Get the message across and show your passion!" They will energize every moment of your presentation. What you will say will come from the heart and thus personalize your remarks (Stella Adler's "make it your own") so that you seem perfectly natural up there. To move people to take action, not only does your message have to be authentic ("Buckle up for safety!") but you have to be, too. That will happen only if you believe in your message and convey your convictions to the audience. But remember: Audiences can spot a phony from the back of the balcony, and they will not follow a phony into battle.

The challenge is not just preparing a series of persuasive remarks; you also have to perform persuasively.

AUTHENTICITY: YOU ARE REAL ONLY IF YOU ACT REAL

I have often been asked after a performance, "Were you acting, or did you really mean it?" My answer is always the same: "I was acting, *and* I really meant it."

Even when an actor plays a bad guy, the challenge, as always, is to bring that character to life, and one way to do that with a character whose behavior you would despise in real life is to find a way of justifying such a person's actions. It is not as difficult as you might think. We human beings find ways of rationalizing even the most heinous acts. Others may view a Mafia don as a vicious criminal, but Marlon Brando never played the god-father as evil incarnate; his Don Corleone was the ultimate family man making sure his sons would take over the family business. As the cliché goes, "One man's terrorist is another man's freedom fighter or head of state" (Ireland's de Valera, Egypt's Sadat, Israel's Begin, and Cuba's Castro, to name just a few twentieth-century leaders who began their political careers in violent opposition to their governments). For the actor, the hardest challenge is playing a monster. Robert Duvall has actu-ally played two of the twentieth century's indisputably evil men—Joseph Stalin and Adolf Eichmann. Proof of Duvall's tal-ent is that he was able to play the dark human qualities of a murderous Communist dictator and a Gestapo chief in a way that made both men seem recognizably real but no less chilling.

Imagination is not limited by moral code. The techniques I have laid out for persuading an audience can be used for bad ends as well as good. It all depends on your objective and how effective you are at making your listeners as passionate about an issue as you are. Too many speakers are absolutely committed to what they are saying, but their public performance doesn't measure up to their private passion.

MOVING AN AUDIENCE TO MOVE INTO ACTION

How do you get an audience to be as devoted to an issue as you are? Anyone who has tried to persuade people to write a check to a favorite charity, or inspire them to join a political or moral cause, knows exactly the kind of frustration I am talking about. There are a lot of worthy causes out there that deserve help, and their challenge is to convince you to write a check.

I've had some experience with this kind of persuasion. My wife and I have been involved in fund-raising for an animal-rights organization called Shambala, headed by the actress Tippi Hedren, best known for her unforgettable performance in Alfred Hitchcock's classic *The Birds*. Shambala (which means "a meeting place of peace and harmony for all beings, animal and human") had become something of a victim of its own success at rescuing animals. When visitors thought back on the organization, they remembered seventy big cats of every variety (lions, tigers, leopards, panthers, cheetahs) and a couple of elephants in a beautiful setting, eating well and receiving the extraordinary care that Tippi and her staff provide. The reaction of many potential donors would often go like this: "Well, that's a nice thing Tippi Hedren is doing. We like to keep the animal kingdom happy, and we're willing to donate some money. But then again, there are kids dying of cancer, homeless people in the streets, great tracts of land that need to be protected or conserved . . ."

There are presently more than fifty thousand wild animals being held in captivity in this country for purposes of breeding and selling. Even though there are already thirty-four laws on the books to prevent such practices as abuse, abandonment, and neglect, the mistreatment of animals is still rampant. All of the animals at Shambala have been rescued and rehabilitated. But the problem is not apparent in this idyllic setting; you see only the results of protection and care. Shambala needed another image to trump people's preconceptions, something that was both true and powerful. Tippi realized that she might be able to mobilize potential donors around another issue that Shambala and other animal-rights organizations were tackling: "canned hunts," the practice of releasing animals into a restricted area where they can be hunted and killed for fun and profit. She asked my advice, and I agreed that she had found her issue. Faced with vanishing ranges and herds of wild animals, hunters have turned to private preserves, many of which are advertised

on the Internet and in hunting magazines. Some even offer a
"no kill, no pay" policy. To make sure the preserves and hunters
profit from the experience, the deck tends to be stacked against
the prey—increasingly exotic species of rams, leopards, and
lions on sale in the open market. Typically raised in captivity,
these so-called wild animals have little or no sense of man as
predator; some are even drugged. For any animal lover, the
canned hunt is a sickening, morally outrageous event. The challenge was to persuade a sympathetic Hollywood audience that
battling this growing phenomenon was worthy of a considerable chunk of their giving.

Tippi and I talked about how to accomplish this. She is a seasoned and very effective spokesperson for animal rights, and
she knew she couldn't get away with simply saying that this
kind of hunting was wrong. She wanted the audience to draw
that conclusion from what they heard. She had to do more than
recite facts and figures. She needed to plant a powerful and unforgettable picture that would convey the evil of this practice. I
suggested that she build more emotion into her pitch, and said
she might be able to do it in the following way:

Talk about three beautiful lions by name, in the same way
you talk about the big cats at Shambala—a mother and her
two cubs (Mary and her children, Penny and Joe). Personalize
them; talk about how the mother related to her offspring; use
an anecdote or two, based on your experiences with lions, just
like the funny and touching ones you've related to me. Then
describe them being slightly drugged and let out of their cages
to roam "free" in a big fenced-off area in Texas so that a bunch
of guys with guns can pay for the pleasure of entering the
area, "hunting" them down—these lions with no sense of their
surroundings who we have come to know as Mary, Penny,
and Joe—and blowing that mother and her children away.

Who would not be sickened and outraged by such an image? Notice how easy it is to heighten the emotional effect of your case by changing the picture slightly. Defenseless wild animals is one thing, but a mother and her children being led to slaughter is quite another. The cruelty can be driven even closer to home by pointing out that the murdered lions are skinned and stuffed for "trophies." What a conquest! You don't even have to be an animal lover to recognize there is something wrong about killing drugged and defenseless animals for fun and profit. It's like drugging a boxer and putting him in a ring to be beaten to death.

At the fund-raiser, Tippi painted a vivid picture of this morally obtuse practice, using her own version of what we had discussed. No one can convey love and concern for the animal kingdom better than Tippi Hedren, who, along with being a passionate advocate, is also a fine professional actress skilled at sharing her emotions while keeping them under control. All Tippi had needed was some additional persuasive power to get people to reach for their checkbooks, and I was pleased to assist her in conjuring up an image that helped to make a difference.

It has already been a couple of years since I first tried to help Shambala on the canned-hunt issue, and hunting preserves are still booming around the United States—as many as two thousand may exist, according to a recent report in *Time,* with five hundred in Texas alone, where the industry brings in $1 billion a year. Animal-rights groups have been lobbying state legislatures to ban or restrict canned hunts, and as I write, both the U.S. House and Senate have bills that would at least try to control trafficking in wild animals. Nevertheless, I would wager that the kind of speech Tippi gave, with a few minor adjustments, would work on audiences a lot more resistant to animal rights than the generally liberal Hollywood crowd we were wooing.

When the issue is posed in terms of fairness, cruelty, and the genuine sporting chance of hunting in the wild, surely all but the most stone-hearted hunters are bound to concede that shooting fish in a barrel has never deserved the name "hunting."

Assignment #6

Prepare a "call to action" speech. Base it on an experience from your own life that taught you a lesson—one that others should also heed. Explain why others should jump on this bandwagon, why it is in their interest, and, above all, how they will benefit from doing what you are advising. Again, the presentation should last no more than two minutes.

If you are stumped for subject matter, I would take the seat-belt and animal-rights issues as models. What are your favorite hobbyhorses, the issues that raise your blood pressure? There are all sorts of causes and controversies to pick from: public education, community spirit, the disintegration of values, pro-tecting the environment, poverty, public housing, zoning, the homeless, AIDS, the disabled, women's rights, children's rights, civil rights, human rights. When I set this assignment for my Har-vard students, more than half the class delivered outstanding speeches. Fifteen years later, I still remember many of them. One in particular, however, stands out because it was so powerful.

It came from a student who had been battling her shyness and performance anxiety from the first day of class. She chose to speak about Amnesty International, a nonprofit Nobel Prize–winning group that seeks to free political prisoners around the world, end torture and political killings, and abolish the death penalty. Her presentation was packed with interesting informa-tion about the organization's work in various countries where political dissent is rewarded with long prison terms. She spoke passionately about the importance of Amnesty International's work and about her personal commitment to it. She was even funny, in a self-deprecating way, about the intensity of her devotion to the cause. She concluded her speech with a fiercely passionate call for support among her fellow students that was indelible. Though the emotion beneath every word was apparent, she kept it under control right to her last word—when the class jumped to their feet in spontaneous applause, yelling "Bravo" for the remarkable power of her presentation. If an Amnesty International rep had been on hand, the entire class, me included, would have signed up. It was that good.

My satisfaction in watching a student excel was immense (and probably contributes to my vivid memory of the moment). This student had improved remarkably during the semester. But so had most of the others. At that point they each had been required to appear before their classmates four times. They knew their audience, and their audience knew them. Gone was the flop sweat from fear; the tension in their voices and bodies had also disappeared, along with the fumbling for words, the obvious insecurity, and hollow bravura with which they had tried to mask their fear and insecurity. Most important, they were talking with sincere feeling and confidence. They were definitely not faking it. In fact, they were acting and really meant it.

By now you should recognize that the kind of inspirational call-to-action speech I have been discussing is a repository of all the advice I've offered from the beginning of this book:

- Prepare a subject that you know well and are passionate about, and it will help stifle your fear.

- Clarify your objective, because to get action, you must play the actions—everything you do, from moment to moment, serves your overall objective.

- To win the audience, you must make an emotional connection.

- If you are totally prepared and focused on a clear objective, full of real feeling, there is no way you will go to Cleveland, even without notes.

- The series of actions that you perform (for example, clicking that imaginary seat belt) will make your message—and you—come alive.

- That sense of reality will impress your audience, open them to your message, and help persuade them to act accordingly.

Take a couple of days to work on your powers of persuasion. When you return, I will show you how what you've learned about public presentation can be applied to virtually any kind of performance you will be called upon to make.

7

TAKING YOUR ACT INTO ANY ROOM

You now have the basic tools to become a very good speaker in any situation. I am confident of that. Let me explain why. When I was preparing for my Harvard course, I looked through a pile of books about public speaking. I soon realized that they were telling me both too much and too little. While the books were filled with information about how to open a talk, close a talk, pick a subject for a talk, outline a talk, and deliver a talk in a loud and clear voice, they spent little if any time on the issue of why certain people were good on their feet and others bad. One book went on at length about distinctions between speaking early in the morning as opposed to late at night, between remarks at a breakfast meeting and those at a cocktail party, between speaking at lunch or a big banquet. Others devoted sections to different kinds of public appearances, from running a meeting to making a pitch, from going on a sales call to sitting for a job interview. Such fine distinctions left me bleary-eyed. I just wanted their take on what made a speaker impressive and how an ordinary person might get some of that. To be fair, a few of the books addressed my issue, but only incidentally. One of the best, Lilyan Wilder's *Talk Your Way to Success* (1986), actually has a chapter called "The Key: Being Real." I agree: That is the key to being an effective communicator. What mystified me was why Ms. Wilder devoted only fifteen pages of her three-hundred-page book to a series of suggestions on "how to be real" that were more enticing than helpful (including a page and a half on an "emotional recall" she picked up from the acting teacher Lee Strasberg).

Those books only confirmed for me that I was onto something. Initially, I thought my method would be most helpful to people who were good in private but tended to freeze in public. I knew I could help them bring their best selves to the podium. But when very smart and successful friends confided to me that confronting even one person in a meeting or interview unhinged them, I began to realize that most people didn't think they were good, even in private. My inexperience was showing: Frankly, apart from summer jobs as a student, I have never held a "real job." My only profession has been showbiz, and my experience as a performer has been limited to acting, singing, playing the role of host or master of ceremonies, and giving speeches to relatively large audiences. I have never made a sales pitch to a client, a presentation to the head of advertising, or a report to the boss. I have never even been on a proper job interview. But I have many friends who make their living in the real world, and I've talked to many others, with all sorts of jobs in the private and public sectors, about the different settings they must shine in to succeed in their careers. I came to realize that they were anxious about these mini-speeches for the same reason I was shaking on opening night: Blowing a pitch or a presentation to the boss, or even being unimpressive in a job interview, could derail a promising career.

I thought my method for improving public speakers could help in those situations, too. While the approach to a job interview might differ from preparing a big speech, and making a pitch might require facts and figures that would be irrelevant to a job interview, they share the same challenge: impressing your listeners. My own experience as a speaker has convinced me that the ability to get real is as useful in the morning as the evening; whether at a breakfast meeting with a small group or a late-night fund-raiser before a packed hotel banquet room, the acting techniques and careful preparation required for making your remarks seem alive with real feeling will impress any audience. If I am looking to make a speech before a large audience seem conversational, then my method should be effective in a genuine conversation, whether it is called a job interview, a sales meeting with a client, or a conference with my boss. As I have tried to show, what distinguishes great communicators is that they can take their personal charm and eloquence to the podium. In the presence of great speakers, people often say, "I felt as if he were speaking to me."

If you have followed my assignments, you know how preparation has helped you turn your anxiety into a kind of energy that makes you a better performer; you are better at setting the objective for your remarks and preparing to achieve that objective; you have a few techniques for locking what you want to say into your memory. You have also worked on bringing real feelings with you into the public arena and experienced how they move an audience. It's powerful stuff, right? But let me remind you of something you must keep reminding yourself: *This is just the beginning of your career as a good speaker.*

If you have improved even a little, that is probably a big step forward. Evaluate your progress, then consider how much better you can be a year from now, or ten! As you improve, you shouldn't have much trouble bringing your confident self before any audience, large or small. But even as a beginning speaker, you have more experience than you know.

YOU KNOW WHAT WORKS BECAUSE YOU'VE BEEN THERE—IN THE AUDIENCE

When I am rehearsing a role or a speech, I often think, "This is going to be on a TV screen, and as someone used to watching TV, I certainly know what doesn't work. If, for example, I deliver a speech as loudly as I might onstage, it will be too big and too theatrical for the TV camera." Similarly, if I'm preparing to speak at a banquet, I will refer to my experience as an experienced banquetgoer who knows what it is to sit out there and watch someone carry on for too long.

As longtime audience members, we are all experts in what does not work. Everyone enjoys being a critic, at least of other people's work. For me it was the biggest problem of acting classes. Students would sit back and criticize what they saw up there. They were usually right: The actress had made a bad choice, what she was doing was wrong for that particular character, not real, and so on. What irked me was that we spent very little time reacting to and discussing what was going *right* in a performance. To be fair, it is not always easy to know what to say. A good speech will have a simplicity that's hard to analyze. "He got up there and talked to the audience as if he were sitting in your living room," someone says. What's so amazing about that? What's amazing to anyone who has done some speaking is how much work it takes to make it look so easy, so natural. The speaker moves from one subject to the next, the story soars, feelings spread through the room, and all at once everyone is applauding. They couldn't help but be affected by that "easy" speech.

It is the same with brilliant acting. Every year when the Academy Award nominations come out, actors shake their heads at the performances that don't even get nominated. Typically, an actor who wins will have done something very different from what we are used to seeing her do; the role stretched her abilities, and she pulled it off. And such a performance is prizeworthy. But what about that small group of extraordinarily talented actors in every generation who deliver a remarkable performance in practically every movie they are in? Certain actors are so good that most moviegoers take their brilliance for granted. Often they play minor roles, but rarely the same ones. In one film an actor plays a general, and in the next he's an equally convincing critic of the military; she's a loving mother in this film, and in that a pathological murderer. These are not the actors who fire the imaginations of the editors of *Vanity Fair* or *People.* Audiences barely notice them. But those of us in the business know how important those supporting players are to making the performances of the stars work. "Well, they're not really acting; they're just playing themselves," people will say. If you met those actors in person, you'd probably wonder how that gentle soul could play a general or that lovely woman could play a murderer. But the explanation is quite simple: They are actors who have learned their craft, put in the time on that role, and what you see is so convincing that you forget they're acting. It is also true of the great popular singers and talented dancers who make it look so easy that even the best critics forget how much technique and art it takes to create the illusion of simplicity.

One of the reasons I often use golf analogies is that I have been struggling to get better for decades. If I could play golf half as well as I can act or speak in public, I would be a fulfilled human being. So I keep watching the best players to find out what they share that I can appropriate. It is exactly what Stanislavski did to come up with his method for modern acting. I would bet that the speakers who have impressed you the most also share the kind of spontaneity, ease, physicality, feeling, and reality that inspire you to clap. Behind every display of performing genius is talent, but less than you might think—and a lot more experience, trial and error, and preparation for the current show. I am a much better actor and speaker today than I was twenty years ago. "Of course," you say. But then why is it that so many people think they should be able to give a decent speech without spending days thinking and preparing and practicing?

By now I should be preaching to the choir. You have been perfecting the fundamentals of effective performing; your attempts at public speaking have already benefited from careful and lengthy practice. Once you learn how to prepare yourself for the role of public speaker, you will be able to move fluidly into any situation, from addressing a roomful of blue-haired old ladies at lunch to a hall of beefy teamsters in the evening. Let me try to prove this point by reviewing several of the public situations in which most people are called upon to say something—with a lot riding on their performances.

THE INTRODUCTION (FOR YOURSELF)

In meetings, retreats, or interviews—virtually every time you find yourself in a roomful of strangers—you will have to introduce yourself. "Let's go around the table and let everyone introduce themselves," says the host, and you can either have something prepared or mumble through your name and job, feeling as uncomfortable as everyone else in the room. But if you have done my homework, you are already prepared to introduce yourself with self-confidence and verve. The first assignment was to prepare an introduction of who you are and what you do, along with an interesting anecdote. So you should already have a version of this introduction, which you can fine-tune or adapt for any situation.

The self-introduction is a seminal speech, a seedling for every kind of public presentation, and thus proves my point most readily. The goal is to make it short and sweet and as spontaneous as possible. Everyone else will be squirming in their seats, while you will be impressive because you have come prepared to be off-the-cuff. And how good do you have to be if everyone else is awful? Keep that in mind, and the task of addressing audiences large and small will get a lot easier.

THE INTRODUCTION (FOR SOMEONE ELSE)

A snap. It's the same as above, albeit with another person's name and biography attached. But filling in those blanks shouldn't be a problem. If you're asked to introduce the guest at a formal meeting or lecture, someone will give you the appropriate information. If you work with the person or are acquainted in some other way, you might have an anecdote; or you can get on the phone and ask a family member or colleague of the person you're introducing for a good story. If the person is well known in your community or industry, you can do a little research. These days the Internet makes this kind of thing as simple as typing a name in a search engine and clicking on "Go."

Few introductions need to be longer than a minute or two. The secret weapon is—what else?—preparation. If you put in a total of a few hours over a couple of days or even a week, imagine how good your talk might be. As experienced audience members, we have heard a lot of introductions. Try to surprise your audience a little, and you will be hugely impressive. In my experience, the main obstacle to success in even the briefest remarks is trying to put together something the same day. No matter how brief my remarks might be, I always prefer at least a couple of days' notice so I can prepare and then let my remarks settle into my mental computer.

THE TOAST OR PUBLIC THANK-YOU

The toast is another twist on introducing someone. Since everyone in the room probably knows the person whose health you're drinking to, all you have to do is come up with a funny (or embarrassing) story, or an anecdote that may be otherwise moving. Maybe you simply want to thank that person (here's the overlap in these two mini-speeches). The ability to bring forth some emotion might be very useful. Some of the most moving remarks I've heard have been from wedding toasts or parties for someone retiring or leaving for a new job.

I have done my share of this kind of speaking. The television series I am currently in recently wound up the first season's production, and one of the producers warned me that I would be handed a microphone at the wrap party to say a few words. I decided to focus my remarks on the people who made it all happen: my fellow actors, of course, but mainly the creator and executive producer, Tim Kring, and the crew. I reminded everyone that when my agent first alerted me to the series, it was known as "The Tim Kring Project"; without him, we wouldn't be there. I did my first TV series in 1973, but I never cease to be amazed that one can evolve from an idea in someone's head. All at once there's a script, actors are hired, sets are built, and 120 or so men and women are there early every morning, setting up to film this figment of a writer's imagination. Almost as indispensable to any film project is the production crew. Anyone who has ever been on a film set knows that an actor has a lot of hanging-around time waiting for new camera setups, lighting changes, hair and makeup fiddling, and the rest of the many but essential variables to getting a story on film. In TV we essentially do half a movie every eight days, and it takes about as many technicians as a movie does. After ten or eleven months of the twelve-hour-plus days it takes to film a twenty-two-episode series, you have a pretty close-knit team, even a family if you're lucky. We were lucky on *Crossing Jordan,* and I wanted to thank the crew. I worked hard to make sure I had all of their names straight.

The night of the wrap party, I spent about five minutes celebrating the people who made it all happen. Needless to say, the crew especially enjoyed being acknowledged by name. Probably no one except my wife realized that to get those five minutes right, I had to spend several hours, off and on—my memory no longer what it was—preparing what I would say and brooding about it right up to the moment I was handed the microphone.

THE INTERVIEW

Though I have never interviewed for a regular job, I have been required to do many auditions over the course of my career. I have known very successful businessmen, lawyers, and doctors who have had one or two job interviews in their entire careers. Some very good actors are not so good at auditioning. But we all know that you will never be able to show your stuff onstage or before a camera unless you get the job first. Most actors work hard at auditioning. That is the first and maybe even most important thing job seekers can learn from actors: Getting the right job can be the most important event in your life. So why would anyone stroll into a job interview without being armed with as much preparation as possible? Here's what to be ready for:

· *Make the right first impression.*
No matter how much lip service we pay to judging people by, in the words of Martin Luther King, Jr., "the content of their character" and not according to superficial things like how they look, most of us make snap judgments all the time. According to recent studies, we tend to make up our minds about other people within the first thirty seconds of meeting them.

Actors must master the art of walking into an audition and impressing a director or producer quickly. The director will have an image of the character already in mind, and an actor must endeavor to replace that image with his own. Typically, the director auditions several actors, and each has to persuade the powers that be that he brings something to the role that the others cannot. I auditioned a couple of times for my current role as Max Cavanaugh on *Crossing Jordan.* My primary objective was obvious: I had to convince Tim Kring and then NBC that I was Cavanaugh. For TV auditions, actors are generally asked to show up prepared to do a scene or two from the script, with a casting director reading the other characters' lines. I like to be so well prepared that I am ready to shoot the scene, which means that by the time I walk into the room, I am in character. For the Cavanaugh audition, I arrived wearing what I thought a retired cop in his late fifties might wear: a windbreaker, jeans, and sneakers. I also brought along a Boston accent that I had worked on in 1984, when I played the stage role of another former Boston cop in a new comedy thriller by Bernard Slade. While I was preparing for that play, I made a point of spending some time on the phone with an old college friend who has a strong Boston-area accent. I probably even got him to say a few phrases so I could get the right music in my ear. For Max Cavanaugh, I was able to revive the accent I had already perfected—another example, incidentally, of making something your own. My plan was not to try to do the whole audition in Bostonian, just a word or phrase here and there, particularly Max's daughter's name, Jordan. I just wanted them to know that I could do a good Boston accent if they needed one.

For a job interview, you, too, should talk and dress the part. What to wear used to be easy: a suit and tie for men, and a dress-for-success outfit for women. But the fashion story has gotten a lot more complicated, and your interview outfit might require some thought. If you're a creative type—an ad-copy writer, say, or an art director, architect, designer, fashion stylist, software wizard—then the clothes you wear become a walking résumé. Edgier fashions might be in order, not to mention that tattoo or green hair. It is your call. Whenever in doubt, use common sense. Professions are a bit like tribes, each with its own culture, value system, and fashion story. Businessmen in most major cities of the world still wear suits and ties, but in Hollywood the only people who wear fancy suits to work are agents. A screenwriter who shows up at a meeting in a $2,000 Italian suit might look terrific, but chances are that everyone in the room will not think he is as "creative" as the previous guy, who was wearing jeans and a baseball cap. A Washington writer, however, who showed up for an interview in the nation's capital wearing jeans and sneakers might have trouble getting through security.

Remember: Whatever job you're interviewing for, you have to show the employer you can play that role.

· *Be enthusiastic or passionate.*
Just about every book on leadership will describe the top managers and CEOs in the nation as "passionate." Companies want

to hire someone who is not only eager to do a good job but can convey his enthusiasm for the company, its products, and its mission to employees, customers, the media, and Wall Street. An experienced corporate interviewer can spot "dull" coming through the door. In fact, she will have already inferred a lot about your personality over the phone. To walk into the room and appear dynamic requires getting yourself pumped up beforehand. Here's where those exercises in sense memory can prove golden.

· *Be entertaining.*
"The best candidates tend to be entertaining," writes Jeffrey E. Christian in his book *The Headhunter's Edge.* "They like to tell stories." For Christian, who has been a headhunter for more than twenty years, working with and recruiting some of the top managers in America, this anecdotal style is evidence that candidates are confident and comfortable with themselves. Christian advises managers to press candidates with probing questions to tell stories about their "most important decision" or "their biggest challenge," listening carefully for the information and detail that only someone involved in the deal will know.

Such expert evaluations of a good interview bring a smile to my face, and they should have you grinning, too. Central to my method of applying acting techniques to public speaking is the idea of entertainer as a storyteller. Corporate headhunters may run into their share of natural entertainers among their best candidates. But you and I know that preparing to be entertaining is what performing is all about—whether you are an actor-entertainer or a public speaker.

· *Be a team player.*
Hirers want to hear the word "we" a lot: "We turned around the marketing department . . . we built a team, and we changed the

way we did business. . . ." Anyone who acts as if he did it alone will not only lack credibility, he will also send the wrong message. The best managers are confident enough to admit they do not know everything, and they surround themselves with people who fill in their own gaps of expertise.

· *Ask a lot of questions.*
Your interviewer wants to know not just what you have done but how you *think*. Talented people tend to be inquisitive and creative, and the questions they ask reveal how their minds work. The more incisive your questions are, the more impressive you will be. That will require some homework.

· *Do your due diligence.*
You ought to know as much about the company as possible, and not only to impress the interviewer. Today's successful company may have some problems brewing that will send it downhill quickly, and you'd better know what's cooking. Is the management stable? What about the competition? Are there new products in the pipeline, or are the company's days of innovation in the past? To answer those questions and raise others, read up on the industry and look at the company's annual reports. If the company is a major player, *The Wall Street Journal* and business magazines such as *Fortune, BusinessWeek,* and *Forbes* have probably done stories on it and its management. Go to the library or do a search on the Internet. Most companies now have websites that feature their annual reports as well as recent news articles. The magazines, too, allow access to their archives via the Internet, usually for free or a nominal charge.

· *Have the answers ready for some inevitable questions.*
While no one can anticipate all the questions an interviewer will ask, you can bet she will want to get a bit deeper than the job

titles you've listed on your résumé. Employers want to know what kind of employee you are; specifically, they will be interested in how you think, how creative you are at solving problems, and how good you are at working with other people. Be prepared to talk about what you have done, particularly your successes. (If you don't have some positive things to discuss, then your career is in trouble, and you'd better start working to line up some wins before you hit the interview trail.) Here are a few obvious questions that human-relations departments are likely to ask:

- What are your strengths?
- What are your weaknesses?
- What was your biggest achievement in your current job?
- What about a failure, and how you handled it?
- What was your biggest strategic decision, and how did it play out?
- What would your current boss and colleagues say about you?

There are many variations of these questions; compiling a list of related questions will be a useful exercise for you. By preparing answers, you will be miles ahead of most of your competition. An average job interview will last forty minutes or so, and you don't want to be stumped for something to say. The biggest interview killer, according to headhunter Jeffrey Christian, is saying, "That's a good question. Let me think about it." The interviewer is now thinking: "It's an obvious question, and the kind of person I'm looking for would have a good answer." Typically, interviewers want to probe deeper into the facts of your résumé to get a feel for such leadership skills as intelligence and work ethic. Definitely go into the details, but stick to the point and don't ramble. Again, avoid saying "I . . . I . . . I . . ." Share the credit.

· *Make an emotional connection.*

If they hire you, they will have to work with you day in and day out, maybe for years. Companies want people who are not only talented but likable and team players. Try to establish a rapport with your interviewer. This is dangerous territory— an ice floe between being too cold and too cool. You are better off erring on the side of businesslike than being so ingratiating you come off as a jerk. There is also the danger of seeming like you are faking warmth or interest. If you see a photograph of your interviewer standing on his boat with a gigantic fish or sitting in her classic Mustang, you'd better not start discussing boats or fishing or cars unless you know what you're talking about.

The one thing I keep in mind when I walk into an audition is to look everyone in the eye when I'm talking. That helps me seem more confident, and it turns a formal and stressful situation—for both sides—into more of a personal conversation. In my roles that required lots of big speeches, such as the leads in *Equus* and *End of the World with Symposium to Follow,* I learned that I was more effective when I addressed my words to specific people in the audience rather than speaking to the theater. In my experience, nothing connects better than exuding a sense of self-confidence and ease. We all know how excruciating it can be to watch a speaker fall apart or go to Cleveland. Interviewers will also have an inevitable bias toward a candidate who seems in control and knows what she's talking about. Your research, memory, and emotional preparation should increase your confidence that you can answer any question. Since most of your competition will be nervous and unprepared, you will have increased your odds for getting the job just by walking into the room ready to handle the first question.

THE PITCH OR SALES SPIEL

This is an easy one. As we saw in the previous chapter, virtually every speech you prepare is about persuading people to do something. We spend much of our lives convincing our spouses, kids, neighbors, and colleagues to do things. What was that conversation I described with José Ferrer but a pitch for staying with the show? When we talk to people in public, we sell ourselves. Again, self-confidence and a general ease with your material are most of the ball game, and an effective pitch is about marshaling all your acting skills to appear as passionate about what you are promoting as you already must be. If you have a pitch coming up, review the previous chapter with that objective in mind.

THE QUICK PITCH

Some business friends of mine also call this the "stairway pitch" or the "elevator pitch." This is the minute or two-minute version of your message that you can deliver on your way to or from the elevator or out the door. Sometimes you have to pitch someone on an idea or project to get a meeting for a formal presentation. This is all about preparation. A version of these remarks can also work over the phone.

THE TELEPHONE CONVERSATION

I know people who are charming and gregarious in public, but when they have to make a business call, they freeze. Some are freaked by not being able to see the other person reacting;

others are just uncomfortable with the artificiality of talking into a device. The telephone, however, is an unavoidable tool in doing business. Often the only way to get an appointment for an interview or pitch is to talk to someone on the phone. So much business gets done on the phone that top managers take lessons on their telephone style. My methods for impressing people in person can help you appear equally confident over the telephone.

Take advantage of the fact that the person on the other end of the line cannot see you, but make sure she can hear you. You can use all the aids you need: notes, facts and figures, even an outline of what you want to say. I suspect you already know what I will say next:

> *Don't ever read what you want to say—at least*
> *if you want to avoid sounding like a telemarketer.*

As soon as you start talking, the person on the other end will already be building an image of who you are. Your challenge is to make sure that image is positive. You must be well organized and know what you're talking about. Be specific but brief. Assume that you're talking to a busy person. The more blathering you do, the more likely he is to get annoyed or toy with his computer or try to get off the phone. Finally, you will be at the mercy of your voice and how comfortable and strong it makes you sound. Work on your telephone style by adapting the techniques I outlined in the previous chapters to speaking to people over the phone.

A couple of caveats: You want the person at the other end of the line to think you are a serious person. Serious people don't eat during a business call. I know it is fashionable among hard-charging young managers to be multitaskers, but even the most dedicated multitaskers on the other end of your line will want to think you're giving them your undivided attention. If you are making calls from home, be sure you won't get interrupted by another call (or even worse, those pesky call-waiting beeps), your kids, or (always a problem at our place) the family dog or dogs. All this should be part of your preparation. If the call is important, do everything in your power to convey that.

GENERATING "LEADERSHIP PRESENCE"

This is one of those phrases that businesspeople throw around without being able to define it, never mind explain how you can create it. Some men and women seem to have an aura about them, a kind of electricity that affects everyone in the room. For a few lucky people, it is a natural part of their personality. More often than not, however, this kind of energy field is just the product of a big reputation or a high office. Presidents of the United States seem to glow when they walk into a room. When legendary CEOs like General Electric's Jack Welch or IBM's Lew Gerstner walked down the street in Manhattan, they looked like thousands of other well-dressed executives in the September of their careers. But when they walked into a conference room at corporate headquarters (or any other place of business where they were known), their personalities filled the room.

Top managers are known for their intelligence, energy, and ability to make their own enthusiasms contagious. (Gerstner also has a reputation as one of the best public speakers in the business world.) But a good actor should also be able to play a CEO or major politician. I have explained how to make yourself come alive in a public speech. There is no law against using the same techniques for lighting yourself up before you enter a presentation or meeting. I cannot make you into a great leader, but I have given you skills that can help you act like one.

Assignment #7

It is now time to take your act on the road, to any spot where you can find an audience to impress.

Prepare intensively for your next presentation, pitch, business meeting, community meeting, job interview, or phoner. Apply what you've learned in the previous chapters. Really work on it, for hours over several days, and then get out there and see what happens.

By now you know what works. The well-informed, confident, conversational speaker, the person who knows how to tell a good story that moves or amuses, impresses every time.

I have repeatedly reminded you that the crucial elements to improving as a speaker are time and preparation. By simply speaking in front of as many audiences as possible, you will get better. These meetings, interviews, and other mini-speeches will be a particularly useful test of how well you have prepared; unlike most speeches, your listeners can be expected to interrupt you with a question, and you'd better be ready with a good answer. This ability to improvise will also help you take your ability to speak in bigger, more formal situations to the next level. To be as impressive as a skilled speaker can be requires more than hard work. The best performers love to get out there and show how good they are. At some point they know they must stop rehearsing, step into the limelight, trust their preparation, and let the performance happen. That ability to let go is what can make speaking in public an enjoyable, even ecstatic, experience. I will explain why in the next chapter.

8

LETTING GO

One night during the run of Laurence Olivier's legendary 1964 performance as Othello at London's National Theatre, he was especially brilliant. After the play, Maggie Smith, his Desdemona and herself an immense talent, charged into his dressing room to congratulate him. "My God, Larry," she said, "You were extraordinary tonight . . . on some other level . . . sublime!" Olivier, the consummate technician, sat with his head in his hands, inconsolable. "What's wrong?" Smith asked. "You were wonderful." His answer: "I know . . . and I have no idea how I did it."

Olivier had achieved what psychologists call a "peak performance," an experience that is as mysterious as it is wonderful, for both the audience and the performer. I have heard actor friends who would not call themselves religious in any conventional sense describe the feeling as spiritual. I can live with that. I have also heard it referred to as a "white moment" or a "trance-like state." I like those descriptions, too. But the peak performance is an experience that you have to undergo to fully appreciate the feeling, like fear in battle or love at first sight. I have been there, as an actor, a speaker, and an athlete. Something happens—a kind of calm settles over you, and you feel in control. It is as if you are having an out-of-body experience, hovering above yourself and watching everything; you are the writer of your own play, anticipating every twist and turn, not only delivering an outstanding performance but enjoying every second of it. Athletes will recognize what I am describing as being in the Zone, that moment when every move you make feels spontaneous and perfect—your bat strikes the ball without effort, the basketball heads directly into the hoop as if by radar, the golf ball moves to the hole as if drawn by a magnet; the crowd seems to have disappeared, you are alone in your excellence, and life is sweet. Some would argue that this ability to frequent the Zone regularly or stay there longer than anyone else is the definition of the superstar, and the amazing ability of certain people to stand out among so many talented performers so often—basketball's Michael Jordan, for example, or golf's Tiger Woods, or Laurence Olivier at his best—seems to back them up. The economic benefits of making the peak performance as repeatable as possible are obviously substantial, and over the past twenty years, professional psychologists have focused on the ups and downs of athletic performance, including the mysteries of the Zone. Their colleagues have explored peak performances in areas outside of sports, and the result has been a new psychology of "optimal states" (along with a shelf of books about this phenomenon).

Speakers, too, can find themselves in the Zone. When that student of mine who spoke so eloquently and persuasively about Amnesty International finished, she seemed stunned by the raucous applause of her classmates. She was so caught up in the passion of the moment that I suspect she'd forgotten she

was even in a classroom. Her audience knew they had witnessed something extraordinary. I recognized it as a peak experience. Like Olivier, my student had no idea how it happened.
But I did. On my occasional trips into the Zone as an actor (to a
region, I would add, far below Laurence Olivier's), I knew exactly what had gotten me there: The emotional connection between my own life and my character had ignited, making me
come alive in a way that the audience could not miss. My student, too, had managed to combine her belief in human rights
with her role as public speaker, and the result was something
the rest of us couldn't take our eyes off.

This kind of public nirvana is a rare thing. I cannot give you a
ticket that will get you into heaven every time you stand before
an audience. Only that one student in my class experienced
what I would call a genuine peak performance. But by the end
of the semester, many students had made excellent presentations and afterward remarked about how amazing it felt, if only
for thirty seconds: "I was in total control," one said. According to
another, "It was incredible—I was on this roll and knew it!" I can
promise you this sensation of holding the audience in the palm
of your hand—if you keep working on the techniques I have offered in this book. As you practice what I preach, and get more
experience speaking in front of colleagues and strangers, you
will not only gain confidence but also find yourself enjoying it.
You, too, will find yourself more frequently on a roll, being in
such total control of your material and circumstances that you
seem to be floating above the fray, reacting to your audience,
shaping their response, and watching yourself excel.

Bobby Lewis used to describe that payoff for all the hard
work as "the little birdie on your shoulder." I performed in my
first movie with Liza Minnelli (*Tell Me That You Love Me, Junie
Moon,* directed by Otto Preminger). We became friends, but I
also became a big fan. We often talked about performing in

front of audiences, the similarities between acting and singing, and the emotional exchange that takes place between the performer and the audience. She explained that when things were going really great for her onstage, she, too, had the sense of being separated from her singing, dancing self and watching her performance. She had even dreamed up a new word to describe the experience—"wafting."

Wafting is, I believe, an example of pure creativity that is open to every speaker, at every level of the game. But it will never happen unless you step out in the limelight, armed with all your preparation, and then let yourself go.

LETTING GO: PREPARING TO BE SPONTANEOUS

When I say "let go," I do not mean for you to forget everything that you have learned. On the contrary, it should be so ingrained through your hard work and practice that you don't have to think about it anymore. When the lights come up, you begin, and the rest will be there. After years of practice and performing under pressure, the downhill ski racer does not stand at the Olympic starting gate thinking about how to ski; she's not even thinking about getting through the final gate. What's on her mind is only: Start fast and go fast! Her training will have prepared her to adjust to the contingencies as she flies down the mountain. The Major League shortstop may have been practicing his fielding for hours the day before, but when the ball is hit to him in today's game, he is not thinking about infielder mechanics; he is simply watching the ball go into his glove. Only when he has the ball will he consider the next step in the shortstop equation: Throw the guy out. (The fielder who gets ahead of himself, thinking "Throw" before he catches the ball, inevitably bobbles the play.) The training and practice have their place, but once the contest begins, it is time, as professional golfers are fond of saying, to "trust your swing."

As a speaker, you are not in a position to let go unless you've done the work and built up some experience as a speaker. When Professor Nesson asked me if I could do a version of my course in a series of long seminars over a couple of weeks, I resisted, explaining that the only way people improve as communicators is over time. There is no such thing as "How to Become a Great Communicator Overnight." Most of my undergraduates had made huge improvements, but it took three classes a week for an entire semester. Think back to your sonnet and your ability to say it at double time. You know you couldn't have accomplished that even if you spent the whole workday trying. You must take time off; you must step away and go about your business to allow the brain to do the important work of locking the words into the hard drive for instant replay. The first time I do a speech, I am like a beginning driver behind the wheel, thinking hard about what's going on inside and outside the car; it's a struggle to stay on the road. But once I've done the preparatory work, I become more like the experienced driver who seems to be doing everything, as we say, "without thinking." The objective of my speech is clear, and everything I do and say serves it. It's all just there. So are my emotions: I am already sitting on my great-grandmother's porch, or I am thinking about those New York City firemen rushing up the emergency stairs as everyone else is rushing down. I have been working on re-creating those feelings for weeks. The more prepared you are, the more times you have practiced your remarks at home, the more dry runs you have been through, the more in control you will be. Actors learn this from long runs, doing a play night after night, week after week. No matter how brilliant you might have been on opening night, a hundred performances into a run a kind of understanding and freedom within the role evolve. Having been in the heat of battle so many times, you've not only put a lot of yourself in the role; you've become the role. Once the prep work is done, your subconscious will take over and get creative. That is the art of it, and the fun.

I suspect that by now you, too, have at least an inkling of the fun of performing and winning an audience. If you have followed my method and attempted my assignments, you have become a much more experienced communicator: You have done a one-minute introduction explaining who you are and what you do; you have prepared a two-minute how-to that was as physical as possible; you have worked at structuring a clear message; you have memorized one of Shakespeare's sonnets and another piece of poetry so well that you can recite it right now (try it); you have learned how to hold a mental map of your entire presentation in your head without notes; you have reached into your past for an emotional moment as well as a funny one, then tried to use such sense memories to enliven a short speech; you have prepared a brief speech aimed at persuading others to mount the ramparts. That's at least nine presentations (without even counting all the practice and test drives). Some of you might have already experienced the pre-Zone phenomenon of being on a roll. I repeat:

This book is just the beginning.

You must keep working at my method, and as you do, you will find yourself polishing the details—getting the phrases and emphasis right, the gestures you need, the timing between what you say and what you do—and you will get better and better. The fine touches are never there in the beginning. You must make them part of your biography, so that they will eventually come from inside. Only after doing the work will you be ready to step into the limelight—and let go.

LETTING GO—AND READY TO RESPOND
TO THE AUDIENCE

Letting go is not just something you do, it is also a state of mind, a state of being. The confidence that accompanies being well prepared allows the performer the freedom to trust his learning and ride his abilities without a second thought. When you are focused and prepared and confident, you will take a sensual pleasure in appearing before people, anticipating their responses, and trying to shape their reactions.

Actors are often asked what they look for in another actor. I am looking for an actor's ability to listen to the other actors onstage. The "other" that the skilled speaker should be listening to is the audience. You are always talking directly to the audience, and success lies in listening and reacting to them from moment to moment. This readiness to react is another reason why the speaker cannot be a slave to a script. Reacting to the audience's mood and responses to what you are saying—the applause, the laughter, or even the resistance to your message—should determine how you will proceed. Ride the applause and laughter, take advantage of their good mood. If they are resisting, you might have to turn on the persuasion. By reacting to this moment, rather than to what you are saying, you will become more alive, more focused, and closer to the Zone. When good actors perform a scene, even though it is "my line, then your line, and my response, and your response," the audience has the sense of a conversation taking place, that the characters are ready to answer anything that comes at them.

The same must be true when you are speaking in public. For example: I make sure that I am always open to someone interrupting me with a question. I am even prepared to put a question to my audience: "Are people cold in here?" "Are you following me on this?" People will nod, and I will go on. But by diverging from my prepared remarks to make a genuinely spontaneous remark, I have increased my reality in the eyes of the audience. If I notice people nodding, I can feel confident about pressing my point a bit more or maybe going on to my next one. If they're laughing hard, I might throw in another funny line. But if they're shaking their heads in disagreement, squirming, or whispering, I will have to deal with these signs of resistance. This is how a speaker can be in the moment. Ignoring a major interruption or trying to finesse a provocative question will wipe out any impression you've made of being real. In the 1988 presidential campaign, Democratic candidate Michael Dukakis might have blown his chances for the White House with his response to one tough and intentionally provocative question. Asked during a debate what he would do if his wife were raped, the liberal governor of Massachusetts gave a typically measured political response that followed the party line on the issues of law and order and capital punishment, instead of expressing the kind of anger and passion that most people would feel in such a situation. Right then many voters decided that they did not want a president so cut off from his feelings. In my terms, Dukakis's response was too unreal. Instead of being in the moment and showing his anger (either at the imagined rape or the journalist baiting him), he decided to stay on message and came off a total wimp. He had also failed to address the question, and his answer, from the audience's point of view. It is, as my friend Tom Sullivan calls it, taming the beast, and no speaker is more tuned in to the "feel" of an audience than he. Tom immediately senses the mood in the room and plays to it. He also understands that while an audience is made up of individuals, it can respond as a crowd. Both applause and laughter can be contagious, and with that in mind, Tom never allows his audience to be scattered throughout a large room. The closer they are to one another, the more susceptible they will be to joining their neighbors in laughter or applause.

LETTING GO—BY BEING FOCUSED
ON WHAT YOU MUST DO

Young actors tend to associate being real onstage with barely trying, or being laid-back—two sure ways, in my opinion, to fail. To perform well, being keyed up is crucial; so is being absolutely focused on what you have to do moment to moment. Everyday nonchalance onstage comes off as discomfort; the person seems disengaged—mainly because everyone else is acting like mad. Whenever a nonactor tries to be himself onstage or before the camera, the result is usually embarrassing. Something is missing. In being real, they seem unreal. Before you can feel free enough to be genuine, you have to prepare yourself in such a way that you can be not only real but also what is often called "larger than life." This is particularly true with your movements and gestures. The things you do while speaking are crucial components in creating the impression of spontaneity. Most people, however, are flummoxed by the prospect of adding gestures and movement. They become so self-conscious that they end up looking like someone is pulling the strings.

As usual, the solution is more practice. But be careful to practice in the right way. Acting natural does not involve mimicking the gestures and the moves that you think are appropriate to what you are saying. You cannot perform by the numbers. You have to prepare in a way so the appropriate gestures come out naturally. They must appear as your own, sometimes big and sometimes small. Occasionally, shout out a word and wave your hands; other times a quieter tone will make the same word possible. Consider saying the word "no." A friend of mine recently told me a story about how he heard that his house was on fire. He was at a birthday party for a friend four houses down when he got a call from the baby-sitter, who informed him that the fire had broken out; she had rushed his daughter from the premises to a neighbor's house and called the local volunteer fire department. My friend grabbed his wife and ran up the street with all his friends from the party behind him. When he arrived at his burning house, he saw a fireman with a large ax about to chop down the elegant nineteenth-century front door. "NO!" he shouted at the ax-wielding fireman. As my friend told me this story, he actually raised his hand and shouted this "No!" just as he had done at the time of the fire. Raising his voice was perfectly natural, conveying the passion of the moment from the fire (and in the telling). But if you were the leader of a nation and a reporter asked you whether you would abandon your fight against terrorism, wouldn't a quiet and resolute "no," without any gestures, be enough to make the point?

I notice in my *American Heritage Dictionary* that the primary definition of "entertain" is "to hold the attention of." That means whether we are singers, ministers, salesmen, or public speakers, we are all entertainers. If we lose our audience, we have failed. As speakers, we are our message, and we have to sell that message—and ourselves. I was a singer before I ever acted, and I now realize it was that experience that opened me up to the possibility of acting for a living. It was singing where I first felt the joy of being "on" and winning an audience. Singing has also helped me become a better speaker, and I believe that understanding what popular singers do to hold an audience can help anyone become a better communicator.

LETTING GO—LIKE AN ENTERTAINER

Like many singers, I admired Frank Sinatra's ability to sell a song. Whatever you thought of his lifestyle, his swagger, or his politics, Sinatra as a singer delivered a kind of emotional charge that few performers have matched. He could create the intimacy of a living room in a cavernous auditorium; from the audience, you had the sense that whatever emotion he was experiencing, he was sharing it with you. When Sinatra was really cooking on-stage, he seemed to be allowing you a glimpse inside himself, and you kept wanting more. As an actor, too, his easy physicality caught your eye. Even dancing with Gene Kelly in the classic movie musical *On the Town,* the skinny Sinatra held his own. When he performed, you couldn't take your eyes off him. At least I couldn't. And I wasn't sure why.

In 1968, during winter vacation, I drove to Florida with another Yale drama school student to get a bit of sun. Frank Sinatra happened to be appearing at the Fontainebleau Hotel in Miami Beach, and I had to see him. My Yale friend did not share my enthusiasm. It was the late 1960s, a politically charged time, and Sinatra had moved into his ultraconservative chairman-of-the-board you-mess-with-me-and-two-guys-named-Vinnie-will-be-knocking-on-your-door mode. But this was my opportunity to see Sinatra in person, so my friend humored me by coming along to catch his act in the Fontainebleau's La Ronde Room.

The man was in total command. He swung through his repertoire of old favorites, and the audience responded as if they were the first people ever to hear him sing. The women in the audience gobbled it up, but so did the men. It was an amazing performance, especially considering Sinatra was fifty-two years old. When he finally got to singing "It's quarter to three / There's no one in the place except you and me," you knew you were watching a genuine artist creating something before your eyes. Even my reluctant friend was impressed. As acting students working every day on the art of performing, we knew we had witnessed a moment of terrific acting. Sinatra's act was perfectly shaped, right down to the slightest gesture. Some of those songs he had been singing for decades, but he gave each of them an emotional charge. A lifetime of feelings looked to be contained in the smallest gesture—a sway of the microphone, a turn of the shoulders, a quick glance to the audience. When he sang "It's quarter to three," he was on a stool with a cigarette in his hand; he looked around and shrugged, with a little smile on his face— the shrug of a lonely guy in a bar. Sinatra the performer, the American icon, was there, but so was the real, feeling person. Or so it seemed—because he was such a brilliant actor. What we were seeing that night was the essence of acting. For every song, he had his objective, whether it was that lonely guy closing the bar or another guy who had "the world on a string"; his cadence and tone embodied the feelings of that man, and so did his gestures. Sinatra never just sang a song. Each one had a point of view.

Ironically, the fact that Sinatra had sung those songs so many times made it easier for him to make them come alive. They were part of him. You got the sense that you were hearing his thoughts, that they were coming from him and not the song-writer. And Sinatra was no more likely to forget the words to "One for My Baby" than you would blank on what town you were raised in. The message was straight, and he betrayed no performance anxiety. He was Sinatra, allowing decades of singing before audiences and a master's technique to shine through —the ultimate in the art of letting go—and the result was not merely great singing and an emotional kick, it was gifted communicating. He was hitting the notes and talking to us. Suddenly, we were in a bar, we became the bartender, and he was asking us for a drink and telling us his story.

As a speaker, your goal is the same as Sinatra's: to appear relaxed and alive and thus absolutely natural. You, too, should seem to be just telling a story. An essential factor in looking like a real person up there is being free enough to behave like one. The main reason people tend to be stiff while speaking is that they aren't doing what they usually do in conversation—moving, gesturing, and allowing their voices and faces to mirror what they are feeling. Happy, enthusiastic people look it. Passionate or angry people behave in a certain way. I am not suggesting you start jumping up and down with glee or pounding the table in anger. But with a few gestures, you will be just you—but you ready to impress the people you are talking to with both your words and their emotional message.

Those gestures, however, must not be tacked on; they must come from inside, from your inner life. If they do, that flick of the hand or shake of the head will break up the monotony of the words. And because your movements seem right and natural to the audience, you also will seem right to them, more alive than the usual speaker or interviewee. Sure, the words can convey some feeling, and the tone of your voice will, too. But what sells it are those gestures and mannerisms, the physical with the vocal, allowing the audience to follow the emotional ups and downs of your message. As a speaker you are a performer, and the essence of performing, as we have seen, is giving a piece of yourself to the audience. How you move can help you do that. It is preparation that will free you from all your other concerns—fear of failure, of forgetting what you are saying, of not winning over the audience—so that you can bring more of yourself to your role as speaker. That is what letting go is all about: trusting your preparation enough to allow your best self to run the show.

WORKING ON YOUR MOVES—LIKE A SINGER

Most nonactors worry that too much gesturing will make them seem theatrical, not so much an actor as a *thespian,* the kind of overacting we identify with old-fashioned drawing room comedies or *Saturday Night Live* skits. Ironically, this justifiable fear of appearing phony turns many speakers into unreal characters reciting words like animatronics at a theme park. How much movement and gesturing is enough? Well, it depends. For example: If you are referring to the bright blue sky in your presentation, it will help to look up and refer to the sky. When you begin practicing that gesture, it is bound to seem big and momentous—after all, it is new and unusual to you—but by the time you get there, it will have turned into something fleeting and subtle and just right. Also, rehearsing that gesture will keep it from looking like an artificial add-on to your performance, like a new suit or hairstyle. The more you practice, the more comfortable you will get with the gesture. It will become part of your performance, and how you move will become an integral part of who you are as a speaker. Once you put in the work, by the time you stand before your audience, the big thespian-like gestures will have become smaller and realer; they will come from within you, and you will appear more real to your audience. You will be *acting natural.*

I saw this over and over with my students. Initially, they felt silly or self-conscious pointing or making a purposeful gesture. I even encouraged them to practice these gestures with big, exaggerated moves. "We were out under a big, blue sky . . ." Reveal that sky with one hand or both hands. Be a thespian, at least in your initial private rehearsals. Soon you will find yourself referring to that sky with a fleeting gesture that will grab the audience's attention because it will help them conjure up that image and its importance to what you are saying.

Singers do this all the time. When Frank Sinatra sang "Blue moon, you saw me standing alone / Without a dream in my heart, without a love of my own," he gestured to the sky, he called attention to himself standing alone onstage, he might even have rested the microphone near his heart. Did he overdo it? Never. When he began working on that song for the first time, he probably tried several different moves, playing them in a big way. Once he made each move his own, as essential to the song as the lyrics and his voice, he was able to go onstage, sing, and move as if he were doing it for the first time, and never in a way that didn't look perfectly natural. But even Sinatra had to learn how to match his gestures to his singing. After all, he first became famous in the early 1940s as a skinny band singer tethered to a stand-up microphone. He was known as "the Voice" before he became the heartthrob of throngs of screaming bobbysoxers who knew his songs by heart from the radio. He made his acting debut in 1943, and ten years later he won an Academy Award for an extraordinary performance as a troubled soldier in *From Here to Eternity*. By the time my friend and I saw him sing in the late 1960s, Sinatra had done another thirty movies, and he had clearly learned a thing or two about how to use his voice and body to create a sense of intimacy in a large room and connect emotionally with the audience. It was not only the voice or the lyrics, it was also what he did onstage—how he *acted*—that sold his message. Sinatra was able to capture the essence of performing live, again and again, by embodying the songs.

As a speaker, you, too, are performing, and like any performer, you will have to consider how your appearance and behavior, what you do and how you do it, affect the audience. They will be sizing you up as soon as you appear. Make sure the message that your body conveys does not contradict the aim of your presentation.

YOUR OBJECTIVE AFFECTS YOUR MOVES

You will often have to fight your own natural inclinations. It is the day of your big job interview or presentation, a career maker, and before you leave the house, you get a call informing you that your aunt Sarah died. You are miserable, but there's no way you can get out of your appointment. Do you walk into the room looking like your favorite aunt just died? Actors and other entertainers must routinely set aside the distractions and even tragedies of their personal lives to do their jobs. The game-show host Chuck Woolery lost a son in a car crash. When he was asked how he could continue to do a game show in the face of such an event, he answered that hosting game shows was what he did, it was his job. "Was I able to shut it out of my mind?" Woolery said. "Yes and no." Most of us have been in situations where we had to play against our real feelings. The experienced performer will try to focus even harder on the task at hand—to give a good interview, to present a forceful motivational speech. Is there a danger that your grief will pop out? Of course, but the importance of the interview or speech is likely to help you get through without revealing how miserable you really are.

How you move communicates volumes to your audience, even before you say a word. For example: It is moments after the Super Bowl, you are the owner of one of the teams that has competed in a game watched by tens of millions. You are a successful zillionaire wearing an expensive suit. One other important fact: Your team won. You make your way to the podium to face the TV cameras. Imagine your elation; feel the bounce in your step. It's one of those moments when people say, "I was walking on air." Now let's change the scenario slightly: Your team lost in the last minute of the game. I don't care how composed or gracious you are, or experienced at speaking in public, your walk to the podium will be different. Actors think about that sort of thing all the time as they create a particular role, always asking, "How would my character act in these circumstances?"

While certain actions, gestures, or behaviors may come naturally to a particular actor, more often than not, just walking across a stage without appearing self-conscious is a challenge for most performers. A good actor can convey who a character is by the way he walks into a room. Is there a John Wayne without that walk? James Dean *is* that hunched-over midwestern shyness waiting for the passion to bust out. When the John Travolta character in *Saturday Night Fever* bops down the street full of attitude and music, you already have a sense that you know who he is. Al Pacino's Michael Corleone walks into the room, and who is going to disagree with him? What made Jimmy Cagney such an unforgettable screen presence wasn't only the distinctive way he talked but the way he moved. He had started off as a song-and-dance man. The next time you catch Cary Grant on TV or video, watch how gracefully he moves through a scene. In *Holiday,* a classic Cary Grant–Katharine Hepburn film, Grant, who was a professional acrobat as a teenager, actually executes a backflip; in *Charade,* another Grant classic with that other Hepburn, Audrey, his amazing physicality is on display when he participates in a game at an elegant party that requires each couple to dance while keeping an orange between them from falling to the ground. Grant manages this feat with an exceedingly buxom woman, pulling off a series of moves that are classic vaudeville.

You must make sure your body language is not out of character and undercutting your message. The way you move will reveal your mood and thus set the mood for your remarks. Too many speakers enter the room and then try to get into the mood. Very dangerous: Getting in the mood will be no match for even ordinary performance anxiety. Like an actor, you must arrive onstage in character. It is now time to allow all that preparation to shine—and not start worrying about your smile or preparing to act passionate. To get yourself in a position to let go, make how you move a major part of your preparation.

WORKING ON YOUR MOVES—LIKE A DANCER

I have danced more than four hundred times in various musical numbers on the Broadway stage, including my solo moves in *Seesaw,* but a hoofer I am not. The ability of professional dancers to make a series of intricate moves, spins, and leaps seem effortless and filled with emotion never fails to astound me. Every performer can learn a lot from dancers, and two things in particular:

1. *Focusing on particular moves.* I once asked a ski instructor what were the fewest number of lessons one of his students took to learn how to ski. "Someone showed up here and in two lessons was careening down hills and making the turns," he said. "It was amazing." That instant skier was a dancer. Tennis coaches will tell you the same thing. Great dancers are athletes, to be sure, but what makes them quick learners is their ability to isolate a part of their body and improve on how it works. "Everything was perfect except for the turnout of your feet," the choreographer will say. "Okay, how about this?" says the dancer, who treats her body parts as if they

were recalcitrant students and keeps fiddling with that particular piece of the dance until she gets it right. The fingers are
too stiff? The dancer tries to loosen them. "Nope, still too
tight. Let's try it again." And so it goes. Each piece of the
dance is worked on until the whole is there, without a seam
showing. Dancers have worked on the details so intently
that when they are finally on the stage performing, they no
longer have to think about those details. This is what letting
go is all about: Every single move just happens, and the
dancer becomes the dance.

2. *Using movement to affect an audience.* When we watch
   dancers, we are focusing only on what they are doing, and
   the slightest gesture can grab us. In fact, the smallest gestures
   can be the most powerful. The late great Bob Fosse turned
   the art of small, quirky gestures into one of the great careers
   in choreography and movie directing (the film versions of
   the Broadway musicals *Sweet Charity* and *Cabaret,* and his
   brilliant autobiographical movie musical *All That Jazz,* to
   name but a few).

We all appreciate genius. But often it is the product of a lot of
sweat and terrific technique. Some artists excel simply because
they have mastered the mechanics of their art better than their
contemporaries. Which brings me to one of my favorite showbiz
anecdotes. Donna McKechnie is best known for her Tony
Award–winning performance as Cassie in *A Chorus Line.* In the
business, however, she had a reputation as one of the best
dancers in the history of Broadway long before that. The hardest, most complicated moves flowed out of her as if she'd been
born doing them. Donna dancing was a picture of fluid movement; the nuts and bolts of her dance, no matter how complicated or strenuous, never showed. When most dancers must

execute a spin or leap, you can see the preparation, the windup. Donna seemed to spin faster or jump higher without even trying.

There was also a mysterious, almost mystical element in her performance that separated her from the other dancers. It was as if she were in a place all her own, and the music was coming not from the orchestra but from Donna McKechnie. I once mentioned that to her, and by way of explanation, she told me about the time Fred Astaire came backstage to meet her. Astaire was extremely complimentary; he also pointed to something she did that he had done as well, and he wondered whether she realized what they had in common. Astaire explained that he always tried to dance a split second ahead of the music. To pull this off, the dancer had to be extremely talented and know the music as well as the conductor, but for Astaire—and Donna—it meant the difference between dancing along with the music and dancing in such a way that they seemed to be creating it. Donna had always admired Astaire and was thrilled to discover that they shared this technique. She had always had the sense that she was dancing ahead of the music. It was a subtle difference in technique, but it made all the difference in the world as to how the audience responded to her, right from the beginning of her career. And Fred Astaire had confirmed it.

I love it when there is a technical reason why someone is better than the rest—something worked on and prepared that makes the magic. But what I really loved about her dancing was the emotion in it. Donna is a very good singer, but she could make an emotional connection to the audience by dancing and not saying a word. She always looked great onstage, and to say she moved well is sheer understatement. But what impressed the audience the most was something that came from inside her. Like every great performer, Donna was brimming with feeling, with meaning in every step. She had worked her way up from being a high school kid in Detroit, dreaming of dancing on Broadway, and what it took to get there helped make her an actress of extreme emotional depth and complexity. With her movement alone, she could convey sorrow, pain, sexual longing, and joy in such a way that the audience also felt those feelings and were personally moved by her dancing. But she still had to have the moves down before she could let go in her dancing to reveal its emotional content.

That's it. I have told you all I know about how the techniques of actors can help you be a more effective communicator. Even the most talented and experienced performers are scared before they go on; they have roles to work on, acts to create and structure, movements to work on and rehearse; they, too, have lines or songs to memorize and chatter to learn; above all, they must move and win over audiences, just as you must when you speak in public. But the one thing that the professional entertainer really knows how to do is to get out there armed with all that hard work, then let it all happen. Here is one of the final assignments I gave my class, which might help you get the feel of what it takes to trust your preparation and let go.

Assignment #8:

Do something different, something crazy, something you've always wanted to do; or, maybe even more liberating, something you've always been afraid of doing. If you're a serious type, tell a funny story. If your previous exercises have tilted toward the lighthearted or humorous, go deep and dark, and speak about something that moves you. If you love to sing, sing. If the inner actor in you has been itching to get out, perform a speech from a favorite play or a soliloquy

from Shakespeare. Whatever—so long as you take a leap of
faith. By now you've tried enough new things to know that
the result will not kill you. Go ahead. Give it a try. Let go.

Like any true believer, I was eager to initiate my students into
the ultimate performer's experience. I could not promise them
the Zone, but I wanted them to do everything that would allow
them to get there. And they already had the experience of
watching one of their own give a peak performance.

As I had hoped, the results of this free-for-all turned out to be
a lot of fun. There were several singers. One student who was
practically tone-deaf sang a song, badly, but with great verve
and enthusiasm, to the delight of the audience. Another sang
"Tonight" from *West Side Story* quite beautifully. (She would
go on to have a successful acting career.) A premed student
crooned "White Christmas" in an imitation of Bing Crosby that
sounded—to my ear, anyway—more like Perry Como, but it was
very entertaining. Another kid played the guitar and sang a series of lyrics he had written about the course with a refrain that
echoed my own: "Practice, practice, practice." A girl from Indi-
ana imitated her grandmother setting her up to date "nice Jewish boys" in a way that was both funny and touching. A guy
who had appeared quite serious throughout the term became a
stand-up comedian, delivering his theory of how all the different
attitudes between the sexes can be understood simply by analyzing the ways men and women respond to a loud, smelly fart
in a small room. Another hopeful actor walked among the class
as Shakespeare's Henry V, rousing his troops for the Battle of
Harfleur with the famous speech "Once more unto the breach,
dear friends, once more" and ending with the line, "Follow your
spirit, and upon this charge / Cry, 'God for Harry, England, and
Saint George!'" as he charged out of the classroom, his voice
echoing back to us from the hallway.

It was great. And the success of these presentations proved that letting it all hang loose should always be part of performing. Those students had come a long way from that first audition, when they were all shaking in their skin. I know you have, too. But everyone can get better. To be able to act natural in public is all about putting in the work. It's that easy—and that hard. I would even go so far as to say that what people often recognize as genius among performers is the result of some genuine talent mixed with years of experience, mastery of technique, and a lot of work toward the current performance. What distinguishes the great ones from even the very talented is that they give themselves as many chances as possible for scoring a perfect ten. Olivier, Gielgud, all the great English actors played the big Shakespearean roles many times in their career. The more they played a role, the easier it was for them to let go and see if they could go to a place they'd never been before. Tonight they are brilliant, and next week they may be brilliant in another way. The legendary politician-communicators, such as Lincoln, Churchill, and Reagan, spent most of their careers giving speeches of one kind or another. Even when they were giving the same speech, it was never quite the same. The audience, the room, what happened that day in the news, all sorts of things could add a different twist. Over a long political career, each got better at playing himself. These were politicians who could take their message into any hall, before any kind of audience, and start talking.

Which reminds me of one final anecdote. In the early 1970s, President Richard Nixon invited Elvis Presley to the White House. Nixon was reportedly eager to connect to the nation's youth, and Elvis was equally eager to gain respect from the Establishment, and thus a summit meeting was arranged between the president of the United States and the king of rock and roll. The singer arrived decked out in full Elvis regalia: white leather and gold jumpsuit and cape, jewelry, and major hair. Nixon, in his customary dark suit, white shirt, and basic tie, shook hands with the singer and checked out his wardrobe. "You dress kind of strange, don't you?" the president said. The King replied: "You have your show and I have mine."

Or, as Stella Adler would say: "Acting is what you do." Or, as I have tried to make clear throughout this book: Whenever you step out in public, to seem really real, you must play the role of speaker, delivering your message with your feelings and your gestures to that particular audience, in that particular room, on that particular day. To impress them, you must never forget that you are putting on a show—your show, nobody else's. You must put your best self forward, and the only way to do that in a public setting is to be so prepared that you can act natural.

9

SOME CONCLUDING WORDS

ABOUT WORDS

It's up to you to take it from here—and for me, as a teacher, that is extremely frustrating. With my Harvard class, I could monitor the progress of each student, learn his or her idiosyncrasies, and then tailor my remarks and suggestions accordingly. As the semester wore on, the subject of the course became the students themselves. The more I found out about their particular strengths and weaknesses, the more effectively I could teach them. I cannot do that with you. I can't see you or hear you or coach you on your strengths and your weaknesses. Also, the Harvard class was a regular audience of some sixty strong and thus a constant measure of popular response.

I have personally road-tested every idea, every technique, every suggestion, and all the exercises in this book over some forty years as an actor and a public speaker. The Harvard course presented me with an extraordinary laboratory to see whether my education from Stella Adler, Robert Lewis, and the many brilliant artists I had worked with over the years could help nonactors faced with playing the daunting role of public speaker. The experiment was a great success, and the proof was in the progress that almost all the students made. The differences between their auditions for the class and their final performances were not obvious—and remarkable—only to me but to everyone in that lecture hall. If students worked at my method, if they put in the practice and preparation, they improved as communicators. That was satisfying for them and for me.

I have no idea whether you're improving, though I suspect if you're still reading, something must have gone right. But please do not stop with this book. I repeat: You have to keep working at this stuff. Talking to other people in formal situations does get easier over the years, but it is never easy. And no matter how good you get at impressing a room, you always risk blowing it if you haven't put in a serious amount of preparation and practice.

There is another aspect that I have sidestepped until now, mainly because I believe you first need some experience as a speaker before tackling it. It was a problem that most of my students struggled with at first and managed to gradually overcome to a greater or lesser degree. It was also a problem that they, as audience members, witnessed in their fellow speakers and therefore were able to attack more immediately and effectively than they might have if they had been working alone, as you are. If kids bright and talented enough to be admitted to Harvard were having this problem, I suspected that beyond the walls of higher learning, it was epidemic.

The problem was language—not what to say but how to say it. To get up in front of people and deliver your message clearly and forcefully is a major accomplishment. To use phrases and sentences that your audience applauds and will repeat afterward—that is, to speak eloquently—is another level of skill. Toward the end of his long and illustrious life, Mark Twain spoke at some length about what he had learned from his countless days on the lecture trail: "Eloquence is the essential thing in a speech, not information." What he was getting at was the same problem my students were grappling with: the essential difference between the written and the spoken word in its finest form. Twain probably made more money speaking than writing books, and he's worth listening to on the differences between grabbing an audience on the page and in the lecture hall:

> Written things are not for speech; their form is literary . . . and will not lend themselves to happy and effective delivery with the tongue—where their purpose is to merely entertain, not instruct; they have to be limbered up, broken up, colloquialized, and turned into the common forms of unpremeditated talk—otherwise they will bore the house, not entertain it.
>
> —1907 autobiographical dictation in
> *Mark Twain in Eruption* (1940)*

Mark Twain the great public speaker, had to rein in Mark Twain the great writer. The Harvard students also had to find ways to speak naturally at the podium without sacrificing their educated command of the mother tongue. Many had developed a kind of fumbling patois excessively peppered with "like" and "you know," "awesome" and "lame," and other phrases of their generation. It was their way of being regular and trying to blend into the real world outside of Harvard Yard. But from their written hour exam and term papers, I learned that most of my students wrote quite well. One of my biggest obstacles as a teacher was to help them find ways to bring their most finely honed sense of the clarity and power of the English language to their work as public speakers.

*From *Mark My Words,* Mark Dawidziak, ed. (New York: St. Martin's Press, 1996).

I stressed with them, as I have with you, not to try to memorize a speech verbatim. But that does not mean you shouldn't carefully craft the language of your presentation and make it your own. The goal is to deliver a prepared speech rather than read it. The challenge is to appear to be winging it without really winging it. Mark Twain explains such a process in a letter to his contemporary William Dean Howells:

> Get your lecture by heart—it will pay you. I learned a trick . . . by accident . . . I came on . . . then remembered that the sketch needed a few words of explanatory introduction. . . . I talked the introduction, and it happened to carry me into the sketch itself, and then I went on, pretending that I was merely talking extraneous matter and would come to the sketch presently. It was a beautiful success. . . . Try it. You'll never lose your audience—not even for a moment. Their attention is fixed, and never wavers. And that is not the case where one reads from book or MS [sic].

I like the phrase "Get your lecture by heart." I think it captures the feel better than the word "memorize." When I was standing in front of a class, I was able to embody what I was teaching my students (and what I hope I have taught you) in the delivery of my lectures. Nothing about learning the art of performance is as immediate and indelible as witnessing a well-crafted version of the act itself. For performers, it is the food of knowledge. Stella Adler loved to say, "Steal! If you think it's really good, watch it, learn it, and steal it. If you can make it your own, do so. Then it *is* yours. Do it every chance you get." My hope was that the students would steal from me the way I had learned to steal from Stella.

I delivered my opening forty-five-minute lecture without notes. I was able to do this because I had sufficient time to prepare. I also wanted to start out by practicing what I was preaching to a roomful of smart kids who would be casting a cold eye on this Hollywood guy playing the role of wise professor. I will confess, however, that I was not brave enough to face such a tough audience week after week without some backup. As a rookie professor wary of the amount of material I had to cover, and figuring I might be asked to give the course again, I wrote out my lectures and had the text with me at the lectern. While acting work soon diverted me from teaching, those lectures became the basis of this book. A number of those lectures were also recorded and transcribed, and it was interesting for me to see how close I stayed to the text. Though I spent half the time away from the lectern, occasionally I would put on my glasses to read a long quotation or to check a sequence of ideas; sometimes I would look at my lecture and speak the words exactly as I had written them for the intended effect. But most of the time, I was speaking from memory while staying in touch with my audience through eye contact and physical actions, and I was making an emotional connection by endowing what I said with feeling and a sense of purpose. Enrico Caruso, the legendary Italian tenor of the early twentieth century who was revered for his uncanny ability to move audiences with the power of his voice, was once asked what it took to be a great opera singer. Caruso reportedly answered: "You gotta have a biga head, a biga mouth, a lotta da memory, anda something ina da heart."

So much of acting natural in front of an audience is the result of making a genuine effort to get in touch with "something ina da heart." Again, however, that passion is not likely to be on display if you are not prepared. We have all suffered through speeches by people who failed to convey their passion to the audience. Being passionate will not make you appear passionate if you are, for example, scared to death. As we have seen, that is the paradox of performing: You have to prepare to act natural. If you have worked on your speech in such a way that you have truly made it your own, some of what is in your heart is bound to reveal itself. "It usually took me three weeks to prepare an impromptu speech," Twain confessed. "The best and most telling speech is not the actual impromptu one but the counterfeit of it."

I made sure to prepare my own "impromptu" introductory remarks—stories and digressions that would appear off-the-cuff, as well as questions for discussion—as carefully as the rest of my scripted lecture. The result of working this way is that you are always talking to your audience, never reading, and therefore you can stay in the moment with them. Since I already had enough performance experience to instinctively manage a lot of the techniques I was teaching, I spent most of my preparation time working on the language I would use. I have shied away from the role of rhetoric in public speaking. I am convinced that when you try to get better at speaking in public, improving your way with words must come last. I am not teaching speechwriting any more than Stella Adler was teaching playwriting. You do not have to be a good writer to be an effective speaker. Speakers who deliver their remarks in an easy, conversational style will always be more impressive than the speaker reading a beautifully written speech in a monotone. Worrying about writing a wonderful speech becomes one more obstacle to preparing a set of remarks, rehearsing them for a couple of weeks, and then getting up there and doing it.

But when Stella warned, "Don't go to the words," she didn't mean don't *ever*, just not at first and not too soon. First your objectives, your ideas, and your actions, then the words. When all the rest is in place, then and only then come the words, which, of course, become everything. They are the message, and you are now the able messenger delivering them to their very best effect. In Henry Higgins's opening number in *My Fair Lady,* he asks Colonel Pickering, "Why can't the English teach their children how to speak? Oh, why can't the English learn to set / A good example to people whose / English is painful to your ears? / The Scotch and the Irish leave you close to tears. / There even are places where English completely disappears. / In America they haven't used it for years!" I don't wholeheartedly agree with Professor Higgins's sentiment, but there is enough truth in it to ensure a big laugh every time.

As I was drafting this final section, I was treated to a unique example of good public speaking that was so perfectly connected to the content of this book that I cannot resist sharing it with you. The first annual Stella Adler Awards were held in Hollywood on June 1, 2002. I was invited to be one of the hosts of the awards dinner, a black-tie event held in the ballroom above the Kodak Theatre, the new home of the Academy Awards. The job entailed nothing more than saying hello to people who had paid a pretty penny to attend the event and thus help fund the Adler acting schools. That done, I could sit back and watch others conduct the evening's festivities. The Angel Award for supporting the Stella Adler Studio was given to Antonio Banderas and Melanie Griffith, a married pair of talented actors. Banderas's acceptance speech was the highlight of the night, and his wife's remarks added some humor and insight into what he had said. After patiently waiting for the oohs and ahs and screams from his fans in the cheap seats to die down, the Spanish heartthrob carefully thanked by name the people who had put the evening together. He then explained to the audience that because he was still working on his English, he had chosen to write down something that would correctly express what was in his heart. I was so impressed with the speech that I asked

Banderas for a copy. Here's what he said, in just under five minutes:

In 1975 I was a Spanish boy who never left the city in which I was born. Living at the end of a political period that left a strong mark on a whole entire generation of people who related more to dreams than to reality, I was part of a land which was transitioning from a painful dictatorship into a democratic country at the same time that I was trying to develop from being a boy into a man. The first thing was done; I am still working on the second one!

That was the time I saw a theater play for the first time. That was the period in which I discovered the ritual of acting. That was the moment in which I decided to jump to the other side of the mirror and become an actor, not knowing that my decision was going to change not only my professional projection but my entire life.

Many of you, especially the ones who are students today, know the implication of making a choice like that. Yes, it is hard, you feel lonely, you have more questions than answers, and you want to know desperately how to use the most important tool that you have, yourself.

So, what did I do? Well, I went to school. I went to the National Dramatic School of Spain, but going to school was not the solution to all the problems I had at the time. I needed a master. Somebody who could talk to me about the mysteries that I was facing. Someone who could talk to me and give me answers which were coming from the same place where my questions were born. I needed that person to tell me why my body or my voice didn't respond to what my brain was dictating. Somebody who could explain to me what is dramatic rhythm, when I am truth or when I am not.

In that context I heard for the first time the name of Stella Adler. Apparently there was a woman in America who knew the answers to all my acting tribulations. She took the teachings of a Russian man called Stanislavski, and she adapted, reflected, and put together a way to perform and act that would become a revolution and it would change the way we understood this art forever.

But how was a boy in Spain of the mid-'70s, without money, who never left his hometown, going to take advantage of such a system? That was when the magic of Stella's teachings came. I never saw her, I never met her, but like millions and millions of people around the world I saw the result of her work. I saw it through the actors who for many years she prepared. I saw it through hundreds of movies bathed with fresh, natural, poignant, different, convincing actors whom she modulated using years of investigation, hard work, common sense, and love, lots of love.

She was the woman behind those moments in movies that made us cry, laugh, feel, or reflect about life and its complications. She was the woman who analyzed the human nature, its greatness and its miseries, and made actors do so themselves.

And how did that fifteen-year-old boy get to know this? Well, because Stella left printed, in every actor she ever worked with, a little bit of herself. I was lucky I married one of them. Every time Melanie talks about Stella Adler, her eyes shine in a different way. I can tell that Stella has a big room in Melanie's heart, a roomful of respect, admiration, and gratitude. Yes, every time that Melanie talks about Stella, I know she is talking about an extraordinary woman and human being.

Around two years ago Melanie and I hosted a party for the Stella Adler Studio. That day I met with some of the professors from the school and I took the step I couldn't take when I was fifteen. I finally started working with the acting method of that

woman from America who knew the answers. It was like
Charles and Marion, my teachers, put glasses on me. I don't
know if this commitment I assumed is ultimately going to
make me better, but I definitely know I have a way to go. Now
that I am forty-one, I decided to be fifteen again and build
from the boy I once was to become the man I always wanted
to be.

Thank you, Stella, for not dying, thank you for becoming
eternal. Thank you for helping us to be not just one but many.
And thanks for being an angel of the actor's lost objectivity.
Many different fifteen-year-old boys and girls from all over the
world who need your legacy will thank you forever.

As you can see, this is a very good speech, and it was even
better in the telling. It is romantic and a bit melodramatic, but
it expresses the passion of the man quite well and is expertly
crafted to suit the occasion. Even the few phrases Banderas
used that might seem awkward to the American ear—"when I
am truth," "the human nature"—lend authenticity and charm.
Banderas didn't read these words so much as deliver them to his
audience with conviction and feeling and humor. I think the
speech would have been even better if he had been able to absorb and prepare it well enough beforehand to speak without
notes, because he is such a marvelous performer. But since his
English is better than my Spanish (he is also fluent in Italian), he
gets a pass. He most assuredly got one that night as a hush fell
over the crowd. I think people were touched that he had taken
the time to prepare what he wished to say with such care. I
know I was. His tribute to Stella Adler was organized in the form
of a personal story about how a young man in Málaga had discovered and pursued acting as a career. His acknowledgment of
Stella's legacy was humbly and artfully stated. People were also
impressed with his command of the English language. When a

fellow actor remarked to me, "He spoke better than anybody else up there," I couldn't help being reminded of one of my favorite tongue-in-cheek rhyme schemes, by Alan Jay Lerner, the great lyricist of *My Fair Lady:*

> Her English is too good, he said,
> Which clearly indicates that she is foreign,
> Whereas others are instructed in their native language
> English people aren.

The impression you leave with an audience, as I have said, is communicated in numerous ways, many of them nonverbal; and no matter how artful your language, if your message isn't clear and well organized, you might as well be whistling. But when all the basic elements we have talked about and studied and practiced come together, when the substance of your speech and its presentation are in place, any fine-tuning you engage in will always revolve around the words you choose, how you arrange them, and your timing. It is language that will boost you to the highest level of the art of communication.

There was a time when public school English teachers required pupils to memorize famous poems and recite them aloud in class. For many young Americans, particularly the children of immigrants who did not speak English at home, it was their first (and maybe only) experience with the glories of the English language. My father, born in 1916, would regale me with recitations from his schooldays, and other bits of poetry he committed to memory just for fun as an adult: "Under the spreading chestnut tree / The village smithy stands; / The smith a mighty man is he / With large and sinewy hands," he would begin, or "There was three kings into the east, / Three kings both great and high / And they hae sworn a solemn oath, / John Barleycorn should die!" He would continue to recite the entire poem as if making it up as he went along. He knew a remarkable assortment by heart, and as a child I would listen, enraptured by the music of the words and the images they conveyed. Along with Longfellow and Burns, there was Blake—"Tiger, tiger, burning bright / In the forests of the night, / What immortal hand or eye / Could frame thy fearful symmetry?" and Tennyson—"Cannon to right of them, / Cannon to left of them, / Cannon in front of them / Volley'd and thunder'd; / Into the jaws of Death, / Into the mouth of hell / Rode the six hundred," and, my personal favorite as a young boy, Rudyard Kipling:

> And the end of the fight is a tombstone
> white with the name of the late
> deceased,
> And the epitaph drear: "A Fool lies
> here who tried to hustle the
> East."
> —*The Naulahka* [1892], chapter 5

So much of who we are comes from memory and mimicry. Patterns of behavior, likes and dislikes, the way we relate to others, the interests we develop, and, yes, our speech habits and use of language come largely from observation of our parents and teachers. But our personalities also evolve from doing. Kids are constantly trying out various styles and lingo. I realize that I had a head start of sorts as a performer because I developed a love of the English language and heard it spoken at its best from an early age. However, it wasn't until my late teens, when I began singing and acting in plays, that I filtered the well-crafted language of poets, playwrights, lyricists, and historical figures through my own sensibility as a performer. Looking back, I am convinced that processing such heightened language in this way, speaking it aloud and hearing myself do so, was the key to my own development as a public speaker.

It is the old-school way of learning the language, but anything that produced such masters of the spoken word as Mark Twain and George Bernard Shaw and Winston Churchill shouldn't be dismissed simply because it's old. There is a reason for the tradition of requiring acting students to perform the classics of the stage. Immersing yourself in the words of such masters as Aeschylus, Shakespeare, Shaw, Ibsen, and Chekhov not only builds a respect for the language but also helps you develop a presence and authority that will strengthen your emotional impact as a performer. Speech teachers, too, have historically relied on the best examples of their art to instruct and inspire. The Romans looked to the Greeks, and medieval teachers of rhetoric relied on such Roman masters as Cicero, who believed that philosophers had to be skilled at persuading others to adopt their views. By the eighteenth century in England, a man was considered literate only if he exhibited proper command of the Bible (King James version, of course) and the complete works of William Shakespeare and John Milton. Everything else followed. The English oral tradition came out of language spoken from the pulpit and the stage, out of prose and poetry that had majesty and grandeur. "It's the greatest possession we have," Henry Higgins explains in *My Fair Lady* (which, I should mention, was adapted from George Bernard Shaw's *Pygmalion*). "The noblest sentiments that ever flowed in the hearts of men are contained in its extraordinary, imaginative and musical mixtures of sounds." And when educated Englishmen emigrated across the Atlantic, so did this oral tradition. The public-speaking guru Dale Carnegie used selections from the American masters of the podium, Abraham Lincoln and Mark Twain, to illustrate his lessons.

What is at the heart of this tradition is not a use of the language that will send listeners reaching for their dictionaries. Nor is it born of a fanatical adherence to grammatical structure even when it doesn't suit the sound and sense of the naturally spoken word. When Winston Churchill, arguably the greatest exponent and proponent of spoken English in the modern world, was chastised by Lady Astor for ending a sentence with a preposition in a speech before Parliament, he put the lady in her place with the witty rejoinder, "This is a criticism up with which I will not put!" Language is amazing not because the words are big and difficult but because they are moving or inspiring. In 1940 Churchill, as the new wartime prime minister of England, made a very short statement to a divided House of Commons:

> I would say to the House, as I said to those who have joined this government, that I have nothing to offer but blood, toil, tears and sweat. We have before us an ordeal of the most grievous kind. . . . You ask, what is our policy? I will say: it is to wage war, by sea, land and air, with all our might and strength that God can give us: to wage war against a monstrous tyranny, never surpassed in the dark, lamentable catalogue of human crime. That is our policy. You ask, what is our aim? I can answer in one word: It is victory, victory at all costs, victory in spite of all terror, victory, however long and hard the road may be; for without victory, there is no survival.

Churchill's call to battle against Hitler's Germany contains several phrases that reverberated through the coming decades. It is often referred to as the "blood, sweat and tears" speech, but Churchill's actual offering of "blood, toil, tears and sweat" is better, tougher; his arrangement of the words insists there is hard work to be done and a fight to be fought. You can almost hear the old bulldog barking "sweat" in defiance of the custom of using "perspiration" in polite company. That word is more moving than ending with "tears," don't you think? His description of the Nazis as "a monstrous tyranny, never surpassed in the dark, lamentable catalogue of human crime" remains, I believe, indelible and without equal. Finally, his repetition of the rallying word "victory" five times in his final sentence is the stuff of legend, a battle cry for the ages, the ultimate call to action.

Say this speech aloud with all the quiet conviction you can muster. Go ahead. Do it now. See what it feels like to say Churchill's words, what it sounds like to hear yourself saying them. Try it again later. You will be amazed at how much confidence you can gain in your own ability to use your full command of the English language. Churchill uses no ten-dollar words. Perhaps "grievous" and "lamentable" are slightly outside what some might consider colloquial, but they are definitely the right words in context and certainly understandable to all. Let me remind you one final time: No one can play you as well as you can. But nowhere is it written that by expanding and improving your appreciation and usage of the English language, you will damage your own authenticity. Yes, there are those who would cluck that the person who dramatically improves his speech is pretentious or has forgotten where he comes from. Ignore them. Work on your speaking, improve your way with words, get better and better as a communicator, and when you give an impressive, moving speech, you will find that even those naysayers will not be able to resist.

And then keep working at it, improving. The best performers, whether they are singers, musicians, dancers, actors, or athletes, keep their edge by continuing to develop their skills. You are now one of them—a performer. We started with baby steps and progressed to the point where you know how to prepare and get up in front of a group of people without falling apart. You have your survival techniques in place, you can get yourself down the hill without falling, you are no longer frozen with fear at the prospect of speaking in public. In fact, you have probably developed some real confidence as a speaker; you may even have visited the Zone. Experienced performers of all sorts, however, know that no matter how gifted they are, they do not always turn up with their best game. Under certain circumstances, you, too, will have to resort to your B game, the one with which you can at least get through a performance without making a fool of yourself. Occasionally, I still find myself scrambling to avoid embarrassment. But the more experience you have under your belt, the more confidence you will gain, and the more you will bring your A game to the platform in the years to come. I know this not only from my own experience but from a number of my former students who have assured me over the years that the foundation they got from "The Self and the Role" endured the test of time. I ran into one of them six years after the course, and he told me how much it had helped him prepare for an appearance before a moot court in law school. Several others have reported how preparing presentations required for their jobs and understanding the value of practice over time have often set them apart from colleagues. This kind of positive feedback is no small part of the joy of teaching. I look forward to hearing from you about your progress.

I have tried to organize this book in such a way that it may also serve as a reference work as you progress. To that end, and to help you begin working on improving your way with words, I have attached an appendix featuring several of the greatest speeches in history. I begin with Shakespeare, considered by many the creator of modern English, and then I move on to one of his most devoted students, Winston Churchill. And to prove Henry Higgins wrong—English *is* alive and well in America—I have also included stirring words from Franklin Roosevelt, John and Robert Kennedy, and Martin Luther King, Jr. I urge you to read these speeches and study how they employ the lan-

guage to make their point. Analyze the interplay of words, notice how they tell a story, how they create memorable images
and phrases. I encourage you to read them aloud, savoring their
language, their poetry. Commit chunks to memory and recite
them. The goal is to understand what makes a particular speech
so great. Pick out the phrases that ring in your ear, the images
that stick in your mind. The best speeches tend to have an emotional punch. What is it about the language, the images, and the
context that is so moving? Above all, you want to answer the
question "What is in these speeches that I can use?" Make them
your own. As speakers striving toward a certain eloquence, we
can be inspired by the lines of others and use variations of what
worked for them; in certain formal occasions, we can enhance
our eloquence by quoting the shiny phrases of others. I am convinced that getting as much great language as you can into your
head is bound to improve your own efforts at communicating.

I wish you well on your journey, which, when taken in the
right spirit, has no end. Not surprisingly, Winston Churchill has
already made my point much more eloquently than I ever
could, so I cannot resist letting him sign things off: "Now, this is
not the end. It is not even the beginning of the end. But it is,
perhaps, the end of the beginning."

I also cannot resist being in Churchill's presence and getting
in the last word: Good luck!

APPENDIX

LEARNING FROM THE GREATS

The only thing we have to fear is fear itself.
—President Franklin Delano Roosevelt

Roosevelt uttered those famous words in his first inaugural address in 1933 to buck up his fellow Americans, by then into their fourth year of the Great Depression. It was a terrific line (certainly appropriate to our subject) and slightly better put than what the great French essayist Montaigne wrote in 1580: "The thing I fear most is fear," though to be fair to Monsieur Montaigne, his line has a more Rooseveltian rhythm in the original French (*"C'est de quoi j'ai de plus de peur, que le peur"*). Did FDR pinch the comment from Montaigne? Probably not, unless he had a French major among his speechwriters. There was Francis Bacon's "Nothing is fearful except fear itself," but Bacon originally wrote that in Latin (*"Nihil terribile nisi ipse terror"*). Roosevelt enjoyed reading history, and maybe he knew that the duke of Wellington, the man who provided Napoleon his Waterloo, had said, "The only thing I'm afraid of is fear." Or maybe when FDR was at Harvard, he had read Henry David Thoreau's *Journal,* where the former resident of Walden Pond had written, "Nothing is so much to be feared as fear." I don't know about you, but to my ear, Thoreau's version sounds like a direct steal from Bacon, the sort of Enlightenment philosopher-scientist that Thoreau might have been attracted to while at Harvard in the 1830s. Then again, all of the above probably plucked the idea from the Bible, where Proverbs 3:25 declares, "Be not afraid of sudden fear."

Great speakers tend to borrow from others, sometimes even unconsciously. For those of you with a passion for originality, rest assured that there is hardly anything you can say that has not already been said before and better, usually in the Bible or by Shakespeare or by the American classic, Abraham Lincoln. Though Lincoln, too, was not above expropriating a sweet line when it fit his purposes. Remember the final ringing line of the Gettysburg Address: "we here highly resolve . . . that government of the people, by the people, for the people, shall not perish from the earth."

It is the classic picture of American democracy. But "government of the people, by the people, for the people" is hardly an original picture, and Lincoln knew it. According to William Herndon, Lincoln's biographer and one of his law partners, several years before the president's appearance at Gettysburg, Herndon had given him a copy of the speeches of Theodore Parker, a well-known abolitionist who died in 1860. Herndon claimed that Lincoln had marked the portion of a sermon Parker gave in Boston in 1858 before the New England Anti-Slavery Convention. It stated, "Democracy is direct government, over all the people, by all the people, for all the people." Lincoln was a great favorite of Dale Carnegie, who noted that Parker himself may have borrowed the phrase from Daniel Webster, who, four years earlier in a famous reply to a senator from the South who was an advocate of states' rights, had referred to "the people's government, made for the people, made by the people, and answerable to the people." Carnegie noted that Webster may have appropriated the phrase from President James Monroe, who had voiced the same idea a third of a century before, and Monroe may have been influenced by John Wycliffe (c. 1330–1384), who, in a preface to his translation of the Bible, wrote, "This Bible is for the government of the people, by the people, and for the people." The classically educated Wycliffe probably was not unaware of Cleon of Athens's description of the ideal ruler as "of the people, by the people, and for the people."

My point is—well, once again Winston Churchill said it better than I could:

> It is a good thing for an uneducated man to read books of quotations. *Bartlett's Familiar Quotations* is an admirable work And I studied it intently. The quotations when engraved upon the memory give you good thoughts. They also make you anxious to read the authors and look for more.
>
> —*Roving Commission: My Early Life* (New York: Charles Scribner's Sons, 1930)

I am not suggesting that you create a speech by stringing together a series of famous quotations. But I do believe strongly that aspiring speakers can benefit from the inspiring language of the past's remarkable speakers. Effective speeches, as we have seen, are a combination of words, gestures, and emotion. Most of us can use as much help as possible in the word department. Now that you have some experience with preparing and delivering various kinds of speeches, my advice is to spend some time reading history's speeches. Read them, recite them out loud, and then analyze what makes a particular speech so amazing. Pick out the phrases, the images. The best speeches always have an emotional punch. What is it about the language, the images, and the context that is so moving? Above all, you want to answer the question "What is in these speeches that I can use?"

Your local library is bound to have several collections of speeches on the shelves (William Safire's *Lend Me Your Ears: Great Speeches in History,* for example, or *The Penguin Book of Twentieth-Century Speeches*). The Internet is now an indispensable source for not only the texts of famous speeches in the public domain but also audio versions. To spur you on (and deprive you of excuses), I would like to introduce you to some of my all-time favorites, in addition to the Gettysburg Address, which I have already cited. The following selections belie my age, but I like to think that they have stuck in my mind because of their emotional power, and that they will stand the test for the outstanding oratory of any time. I suspect that you are familiar with most of these speeches, even if you've never read or heard them before. All are so famous that many of their phrases have made it into the common parlance. I will start with the greatest writer of English: Shakespeare. And since our subject is public speaking, I will begin with one of the most famous speeches in Shakespeare.

SHAKESPEARE'S *HENRY V:* "BAND OF BROTHERS"

The play is a sequel to two earlier historical plays, *Henry IV,* Parts I and II, where we first meet the king's son, Prince Hal, ambivalent about his royal future and, much to his earnest father's dismay, spending his time in the streets and pubs on the wrong side of London in the company of the witty and not-so-virtuous Sir John Falstaff, one of Shakespeare's greatest characters. By the end of Part II, the hard-drinking prince has matured into a worthy successor to the throne, though a less interesting and more ruthless character.

In his own play, *Henry V,* King Harry, as Shakespeare now

calls him, seems almost too comfortable with power and eager to regain lands that he believes belong to England. He is preparing to invade France. But there is a problem: The French have an army far more powerful than Harry's, waiting on the other side of the channel. The climax of *Henry V* is the real and legendary Battle of Agincourt in 1415. By Act Four, the English are about to meet the French at Agincourt. It does not look promising. The English are facing an enemy of sixty thousand—five-to-one odds, and, as the duke of Exeter adds, the French "are all fresh." Their fate rests on a recent British innovation in the art of war—the longbow. As the king enters, the earl of Westmoreland laments, "O that we now had here / But one ten thousand of those men in England / That do no work to-day!" The king puts him down:

> No, my fair cousin·
> If we are mark'd to die, we are enow
> To do our country loss; and if to live,
> The fewer men, the greater the share of honour.
> —*Henry V*, 4.24–27

King Harry then proceeds to give a speech extolling the benefits of honor. Anyone who doesn't have "the stomach" for this battle, the king declares, let him leave. Harry will fight only with those willing to die with him. The part of the speech I enjoy most comes as he eloquently explains the upside of triumphing against huge odds:

> This day is call'd the feast of Crispian:
> He that outlives this day, and comes safe home,
> Will stand a tip-toe when this day is nam'd,
> And rouse him at the name of Crispian.
> He that shall live this day, and see old age,

Will yearly on the vigil feast his neighbours,
And say, "To-morrow is Saint Crispian:"
Then will he strip his sleeve and show his scars,
And say, "These wounds I had on Crispin's day."
Old men forget; yet all shall be forgot,
But he'll remember with advantages
What feats he did that day. Then shall our names,
Familiar in his mouth as household words,
Harry the king, Bedford and Exeter,
Warwick and Talbot, Salisbury and Gloucester,
Be in their flowing cups freshly remember'd.
This story shall the good man teach his son;
And Crispin Crispian shall ne'er go by,
From this day to the ending of the world,
But we in it shall be remembered;
We few, we happy few, we band of brothers;
For he to-day that sheds his blood with me
Shall be my brother; be he ne'er so vile,
This day shall gentle his condition:
And gentlemen in England, now a-bed
Shall think themselves accurs'd they were not here,
And hold their manhoods cheap whiles any speaks
That fought with us upon Saint Crispin's day.

(Henry V, 4.45–72)

Read this speech aloud. I would also advise you to watch Laurence Olivier's famous film of *Henry V,* which came out in 1944, during World War II, and rings with patriotic fervor. I would also recommend Kenneth Branagh's recent movie version (1989), which takes a more antiwar point of view. Both men are great Shakespearean actors, and it is an education to compare how they handle the same speeches, particularly "Crispin's Day." This is a beautiful page of language—two sonnets' worth of lines, 240 syllables that have mesmerized playgoers and readers for centuries. The speech is a perfect training tool for actors and speakers, with all the connections between breath and language and thought.

These lines are poetry, but they also constitute an effective speech. In fact, Shakespeare's words have such a powerful, goose-bump-raising force that politicians and business leaders have been quoting King Harry ever since he stepped out on the stage of London's Globe Theatre in 1599. The strong images are there: old men stripping their sleeves and showing their battle scars, feasting and drinking while telling war stories; "the good man" teaching his son about what happened that day in the past; "gentlemen in England now abed," regretting that they were not on the battlefield, where even "vile" (meaning low-born for the Elizabethans) men who fought for England had become "brothers" of the king. Anyone needing to inspire his own "band of brothers"—now you know where that phrase comes from—might consider using a line or two from this speech in one of his own motivational talks.

After the Battle of Britain, Laurence Olivier stepped onto the stage of London's Old Vic Theatre in his naval officer's uniform and recited another of Harry's speeches to an appreciative English audience:

> Once more unto the breach, dear friends, once more;
> Or close the wall up with our English dead.
> In peace there's nothing so becomes a man
> As modest stillness and humility:
> But when the blast of war blows in our ears,
> Then imitate the action of the tiger;
> Stiffen the sinews, summon up the blood,
> Disguise fair nature with hard-favour'd rage;
> Then lend the eye a terrible aspect;
> Let it pry through the portage of the head

Like the brass cannon; let the brow o'erwhelm it
As fearfully as doth a galled rock
O'erhang and jutty his confounded base,
Swill'd with the wild and wasteful ocean.
Now set the teeth and stretch the nostril wide,
Hold hard the breath, and bend up every spirit
To his full height. On, on, you noblest English!
Whose blood is fet from fathers of war-proof,
Fathers that, like so many Alexanders,
Have in these parts from morn till even fought,
And sheath'd their swords for lack of argument.
Dishonour not your mothers; now attest
That those whom you call'd fathers did beget you.
Be copy now to men of grosser blood,
And teach them how to war. And you, good yeomen,
Whose limbs were made in England, show us here
The mettle of your pasture; let us swear
That you are worth your breeding; which I doubt not;
For there is none of you so mean and base
That hath not noble lustre in your eyes.
I see you stand like greyhounds in the slips,
Straining upon the start. The game's afoot:
Follow your spirit; and, upon this charge
Cry "God for Harry! England and Saint George!"

(*Henry V,* 3.3–36)

Even Napoleon seems to have been influenced by the English king in his efforts to install himself as the ruler of France, beginning with the Italian Campaign in 1796. After his troops had removed the Austrian occupiers from the Italian states of Piedmont, Milan, Parma, and Modena, Napoleon tried to inspire his exhausted troops for the final push toward Rome. He congratulated them for their successes but declared to the assembled

forces that "we have other forced marches to make, other enemies to subdue, more laurels to acquire, and more injuries to
avenge" in order to retake Rome. Napoleon assured the troops
that "immortal glory" would be theirs, ending his speech with an
unacknowledged echo of Shakespeare's English king: "You will
again be restored to your firesides and homes; and your fellow
citizens, pointing you out, shall say, 'There goes one who be-
longed to the army of Italy!'"

Shakespeare remains a living repository of the English language, full of phrases we still use. Any speaker who does not
use such a ready supply of emotionally packed lines would be
like King Harry showing up at Agincourt without his longbow-
men. It was the kind of wartime eloquence that did not meet its
match in Olde England until that inveterate reader of *Bartlett's
Familiar Quotations* and Shakespeare, Winston Churchill, was
leading England against its fiercest enemy ever.

WINSTON CHURCHILL:
WINNING THE WAR OF WORDS

Churchill would have been the first to express embarrassment at
being compared to Shakespeare. But in the next sentence, he
would have noted with a twinkle that he did win the Nobel
Prize for literature in 1953. Even if Churchill had died in 1939 at
the age of sixty-five, before he became prime minister, he would
have been remembered as a famous writer. By then he had written three books about his military experiences in India and
Africa; a memoir of his early life; a two-volume biography of his
father, Randolph Churchill, another well-known (and not so
successful) politician; a four-volume biography and social history of his ancestor the first duke of Marlborough; a five-volume
history of World War I; a novel; and several other books about

his experiences and contemporaries. Add to that his regular journalism (as a young man, Churchill was a war correspondent), plus the speeches in Parliament and on the road and a constant stream of correspondence, most notably with his wife, Clementine, and Churchill must hold the all-time record for most words to paper for a modern politician.

Few political leaders have made better use of the language than Churchill. "Shakespeare created the English language," John F. Kennedy wrote in his first book, *While England Slept,* "and Churchill took it into battle." No political leader delivered as many memorable speeches, and according to his son, no politician spent as much time preparing his remarks to appear extemporaneous. The former distinction, I believe, is impossible without the latter. (Remember Mark Twain's line "It usually took me three weeks to prepare an impromptu speech.")

Certainly, Churchill grasped the importance of the memorable phrase. Every one of his wartime speeches seems to have at least one phrase that would stir his audience and write the next morning's headlines. By the beginning of summer in 1940, the war in Europe looked like it was already over. German Panzer tanks had attacked through the "impassable" Ardennes Forest and thus sidestepped the notorious Maginot Line. The Germans then caught the Allied armies in northern France at the town of Dunkirk—338,000 French and British soldiers with their backs to the sea. To avert a massive slaughter, more than a thousand vessels, including Royal Navy destroyers, rushed to Dunkirk and saved the troops. After a few weeks of battle, the Nazi armies had won stunning victories on all fronts. By the end of May, Holland had surrendered, along with Luxembourg and Belgium. Paris fell on June 14 and was making a deal with the Nazis by the seventeenth. The next day Churchill went before the House of Commons. With Dunkirk still very clear in their minds, Churchill's audience knew that the Nazis' next target was England. But he rose to the occasion and wound up his speech in this way:

> What General Weygand called the Battle of France is over. I expect that the Battle of Britain is about to begin. Upon this battle depends the survival of Christian civilization. Upon it depends our own British life, and the long continuity of our institutions and our Empire. The whole fury and might of the enemy must very soon be turned on us.
>
> Hitler knows that he will have to break us in this Island or lose the war. If we can stand up to him, all Europe may be free and the life of the world may move forward in broad, sunlit uplands. But if we fail, then the whole world, including the United States, including all that we have known and cared for, will sink into the abyss of a new Dark Age made more sinister, and perhaps more protracted, by the lights of perverted science.
>
> Let us therefore brace ourselves to our duties, and so bear ourselves that if the British Empire and its Commonwealth last for a thousand years, men will say, "This was their finest hour."

Again, notice the echo in the last sentence of *Henry V's* Crispin Day speech. Churchill's speech was only one of his finest hours; throughout World War II, the prime minister certainly delivered more incredible speeches than anyone in the history of politics or war, at times almost one a week. For example:

- May 13, 1940, three days after Churchill became prime minister, at a Cabinet meeting:

> I would say to the House, as I said to those who have joined this government: I have nothing to offer but blood, toil, tears and sweat.

- May 19, 1940, Churchill's first radio broadcast as prime minister:

  Arm yourselves, and be ye men of valor, and be in readiness for the conflict; for it is better to perish in battle than to look upon the outrage of our nation and our altar.

- June 4, 1940, during the disaster at Dunkirk:

  We shall not flag or fail. We shall go on to the end. We shall fight in France and on the seas and oceans; we shall fight with growing confidence and growing strength in the air. We shall defend our island whatever the cost may be; we shall fight on the beaches, landing grounds, in fields, in streets and on the hills. We shall never surrender and even if, which I do not for the moment believe, this island or a large part of it were subjugated and starving, then our empire beyond the seas, armed and guarded by the British Fleet, will carry on the struggle until in God's good time the New World with all its power and might, sets forth to the liberation and rescue of the Old.

Read the Dunkirk speech aloud a few times, and you will get the feel of the genuine power of some ordinary English words strung together in a certain way.

- Two weeks later, on June 18, 1940, Churchill was back before the House of Commons with another effort to bolster British resolve in the form of his "This was their finest hour" speech.
- July 14, 1940, Churchill spoke to the nation again:

  This is a war of the unknown warriors; but let all strive without failing in faith or in duty, and the dark curse of Hitler will be lifted from our age.

- August 20, 1940, during the crucial Battle for Britain, with all
the nation's air resources up against the odds of the fierce
German attack on the airfields in the south of England. The
English people had only to look up in the air and watch their
fighter planes take on the stronger and better-prepared Luft-
waffe. It did not take a military strategist to recognize that
those fighter planes were all that stood before them and a
German invasion. In his speech before the House of Commons, the British prime minister reported on the first year of
the war. Halfway into the long speech, he made a statement
that would have again called up *Henry V's* words in the
minds of Britons raised on Shakespeare:

The gratitude of every home in our island, in our Empire, and
indeed throughout the world, except in the abodes of the
guilty, goes out to the British airmen who, undaunted by odds,
unwearied in their constant challenge and mortal danger, are
turning the tide of the World War by their prowess and by their
devotion. Never in the field of human conflict was so much
owed by so many to so few . . .

I cannot even write those words without tears welling up. Their
power is in the idea of men putting their lives at risk to save the
lives of their fellow citizens—"so much owed by so many to so
few."

- On December 30, 1941, only weeks after Pearl Harbor and
the entry of the United States into the war, but twenty-one
months into his war with Germany, Churchill gave a speech
to the Canadian Parliament in which he combined his typical
bulldog attitude toward the war with some wit at the expense
of the Nazis. I have heard a recording of it, and Churchill's
timing was perfect:

When I warned them that Britain would fight on alone, whatever they did, their generals told their prime minister and his
divided cabinet that in three weeks, England would have her
neck wrung like a chicken . . . Some chicken! [*laughter in the
house—Churchill milked it, and then*] Some neck! [*huge applause*]

World War II also inspired the American commander in chief
to greater rhetorical heights.

FRANKLIN DELANO ROOSEVELT:
"A DATE WHICH SHALL LIVE IN INFAMY"

Like Abraham Lincoln, Franklin Roosevelt was a leader who recognized the power of brevity in emotional times as he prepared
to ask Congress to declare war on Japan. The reason for finally
going to war had been clarified to all Americans the day before,
in Oahu, part of the U.S. territory of the Hawaiian Islands, in a
place called Pearl Harbor:

Mr. Vice President, Mr. Speaker, members of the Senate and
the House of Representatives:
    Yesterday, December 7, 1941—a date which will live in in-
famy—the United States of America was suddenly and deliberately attacked by naval and air forces of the Empire of Japan.
    The United States was at peace with that nation and, at the
solicitation of Japan, was still in conversation with its government and its emperor and looking toward the maintenance of
peace in the Pacific.
    Indeed, one hour after Japanese air squadrons had com-
menced bombing in the American island of Oahu, the Japa-

nese ambassador to the United States and his colleagues delivered to our Secretary of State a formal reply to a recent American message. And, while this reply stated that it seemed useless to continue the existing diplomatic negotiations, it contained no threat or hint of war or armed attack.

President Roosevelt pointed out that it was clear Japan had been deceiving the United States with peace negotiations while planning a massive attack. The president very matter-of-factly stated the tragic results of this surprise attack, leaving the details up to the newspapers: "The attack yesterday on the Hawaiian Islands has caused severe damage to American naval and military forces. I regret to tell you that very many American lives have been lost. In addition, American ships have been reported torpedoed on the high seas between San Francisco and Honolulu."

And if the news of the enemy so close to the continental United States was not frightful enough for his audience, the president made it very clear that the Japanese efforts to wipe out the American navy in Hawaii were part of a much bigger plan to subjugate the entire Pacific:

> Yesterday, the Japanese government also launched an
>   attack on Malaya.
> Last night, Japanese forces attacked Hong Kong.
> Last night, Japanese forces attacked Guam.
> Last night, Japanese forces attacked the Philippine Islands.
> Last night, Japanese forces attacked Wake Island.
> This morning, the Japanese attacked Midway Island.

FDR had set the scene for Congress—and the nation. As he put it, "The facts of yesterday and today speak for themselves." U.S. security was at stake, and, "as commander-in-chief of the army and navy," the president assured his audience that he had taken "all measures . . . for our defense." He then put the Japanese on notice in a way that echoes Churchill's promise that the Nazis were in for a long fight:

> No matter how long it may take us to overcome this premeditated invasion, the American people, in their righteous might, will win through to absolute victory.
>
> I believe that I interpret the will of the Congress and of the people when I assert that we will not only defend ourselves to the uttermost but will make it very certain that this form of treachery shall never again endanger us.
>
> Hostilities exist. There is no blinking at the fact that our people, our territory, and our interests are in great danger.
>
> With confidence in our armed forces, with the unbounding determination of our people, we will gain inevitable triumph. So help us God.
>
> I ask that the Congress declare that since the unprovoked and dastardly attack by Japan on Sunday, December 7, 1941, a state of war has existed between the United States and the Japanese Empire.

FDR reportedly drafted this speech himself, though he did ask his speechwriters to come up with a longer version to be delivered over the radio to the American people the next night. The president began his first draft with the line "a date which will live in world history, the United States was simultaneously and deliberately attacked." He crossed out "simultaneously" and substituted "suddenly," a sharper-sounding word; he also put a line through "world history" and inserted "infamy," a slightly archaic usage, but its very strangeness seems to make his description of the attack more memorable. Not a "day which will live in infamy," as so many people have misquoted FDR for decades and, more recently, after the United States marked another date that shall live in infamy, September 11, 2001. (This widespread error is suspected to be due to a very successful book about the Pearl Harbor attack entitled *Day of Infamy*, by Walter Lord.)

The effect of the immediacy of the attack and the need for quick reprisal comes with the president's skillful, quick, and repetitious litany of recent events:

> Last night, Japanese forces attacked Hong Kong.
> Last night, Japanese forces attacked Guam.
> Last night, Japanese forces attacked the Philippine Islands.
> Last night, Japanese forces attacked Wake Island.

He capped that list with "And this morning the Japanese attacked Midway Island." The implication is clear and the call to action inevitable: We have been attacked, and in the most dishonorable way imaginable. While we were negotiating in good faith with the Japanese government, they were planning to destroy us. As commander in chief, Roosevelt had no alternative but to ask Congress to declare war—a war in which the United States would triumph.

PRESIDENT JOHN F. KENNEDY: *"ICH BIN EIN BERLINER!"*

One of the principles of effective communicating that I have stressed over and over is "Know your audience." No politician was better than JFK at connecting to his listeners, whether they were voters or journalists. (President Kennedy famously snowed the press at his regular press conferences, which were classic examples of extemporaneous charm and witty repartee.) As I noted in Chapter Five, one of Kennedy's biggest successes came in front of the largest live audience he ever addressed—more than a million people, who had lined the streets of Berlin, shouting, "Ken-ned-ee, Ken-ned-ee!" Kennedy delivered a brief speech, but I doubt his audience was dissatisfied. Here is the speech in its entirety:

> I am proud to come to this city as a guest of your distinguished Mayor, who has symbolized throughout the world the fighting spirit of West Berlin. And I am proud to visit the Federal Republic with your distinguished Chancellor, who for so many years has committed Germany to democracy and freedom and progress, and to come here in the company of my fellow American, General Clay, who has been in this city during its great moments of crisis and will come again if ever needed.
>
> Two thousand years ago the proudest boast was "*civis Romanus sum.*" Today, in the world of freedom, the proudest boast is "*Ich bin ein Berliner.*"
>
> I appreciate my interpreter translating my German!
>
> There are many people in the world who really don't understand, or say they don't, what is the great issue between the free world and the Communist world. Let them come to Berlin. There are some who say that communism is the wave of the future. Let them come to Berlin. And there are some who say in Europe and elsewhere we can work with the Communists. Let them come to Berlin. And there are even a few who say that it is true that communism is an evil system, but it permits us to make economic progress. *Lass' sie nach Berlin kommen.* Let them come to Berlin.
>
> Freedom has many difficulties and democracy is not perfect, but we have never had to put a wall up to keep our people in,

to prevent them from leaving us. I want to say, on behalf of my countrymen, who live many miles away on the other side of the Atlantic, who are far distant from you, that they take the greatest pride that they have been able to share with you, even from a distance, the story of the last eighteen years. I know of no town, no city, that has been besieged for eighteen years that still lives with the vitality and the force, and the hope and the determination of the city of West Berlin. While the wall is the most obvious and vivid demonstration of the failures of the Communist system, for all the world to see, we take no satisfaction in it, for it is, as your Mayor has said, an offense not only against history but an offense against humanity, separating families, dividing husbands and wives and brothers and sisters, and dividing a people who wish to be joined together.

What is true of this city is true of Germany—real, lasting peace in Europe can never be assured as long as one German out of four is denied the elementary right of free men, and that is to make a free choice. In eighteen years of peace and good faith, this generation of Germans has earned the right to be free, including the right to unite their families and their nation in lasting peace, with good will to all people. You live in a defended island of freedom, but your life is part of the main. So let me ask you as I close, to lift up your eyes beyond the dangers of today, to the hopes of tomorrow, beyond the freedom merely of this city of Berlin, or your country of Germany, to the advance of freedom everywhere, beyond the wall to the day of peace with justice, beyond yourselves and ourselves to all mankind.

Freedom is indivisible, and when one man is enslaved, all are not free. When all are free, then we can look forward to that day when this city will be joined as one and this country and this great continent of Europe in a peaceful and hopeful globe. When that day finally comes, as it will, the people of West Berlin can take sober satisfaction in the fact that they were in the front lines for almost two decades.

All free men, wherever they may live, are citizens of Berlin, and, therefore, as a free man, I take pride in the words "*Ich bin ein Berliner.*"

The crowd roared its delight as only a million people can, and as Kennedy knew they would. He had posed his audience as a living counterexample to communism, within sight of the enemy. West Berlin was freedom, a draw so strong that the other side had to build a wall to keep their people from fleeing west. But what won the audience over entirely was his own personal identification with them: *Ich bin ein Berliner.* For an audience, this kind of emotional connection is irresistible. It should be equally so for every speaker. Any time you can establish yourself as "one of them," do so. The audience will love you for it.

MARTIN LUTHER KING, JR.: "I HAVE A DREAM"

One of the most eloquent speakers of the twentieth century—perhaps Churchill's only competitor—was Martin Luther King, Jr. They came from different traditions: Churchill was the cosmopolitan leader of the British Empire, a member of a distinguished aristocratic family who had polished his speaking skills in Parliament. King was a descendant of slaves, albeit with a Ph.D., who had followed his father into the church and was bred on the bombastic and musical African-American preaching style that he honed to perfection. From his childhood, the Bible had been cooked into his bones. But Dr. King did have one thing in common with Churchill: He seemed incapable of delivering an unmemorable speech. His most famous was made from the steps of the Lincoln Memorial, during a peaceful march on Washington for civil rights in 1963. The address was televised, and no public appearance did more for the cause than King's speech that day. He began:

> I'm happy to join with you today in what will go down in history as the greatest demonstration for freedom in the history of our nation.
>
> Five score years go, a great American, in whose symbolic shadow we stand, signed the Emancipation Proclamation. This momentous decree came as a great beacon light of hope to millions of Negro slaves who had been seared in the flames of withering injustice. It came as a joyous daybreak to end the long night of captivity.
>
> But one hundred years later, we must face the tragic fact that the Negro is still not free. One hundred years later, the life of the Negro is still sadly crippled by the manacles of segregation and the chains of discrimination. One hundred years later, the Negro lives on a lonely island of poverty in the midst of a vast ocean of material prosperity. One hundred years later, the Negro is still languishing in the corners of American society and finds himself an exile in his own land. So we have come here today to dramatize an appalling condition.

King's "I have a dream" speech is a beautifully structured and complex presentation, a genuine work of art. Others with more expertise have studied this speech in more depth than I, but King's effort is so good that even on first reading (and reciting), anyone can learn from it. The one thing that no one can fail to notice about a King speech is its music. Recite his paragraphs, and the music of his words will take over. Not a word seems to disrupt the rhythm. You do not have to transform yourself into a stem-winding preacher to get the feel of how musical language can be. Repeat after King, let his words play their music, feel what poetry can do. And then try putting a little of your own music into your next presentation. Let me point out some other touches in King's most famous speech that you can use.

King began, as every prophet must, with a prophecy: that this demonstration would go down in history. In the second sentence of the speech, however, he used a common technique of connecting immediately to the context of his speech by echoing the words of the man whose memorial stood just behind him: "Five score years ago, a great American, in whose symbolic shadow we stand, signed the Emancipation Proclamation. . . . But one hundred years later, we must face the tragic fact that the Negro is still not free."

Given that undeniable state of affairs, King summarized the goal of his speech: "to dramatize an appalling condition." In the next two paragraphs, using a series of burning metaphors, he explained that he and his followers were in Washington to cash a check: The Declaration of Independence and the U.S. Constitution had promised all Americans equality and justice but had defaulted on that promise to African-Americans. King then made it clear that the time for justice was now—or else "the whirlwinds of revolt" would continue to threaten the nation. It was a violent image aimed at his white audience, particularly those in power and authority. But as an apostle of Gandhi's nonviolent resistance, King was quick to caution his own followers to show their dignity and avoid violence: "Let us not seek to satisfy our thirst for freedom by drinking from a cup of bitterness and hatred." He pointed out that there was no need to distrust all white people, many of whom saw their own destiny tied to racial justice: "We cannot walk alone."

After reminding his audience of past injustices to America's black citizens, he advises them to "march ahead" with their struggle for voting rights and against "the unspeakable horrors of police brutality." King then switches to an even higher rhetorical gear. The result is the English language structured for maximum beauty, feeling, and power. As soon as King's words were uttered, they already seemed carved in stone:

> Go back to Mississippi, go back to Alabama, go back to South Carolina, go back to Georgia, go back to Louisiana, go back to the slums and ghettos of our modern cities, knowing that somehow this situation can and will be changed. Let us not wallow in the valley of despair.
>
> I say to you today, my friends, that in spite of the difficulties and frustrations of the moment, I still have a dream. It is a dream deeply rooted in the American dream.
>
> I have a dream that one day this nation will rise up and live out the true meaning of its creed: "We hold these truths to be self evident; that all men are created equal."
>
> I have a dream that one day on the red hills of Georgia the sons of former slaves and the sons of former slave owners will be able to sit down together at the table of brotherhood.
>
> I have a dream that one day even the state of Mississippi, a desert state sweltering with the heat of injustice and oppression, will be transformed into an oasis of freedom and justice.
>
> I have a dream that my four little children will one day live in a nation where they will not be judged by the color of their skin but by the content of their character.
>
> I have a dream today.
>
> I have a dream that one day the state of Alabama, whose governor's lips are presently dripping with the words of interposition and nullification, will be transformed into a situation where little black boys and black girls will be able to join hands with little white boys and white girls and walk together as sisters and brothers.
>
> I have a dream today.

I have a dream that one day every valley shall be exalted, every hill and mountain shall be made low, the rough places will be made plains, and the crooked places will be made straight, and the glory of the Lord shall be revealed, and all flesh shall see it together.

This is our hope. This is the faith with which I return to the South. With this faith we will be able to hew out of the mountain of despair a stone of hope. With this faith we will be able to transform the jangling discords of our nation into a beautiful symphony of brotherhood. With this faith we will be able to work together, to pray together, to struggle together, to go to jail together, to stand up for freedom together, knowing that we will be free one day.

This will be the day when all of God's children will be able to sing with new meaning "My country 'tis of thee, sweet land of liberty, of thee I sing. Land where my fathers died, land of the pilgrim's pride, from every mountainside, let freedom ring."

And if America is to be a great nation this must become true. So let freedom ring from the prodigious hilltops of New Hampshire. Let freedom ring from the mighty mountains of New York. Let freedom ring from the heightening Alleghenies of Pennsylvania!

Let freedom ring from the snowcapped Rockies of Colorado!

Let freedom ring from the curvaceous peaks of California!

But not only that; let freedom ring from Stone Mountain of Georgia!

Let freedom ring from Lookout Mountain of Tennessee!

Let freedom ring from every hill and molehill of Mississippi. From every mountainside, let freedom ring.

When we let freedom ring, when we let it ring from every village and every hamlet, from every state and every city, we will be able to speed up that day when all God's children, black men and white men, Jews and Gentiles, Protestants and

Catholics, will be able to join hands and sing in the words of the old Negro spiritual, "Free at last! Free at last! Thank God Almighty, we are free at last!"

It is a tremendous speech—filled with metaphor, both mundane and highfalutin; there are allusions to American history, the Bible, and Shakespeare. As phenomenal a speaker as King was, he was not shy about using the words and phrases of others to increase his own emotional power and eloquence. I advise you to do the same.

King was particularly skilled at firing up his audience and then calming them down. He acknowledged the suffering of American blacks but gave them hope. Brilliantly, he took his audience on a quick trip from the ghetto and rural indignities of discrimination that they all knew so well to the mountaintop where, he proclaimed, "I have a dream." The repetition of that phrase—nine times—is powerful. The emotional pictures are emotionally striking: his four children and all those other little black and white kids holding hands as brothers and sisters. It is a picture that is at once heartrending and full of optimism. The use of the lines from "America the Beautiful," a song that many in the audience, black and white, knew by heart from daily recitations in elementary school, was a wonderful touch. Letting freedom ring from those mountains in the South, which he named, one by one, is also a killer. And when you think the speech can't get any better, King ends by quoting from a Negro spiritual that his fellow African-Americans also knew by heart, "Free at last! Thank God Almighty, we are free at last!"

For those of us who watched the performance of Martin Luther King, Jr., that day in person or on television, it was an unforgettable emotional moment. If you have never seen or heard King in action, get a video- or audiotape of that famous speech and others. King was the king of that traditional preaching style of the African-American churches, big and orotund, and I don't recommend trying to imitate his style and rhythm. But everyone can learn from his structure, his repetition of words and phrases to make a point and get the audience with him, his combination of historical and literary allusions, his poetry, and, above all, his emotional connection through images.

Still, as emotional as King's speech was for me, the most moving speech I have ever heard was made by Robert Kennedy in 1968, before a black audience, moments after he had been told that Martin Luther King, Jr., had just been assassinated by a white gunman on a motel balcony in Memphis, Tennessee.

ROBERT F. KENNEDY:
"I HAVE BAD NEWS FOR YOU"

On April 4, 1968, Robert Kennedy was campaigning for the Democratic nomination for president in Indianapolis and en route to speak before a black audience that was unaware of what had just happened in Memphis. The local police warned Kennedy that the crowd was likely to be enraged by King's murder and that they couldn't assure his safety. The senator from New York would have been way ahead of his advisers in calculating the dangers. While the police and even his own aides and security detail were focusing on crowd control, Kennedy would have recalled that as attorney general, he had approved the FBI wiretapping of King. The pugnacious director of the FBI, J. Edgar Hoover, believed that King was a pawn of communist conspirators, and the Kennedy administration had foolishly allowed Hoover to continue his efforts to destroy the black leader. Robert Kennedy, however, faced the crowd hoping that his own personal experience with deadly hatred, via his brother's murder, might help the crowd deal with the shocking news he brought. Kennedy spoke without notes, and he certainly got straight to the point: "I have bad news for you, for all our fellow citizens, and people who love peace all over the world, and that is that Martin Luther King was shot and killed tonight."

It came as a kick to the stomach, but before his audience could catch its breath, Kennedy tried to elevate their thoughts.

Martin Luther King dedicated his life to love and to justice for his fellow human beings, and he died because of that effort.

In this difficult day, in this difficult time for the United States, it is perhaps well to ask what kind of nation we are and what direction we want to move in. For those of you who are black—considering the evidence there evidently is that there were white people who were responsible—you can be filled with bitterness, with hatred, and a desire for revenge. We can move in that direction as a country, in great polarization— black people amongst black, white people amongst white, filled with hatred toward one another.

Or we can make an effort, as Martin Luther King did, to understand and to comprehend, and to replace that violence, that stain of bloodshed that has spread across our land, with an effort to understand with compassion and love.

For those of you who are black and are tempted to be filled with hatred and distrust at the injustice of such an act, against all white people, I can only say that I feel in my own heart the same kind of feeling. I had a member of my family killed but he was killed by a white man. But we have to make an effort in the United States, we have to make an effort to understand, to go beyond these rather difficult times.

My favorite poet was Aeschylus. He wrote, "In our sleep, pain which we cannot forget falls drop by drop upon the heart until, in our own despair, against our will, comes wisdom through the awful grace of God."

What we need in the United States is not division; what we need in the United States is not hatred; what we need in the United States is not violence or lawlessness but love and wisdom, and compassion toward one another, and a feeling of justice toward those who still suffer within our country, whether they be white or they be black.

So I shall ask you tonight to return home, to say a prayer for the family of Martin Luther King, that's true, but more importantly to say a prayer for our own country, which all of us love—a prayer for understanding and that compassion of which I spoke.

We can do well in this country. We will have difficult times. We've had difficult times in the past. We will have difficult times in the future. It is not the end of violence; it is not the end of lawlessness; it is not the end of disorder.

But the vast majority of white people and the vast majority of black people in this country want to live together, want to improve the quality of our life, and want justice for all human beings who abide in our land.

Let us dedicate ourselves to what the Greeks wrote many years ago: to tame the savageness of man and to make gentle the life of this world.

Let us dedicate ourselves to that, and say a prayer for our country and for our people.

There is nothing Churchillian about this speech. Robert Kennedy's language is very simple, very conversational, and, except for the reference to Aeschylus, without any of the kind of poetry that King was famous for. Yet every time I see a clip of this moment, I am overwhelmed with emotion. I cannot even read this speech without being moved. What is it about Kennedy's remarks that night in Indianapolis that made what he said so moving? First of all, it was a dramatic *performance:* Robert Kennedy was speaking before an audience of strangers who he knew might turn hostile. He needed to hold their attention. Like any good actor, he had a clear objective in mind: to inform them of the tragic news and keep them from rushing into the streets and expressing their justifiable anger and bitterness. Everything he said and did before his audience would have to be filtered through that objective. Telling the audience was the least of it; he would have to convey his shock and outrage but also divert them from the natural human desire for revenge.

Robert Kennedy also had an advantage over any other politician when he faced that audience: He carried a considerable personal emotional burden that would connect him at a basic human level to his audience. This was not some white politician keeping them abreast of the news. As soon as Kennedy processed his own shock, King's murder would have provoked in him uncontrollable memories of the shock he must have felt when he learned about his brother's assassination almost four and a half years earlier. At that moment, before that crowd, Bobby Kennedy could not fail to make it personal, and voicing that experience when his own brother "was also killed by a white man" would help him calm the crowd, if only out of respect for two leaders wasted in their prime. Robert Kennedy had suffered just as these people were suffering. He really did feel their pain. Surely, too, the warnings from the local police and his own Secret Service detail (after President Kennedy's assassination, a law was passed providing federal protection to all presidential candidates) were stirring inside him and enlivening his performance. There was nothing forced about it, because Kennedy's feelings—about both the past and the present—were all genuine. You can sense him battling those feelings during the speech. "Feeling follows action," as Stella Adler always said.

Then there was the impromptu nature of the event. There is no way Kennedy could have prepared for this speech. But in a sense, he had been preparing his whole life. Kennedy's political experience, along with his empathy for the level of grief among his listeners, was palpable. He went out before the audience and gave it to them straight, and what he delivered came straight from his heart. Without notes.

In short, everything that I have been talking about in this book was present in Robert Kennedy's brief speech that night in Indianapolis. I had not even anticipated how moving I still found that moment, almost twenty years later, as I stood before my class at Harvard. I had intended only to talk about the impact that the expression of true feeling can have on an audience. I ended up demonstrating it. One student later told me that as I choked up for a second, she noticed that I made a fist with my right hand at my side and pulled it back as if I held an emergency brake. It was this effort to control my feelings that had moved her, she said, because it seemed so real and expressive of what was going on inside me. I do not recall the braking gesture, only my efforts to keep from losing it, to regroup, and to continue my lecture. But my discussion of the Kennedy speech ignited a bunch of emotions that had all piled on me, like an opposing football team on the guy with the ball: The memory of King's death was upsetting; but even stronger, because it took place at an earlier time in my life, was the memory of my emotional response to the assassination of President Kennedy. It was a traumatic event for most Americans of my age, but even more so for the Amherst students who had seen the president dedicate the Robert Frost Library at Amherst College just four weeks before he was shot in Dallas. On top of those two emotional memories was the tragic irony of Robert Kennedy talking to an audience about the murder of one of their heroes when, three months later, he, too, would be the victim of another mad bullet. What my audience was seeing and hearing was human nature on parade—and the power of sense memory.

And that is what it takes to impress an audience. You can learn a lot from studying Robert Kennedy's speech. Churchill and Lincoln are typically cited as examples of eloquence. Both were gifted writers who knew how to hold an audience in their thrall. But for me, Robert Kennedy's speech is also an example of eloquence, where real emotion can infuse even the simplest prose with poetry.

Those are my favorites. I suspect you already have yours. Look them up, listen to them if they're available on audio- or video-tape, and by all means, recite them aloud. You will find that you can enjoy great speeches even more as an aspiring great speaker. The more you read and recite them, the more you savor the language, the more these words will become part of who you are, as a person and as a speaker.

ACKNOWLEDGMENTS

This book would not have come to fruition without the guidance, instruction, and tireless collaboration of my longtime friend Edward Tivnan. "Howard," he said a few years back, "I'm going to teach you how to write a book." It was with his encouragement and support that I began this endeavor and through his journalistic expertise and unerring sense of structure that I was able to complete the task. We had a lot of fun working on this project together, managing to squeeze in more than a few rounds of golf in the process. I am forever indebted to this gentleman and scholar whom I am in the habit of calling "Professor."

I especially wish to express my gratitude to those people in Cambridge, Massachusetts, who were instrumental in providing me with the opportunity to teach "The Self and the Role"—to Henry Rosovsky, who had recently retired as dean of faculty at Harvard University, for patiently listening to my presentation over lunch at the Harvard Faculty Club and graciously paving the way for me to meet his successor, A. Michael Spence, who had the temerity to give me my chance. Many thanks to Professor Charles Nesson at Harvard Law School, who arranged for me to teach "Public Speaking for Lawyers," and then took the course himself. I also want to thank him and his colleague Professor Charles Ogletree for including me in the creation and teaching of a new course in the study of oral argument the following year. I am most indebted, of course, to the many undergraduate and graduate students at Harvard who studied with me and from whom I learned so much.

To Carol Cartwright, president of Kent State University in Ohio; John Crawford, director of the School of Theatre and Dance; and the many teachers and students I worked with there, my heartfelt thanks and appreciation. The thesis I wrote to earn my M.F.A. degree in 1999 became the springboard for diving into this book.

My gratitude also to my publicist, Cynthia Snyder, for her ongoing help; to Karen Rabe for her unwavering faith and encouragement; to Dave Morine for his constant friendship, advice, and support; to Jim Levine, my literary agent and old friend, for his wisdom in putting me with Random House; to the editors and staff of that august establishment, notably Scott Moyers, Beth Thomas, Elena Schneider, Janet Wygal, and Katie Zug, for providing so much constructive criticism and positive input during their shepherding of this project to completion.

I want to thank my pal Erick Keays, computer genius extraordinaire, for his invaluable guidance and support while dragging me kicking and screaming from old-school typewriter to new-world laptop. Last and most heartfelt, my indebtedness to my wife, Linda, for her patience, her cheerleading, and her incredibly fast and accurate typing; her wise counsel and her constancy are beyond measure. Thank you, my love.

INDEX

Page numbers followed by *n* refer to footnotes on those pages.

ABOUT THE AUTHOR

KEN HOWARD is an Emmy and Tony Award–winning actor whose thirty-five-year career includes acclaimed roles on stage, on television, and in film (*1776, The White Shadow, Dynasty,* and *The Thorn Birds*). He is currently starring in the NBC series *Crossing Jordan*. A graduate of Amherst College and a student of Stella Adler and Robert Lewis at the Yale School of Drama, Howard received his M.F.A. from Kent State University in 1999. He lives in Los Angeles with his wife, Linda.

ABOUT THE TYPE

This book was set in Garamond, a typeface originally designed by the Parisian type cutter Claude Garamond (1480–1561). This version of Garamond was modeled on a 1592 specimen sheet from the Egenolff-Berner foundry, which was produced from types assumed to have been brought to Frankfurt by the punch cutter Jacques Sabon (d. 1580).

Claude Garamond's distinguished romans and italics first appeared in *Opera Ciceronis* in 1543–44. The Garamond types are clear, open, and elegant.

DATE DUE